Recovery Happens
Through
Christ

(My Story of Abuse, Alcoholism, and Adultery)

Recovery Happens Through Christ

(My Story of Abuse, Alcoholism, and Adultery)

MARILYNNE HARRISON

ARPress
ILLUMINATING IDEAS
EMPOWERING VOICES

ARPress
45 Dan Road Suite 5

Canton, MA 02021
Hotline: 1(888) 821-0229
Fax: 1(508) 545-7580

Ordering Information:
Quantity sales. Special discounts are available on quantity purchases by corporations,associations, and others. For details, contact the publisher at the address above.

Printed in the United States of America.

ISBN-13:   Softcover   979-8-89330-539-5
             eBook   979-8-89330-540-1

Library of Congress Control Number: 2024901022

CONTENTS

iii

PREFACE

My testimony – June 24, 2008

My name is Marilynne, and I want to share how God in his awesome power delivered me from alcohol, drugs, and a life lived in a lesbian relationship for fourteen years. God is good. Today I can say that, and I know God is real. There was a time when I was not sure there was a God.

While I was growing up, I attended church services with my grandma, and I was even healed from a hearing problem when I was two. My grandma was a woman of God and full of faith. She is the one who took me to the service where God reached down, and I believe He healed me through her faith.

I wish I would have been able to trust someone enough to tell them what was happening to me at age five. I was taught to listen to those older than myself, so when I was told not to say anything to anyone about being touched, I didn't say a word. Trouble became my middle name from that day on. The sexual encounters didn't go away, and, consequently, the little girl I should have been was instead all grown up.

I got into the liquor cabinet. Not much at first, but later my life became consumed with drugs, sex, and alcohol. I began running away. I craved attention. What I really wanted was to tell someone what had happened to me. But grownups knew best, and who was I but a child to them? At age eleven, I felt ready to live on my own. I was a very independent young person, and in my eyes, I lacked nothing.

My dad was a very respected person in the community. What if people had known the truth? But who would tell? Not me! I grew up going to church and Bible camps. I even attended one year of Bible school to try to turn away from my sins. I learned some Scripture, went to class with hangovers, and passed the time away in slumber. Drugs almost killed me at the age of twenty-one, but God saved me.

After getting married, I tired of married life with another alcoholic. What I didn't know was that my choices carried me down a road where I would be no better than he was. Later I entered into what I called a safe relationship where I could not be hurt by men again. I joined in a woman-to-woman relationship, knowing from the Bible that God was not in agreement with that. But I wasn't living for God or anyone else. Whatever I wanted to do I did.

At this point, I did not care about anything. I had walked away from God, the God who took away my cocaine addiction, gave me complete healing with no withdrawals, and restored my body, which was falling apart. I walked away and said, *I want to do things my way.*

Guess what? When you make a choice like that God won't stop you, and He did not stop me from destroying the beauty that he gave to me. I took His love but thought I could do a better job. The years would prove my behaviors destructive. Friendships dropped away, and the relationship with my son broke apart. I wasn't dying from drug addiction. I was killing myself with alcohol, and I didn't know how to stop it. In fact, I knew I couldn't stop. God could save me. BUT I thought His grace and forgiveness had passed me by because of the life I was living.

At the time it was more than I could bear. I tried killing myself many times, and somehow I always lived to face reality. For twelve of those fourteen years, I was in a lesbian relationship. Looking back at this fourteen years later, I praise God for all He has done for me.

I am a recovering alcoholic by the grace of God. When I was drinking, I often asked God to help me, but one day was different. I wasn't just asking him to help me with my drinking; I wanted him to help me with everything, even if it meant big changes in my relationship. From preaching I'd heard I knew I couldn't sit on the fence, but how was God going to fix the damage fourteen years had done to me?

I couldn't grasp that our God is a forgiving God, and His grace was and is sufficient for anyone who desires to live in freedom from a life of addiction and from bondage to sexual immorality. God is truth, and I was living lies from the enemy. Then, in 2003, my new life in Jesus would begin ONE DAY AT A TIME, SWEET JESUS. This is my story of hope.

> *Each time he said, "My grace is all you need. My power works best in weakness." So now I am glad to boast about my weaknesses, so that the power of Christ can work through me.*
> (2 Corinthians 12:9

PART 1
CHILDHOOD

I was born in Torrance, California, and moved to Illinois before the age of two. I had a sister who was older than me as well as a few brothers who were much older than me.

In kindergarten I caused problems in the classroom. At home I disrupted family gatherings. I was always trying to get attention; right or wrong – it didn't matter – just as long as someone showed an interest in my distress. Other than that, I was a normal five-year-old who was looking for something, although I wasn't exactly sure what. A person to trust?

I had speech therapy in first grade, and then had a crush on my second-grade teacher – a woman. She was kind and pretty. I think I wanted to be like her in some way. Maybe I liked school because I was in her class.

In third grade I taunted the boys by doing things like pulling my dress up to them and letting them look at my underwear. I remember being in the hallway while class went on without me in hopes of luring a boy out of class to join me in the hall.

Then I found someone to be in trouble with. The boy was perfect; he flirted back at me. I had a friend. Now it was my turn. Everything I had learned from the sexual experiences I'd had since the age of five, I would

1

teach him. He would be my way to release the tension inside me – with a boy my own age, not a man.

Help me! Inside I was just screaming; outside I was running. At home I was quiet – just going through the routine. I didn't play with dolls. I didn't like too many people around me, in spite of the fact that I craved others' attention. I was very neat. I liked things in order. I observed everything. I acquired skills like cooking and learned responsibility. I watched. I listened. I heard everything. But I was hurting and stuck in a world all my own. I wanted to be grown up, yet I needed to be a child. I dreamed of living in my own place and had goals of being famous. I was in fourth grade but I wanted to be free.

This boy and I wrote a letter to each other and were almost caught together, but we managed to get out of that. We snuck out to the bathroom or other places to be with each other. This was just for us to know, a secret playtime together.

I didn't want anyone to take away my new friend. Was this a bad thing? Someone gave me the appetite for sex, and now I could do the same for this boy and no one needed to know. After all, we both liked each other, or at least used each other.

I loved sports and was good at all of them. As long as I stayed out of trouble I could enjoy sports, but that didn't always happen. More trouble came along when I started smoking cigarettes off and on with a few kids in the neighborhood, but it made me appear cool and grown up.

My pastime was rollerskating every weekend when I had a chance. I enjoyed that and was also good at pinball – even got the best scores. It made me feel important. I became a real shark at shooting pool, even better than those older than me. These places were like a retreat, a place where I was important and got noticed for the skills I had.

Every summer I looked forward to my visits to Grandma's house where things were different than at home. When I was about seven, my sister and I lived at different homes for a short time. It confused me. Why would we be separated? The separation meant another school as well as another home. Once I adjusted, I wanted to stay and never go back home. There were so many things I didn't want to remember. I think I tried to block them out by having a sip of beer along with a cigarette.

After the last visit with my grandparents at the age of seven, I didn't see them for many years and never understood why. I felt like my whole world shattered the day Mom and Dad came to get me. Dad brought me some dresses and insisted I come home. I think he wanted Mom to return, as they had split up during the time I was away.

This memory is fuzzy, but I remember not wanting to leave. Grandma was upset, and I heard a gun go off. I was bawling, and no one would let me see her. But, then I heard her speak. "Marilynne, go with them. I love you. I'm okay."

I went with Mom and Dad but never forgot Grandma's I love you, called to me through the bathroom door. Grandma and Grandpa's was the only place I felt safe, and now it was all gone.

For a time I lived with my aunt and uncle and my new cousins. While I was there, my aunt taught me the basics of caring for babies. I loved to learn. I listened closely to her talk about how to care for them – from bathing to changing them, to helping them with teething, and to learning their different cries like the one for food. I hated to leave this place where I fit in.

At every place I lived I attended church with the people who lived there. Church was a place I didn't understand. Some churches taught Bible verses, and I learned to make things at others. I learned to sing praise songs to God. I wore the new dresses Dad had bought me when he picked me up from Grandma's house. However, we didn't talk about church, and we didn't even mention God much at all. My dad didn't believe in God or church.

Eventually, I went to church alone. I listened and wanted to be saved from the mess I was in. The song Just As I Am would have an impact on me over and over. I still felt like God didn't hear me when I prayed. I tried to find Him. I got on my knees every Sunday and talked to Him, but nothing changed in my behavior, and nothing changed at home or at school. I knew there was a God, His Son died for my sins, and I'm forgiven, but life went on the way it always did.

I could never please my dad. We'd shoot our guns, but if I didn't hit the bull'seye, he'd say I wasn't trying. When I was learning to ride a bike, Dad took my training wheels off even when I wasn't ready. I remember crying because it was raining, and I didn't want to ride, but he made me ride anyway.

When I was nine, I hadn't learned to swim. I had tried a few times, but twice I nearly drowned. Once I got caught in an undertow and thought it was all over when suddenly I felt my hair being pulled. It was Dad. He ran into the water with all his clothes on and his wallet still in his pocket to rescue me. He did care about me, apparently, even though I thought I could never please him.

School was a challenge since I didn't want to be in class, except for art and wood crafting. I enjoyed those classes, but I skipped most of the other ones and went to hideouts where I smoked or just waited until it was time to go home. We were the not-so-perfect kids. To get bullies off my back I started being a bully to some of the new kids to gain the respect of the incrowd. I called it survival.

I did have one good friend, but she got hit by a car and killed. My heart broke. I kind of closed up inside myself and didn't get close to anyone again. I befriended someone else later on, but I used the friendship to manipulate her and use her for what I wanted. Despite the manipulation, however, we still had a special relationship. One day we were called lesbians, and I knew in our neighborhood that was grounds to beat us up or kill us. We denied this accusation – we were only good friends – but it made me think about needing some guy friends to change that label.

So I started to hang out with guys, but it didn't take long before I was called the slut of the neighborhood. I thought if they only knew what started this, they wouldn't be so quick to call me that. I was only doing to them what I had learned myself. I never did tell anyone what had happened to me when I was five and then again when I was seven and then again when I was eleven.

I enjoyed reading, mostly good mysteries, but also books about survival. I read a book called *The Other Side of the Mountain,* about a boy who lived in the woods and made all his things out of what the earth had to offer. The book gave me great expectations of making it on my own. I now planned to run.

I had learned many things in order to survive. I learned about Native Americans and how to shoot a bow and arrow. I was taught how these people survived.

I learned how to camp in extreme conditions, how to shoot a gun and skin an animal, and how to fish and clean fish, all by the age of ten. One time I climbed very high up a tree and the limb I was on broke. I dropped to the ground and the branch fell on top of me and knocked me out. I wasn't hurt bad. I enjoyed all of these acts of "survival." I continued to read about surviving in the wilderness. I prepared to survive in what my mother called a cruel world.

I found a two-story playhouse on an abandoned lot for a hide-away. I decided to make this my place and fix up the inside just like home. I hid away here for short periods of time and brought along a Zombie drink full of every kind of liquor in the cabinet at my house, topped off with Kool-Aid© or soda and a pack of smokes. This was my home-away-from-home and a place I could call my very own. I decided to invite a few friends over to celebrate this new place and do what grownups do: drink and be merry and get sick.

One day I got sick after my Zombie and staggered home. I had to be careful so no one would know. After all, my life at this point was all about secrets anyway.

I had also learned to smoke pot from some boys I met on the school bus during summer school. This was better than drinking because it had a calming effect on me. My worries seemed to disappear, and pot would be easier to hide from Mom and Dad. I dealt drugs to pay for my habits, while my babysitting money went toward buying clothes.

Finally, at the age of eleven, I spent the summer with my grandparents again. They were my rock. I went through some old picture albums Gram and Grandpa had. I wanted to look through these since I had missed so many years of not being with them. I saw my mom in a wedding gown in a couple of different pictures. I thought she only got married once, but I had suspected something wasn't right about the man who had been raising me with Mom. Now I began to make sense of his actions with me.

In anger and confusion, I demanded an answer as to who my dad was. Grandpa told me to talk to Grandma. Grandma told me I was not old enough to know. I thought, *Not old enough for what? Good grief! After all I had already done and been forced to do? You're kid-ding! I'm a woman in so many ways while still in a child's body.* I told Grandma I could handle this. She wouldn't explain, but said I could take a guess, and she wouldn't lie to me.

So I started with all the questions: How old is Mom here? Who is this? What is his name? Where is he? I look like him; is he my real father? Grandma had said she wouldn't lie, but she also said I needed to keep this a secret and never tell anyone who told me. I wouldn't tell anyone. I had already lost enough years of not seeing Grandma.

I needed to understand why I was adopted and my name was changed. I was told it was for good reason. But how bad could he have been? After everything that happened to me, nothing could top all of that, could it?

He was a nice man and very intelligent, as long as he didn't drink. But when he drank he became violent and abusive toward whomever he was with. He was able to get a barber's license after being in the jail system for so long and became a good barber. He enjoyed fishing and was good at making things. I didn't really judge him at all for this, once I finally heard it, as he had never hurt me.

That summer Grandpa taught me gardening and Grandma taught me how to bake cookies and bread. I also went to summer camp and learned about Jesus. I loved praise songs. Grandma had faith in God. She was almost always positive about life, even in difficult times when other people were negative. She would say, *God is here and He has it all in His hands,* just like the song that says, "He's got the whole world in his hands." Grandma was my inspiration, the one I looked up to, and the one who understood me when others didn't. But school would be starting soon and I returned home.

RUNNING

I wanted things to be over at home with the ma-and-pa-pretending-and-divorce games. I became more protective of my younger sister. I didn't think Dad would really touch his own daughter like he had me. I justified his actions with me because I was adopted, so it was no big deal.

I didn't figure it would take much for me to get the ball rolling so he would be out of the house before long and out of the picture for good. I wanted to tell someone what he had done to me, but it scared me to think about the people who would say I wasn't telling the truth. I preferred not to say anything at all than lie.

The divorce between Mom and Dad was finalized with visitation rights granted for my dad to see me. Oh great. Now it would be one-on-one with no one else around. In this new life of divorced parents, I was allowed to drink and smoke. I wasn't upset about what else was happening. I accepted my new life.

I could hardly stand being around Mom, however. It was the guilt and shame I felt, along with being forced into visitations with my dad. On top of this I was put into counseling. I thought this was stupid. All of us sitting in a room with this person I didn't even know, to talk about what my problem is: why I wanted to run all the time, why I was doing drugs and drinking, why I was skipping school all the time. I was expected to talk this out. I just froze and couldn't say why I was acting this way. Fortunately, Dad moved out of state soon after and the visits with him ended. I was free. When I was twelve or thirteen, I made another visit to my grand-parents'. Grandpa asked me to sing a song at church for him. I sang one of his favorites, *One Day at a Time.* Grandpa knew all the trouble I got into at school, and he wanted to see me turn things around. He wanted me to go to the Baptist school and let him and Grandma help me with schoolwork. He had such a way of talking me into what was right that I promised I would go to the school.

By now Mom had a good job and things seemed to be better for her. I couldn't get away with smoking or drinking much. I still tried to be sneaky in doing it and got better at hiding stuff from her.

My sister and I both attended the Christian school. This would have been a good place for me if I didn't stay out so late. I was sleep-ing in class and especially liked the days when a film was shown in class so I could sleep. I rested all day in class and played all night. I didn't make any new friends at the school and mostly hung out with my older-aged friends who could buy alcohol.

In my sneaking around, I would back my mother's new car out of the garage without starting it while Sis was sleeping. I'd start the car at the end of the driveway so the neighbor wouldn't wake up, and take off. I unrolled all the windows so I could smoke, and I always checked the gas gauge to make sure there was enough gas to drive the car back home. I was only fourteen when I did this so I could have gotten into a lot of trouble.

One night I took Mom's car and headed to a party. It turned out to be the worst night of my life. I was raped. I thought I was going to die. But I thought no one would believe me if I told them what happened.

I drove back home in Mom's car that night and cut the corner too close. I kept going and just wanted to get home and go to bed and wake up to find it was all a nightmare. But that didn't happen. I forgot to remove the smoke smell from the car, and I had also forgot-ten to put more gas in the car. I decided to act like she didn't know what she was talking about when she noticed the damage to the car. I made up a story about what must have happened to the car, and as far as I know she believed me, but I never went out with her car again.

By now I had friends with cars. I was usually their driver because they said they liked how I paid attention to the road and played it safe so we never got pulled over for anything. I even learned how to drink and drive at the same time. Shortly after this I learned what cocaine was, from a friend who gave me a mirror with the word cocaine on it, and of course I tried it.

I was still good at some things, like cleaning, crocheting, and keeping things in order. I enjoyed writing poems I hoped one day to put into a book or make into songs. I wanted to be a writer at the age of thirteen, so I started keeping diaries.

All the while, though, I was doing more and more drugs and moved through many different relationships. I ended up in the hospital where the drug problems had apparently removed any possibility of my having children. There went my dreams of being a mom and having ten children. I blew up when the doctor told me this, and Mom and I got into it big-time. I almost told her about what happened to me so long ago. Instead, I only told her about the rape the night I banged up her car and left it at that.

I remembered the times I had spent at Bible camp. I had felt such a peace among the trees there and would sit next to the water and the big rocks and talk to God. I would ask Him why things were so different for me. *How can I get close to you?* I asked Him. I wanted to do what was right every time but constantly disappointed myself and those around me. *How do I read the Bible?* I asked God. It didn't make sense to me. I pleaded with God to save me, and then it was time to go home again. Once I got home, I tried to take my Bible to a secret place and be in the "God way," but inevitably it happened that a friend would show up and we would do drugs or other things together. Time and time again, I put down the very words that could have helped me in those situations. I struggled with what was good and didn't understand how to live right, while in actuality the life I lived was the only life that felt right.

When I was home, I just wanted to get away from home. I would gather some clothes and promise myself I would never return. Noth-ing made me happy there.

I never could find a place where I fit in. I went to a few different churches and attended a Christian school for a year in my teen years. Still, I really was a troubled child with a stepfather who found his way with me, and it seemed I was always running.

I spent time running away and getting into drinking and drugs and sexual acts. I went to the altar on occasion, and still I had no peace. It was a kind of battle, always wanting to do what was right, but trouble always found favor in my life.

I hung around with a "gang" of girls. I felt like I was a protector and no one could hurt me when I was with my gang. I grew closer to one girl than the others. One day after doing a bunch of drugs, she became motionless. We got her to the emergency room, but it was too late. I was upset with her for dying. I had lost my friend. Now I felt like I didn't have anyone.

In spite of this incident, I continued doing drugs, having sex with whomever, and drinking alcohol. I couldn't wait to become a legal adult so I could stop living as an adult in a child's body.

I ran away from home many times. Each time the police were called to come get me, until I was finally put into a foster home. Everything went fine for a while, until they took in another runaway girl whom I knew. This girl ran away. I had to tell the family she had taken off and that I was unable to stop her. I hadn't even tried, because I knew exactly how she felt.

Shortly after this my mom visited me. She asked me if I was ready to come home. I didn't want to leave, but I knew she had to pay for me to stay there, so I agreed to leave with her. School would be start-ing again soon.

When I got home I stayed sober for a while. I made a promise not to run away again. I promised I would stay in school and make myself do the right thing.

Once school started, word got out that I was back. My gang was together again, and they wanted to celebrate. I committed to doing my best to get everything out of school I could.

I enjoyed English and felt inspired by the English teachers. I put my heart into writing poetry and was determined to write a book. My grades were good for the first time in many years.

I also wanted to learn about criminal justice. I had thought about being a detective. I liked mystery stories, and I liked to solve problems. I took adult education courses. I liked everything having to do with nursing and thought I wanted to continue school and become an RN.

I also took typing classes but didn't care for them very much. Math classes were boring.

My favorite and, to me, my most important class was driver's ed. If my grades didn't stay high enough or if I got into trouble again, I would lose the right to drive. That meant I would lose the opportunity for the freedom I needed to travel the world.

The very first time I drove was out in the country where my grandparents lived. Grandpa let me drive down the road to the mailbox. I took my little sister with me. I ended up driving past the mailbox and then when I tried to back up, I ended up in the ditch. The neighbors had to pull out Grandpa's car with a tractor. Needless to say, I lost my driving privileges after that incident.

Eight months into the new school year I was finding it difficult to stay in school. The principal caught us smoking outside, and I was suspended from school and didn't know if I would return.

By age sixteen, I had to put in enough time to get my driver's license, and in my mind that was all school was really good for. I went downhill from here. I partied with my friends, sold drugs, and continued to get in trouble by not going to class. I just wanted to be on my own, but legally I wasn't old enough yet.

Mom signed me out of school so I could start working, even though I still needed my driver's license. I needed to work because my habits were costing me money and I was tired of selling drugs. I went to work at Burger King. I made money, paid for rent, and was able to buy some things. I wasn't drinking or drugging, but I hadn't completely stopped doing these things either. I had saved enough money to get a car, so I bought a big Pontiac Catalina.

One night I talked my mom into letting my younger sister join some friends and I out for a drive, convincing her I would keep my sister safe. My boyfriend this evening was driving, and we had a special road we called the rollercoaster. The faster you could go the higher the car would become airborne and it was as thrilling as the fair. When we came to the stop sign, we were traveling too fast to stop and went through the two-lane highway and right into the ditch. The cops showed up, and because my boyfriend did not have his driver's license with him, he talked me into saying I was the one driving. The next thing you know, I had to go to court.

As my mom and I walked to the courthouse on the appointed day, we met my real father. He was there for drunk-driving offenses. My mom did introduce us, and he asked if he could have a picture of me. I told him "No," and said, "I don't know you! You are a stranger to me." I stared intently at his face to see if I could see any resemblance of myself. But he looked so old and worn out, no doubt caused by all the drinking he had done over the years. He hadn't changed. I had never seen Mom so scared before either. After all the years of wanting to meet my father, I had finally done so. I could put that day behind me now.

My punishment for driving into the ditch was to do community service. I was put on probation and was still able to live on my own. I had learned about the justice system firsthand. I respected the judge and found I liked his side of the law much better than the side I was on. The good that came out of this whole experience in court was that, in almost losing my driving privileges, I decided not to hang out with that crowd of kids anymore.

Caught in the Spiral

My second "adult" job consisted of doing dishes, which I was good at, and I had a new male best friend, Danny. I met Danny in my neighborhood. He was a friend of a friend. We would actually talk! We talked about what we wanted out of life. I told him things I had never told anyone. I also tested his confidence and his sincerity by telling him things to see if he would tell anyone.

I saw Danny as my ticket to a new life. I had everything figured out. We would get married and live happily ever after.

At Christmas he said he had something special to ask me, and I was so ready for an engagement ring, the thing that would make me honest and secure and well again. Instead, he gave me a keepsake and told me he was joining the Air Force. Instead of a proposal and a new life, he was leaving.

The news shattered my hopes and dreams. I didn't want to talk to him anymore. Inside, I just wanted to tell him I was done with him and let that be it. But we talked again one last time before he left. He helped me find a new place to live and a new beginning without him.

As I started my life without Danny, I went in to take a test and passed all the requirements to enter college to become a nurse. My dream would be fulfilled! I would be a nurse! I was only seventeen but I had been accepted! There was just one problem; I didn't have my high school diploma, so I couldn't even get into college to become a nurse. I needed my GED, but I wasn't ready to go back to school to get it.

Meanwhile, I started going with the cook from my workplace who was married and had two children. I thought that was safe and believed him when he promised to leave his wife. He never did. I found out later that he was seeing not only me but also my best friend and another person who worked with us, and he had passed on STDs to all of us. Ashamed and embarrassed, but grateful that it wasn't a disease with a death sentence. My body would recover without long term consequences. I quit working there, bought a smaller car, and moved in with one of my gang girlfriends and her boyfriend in another town and paid them rent.

While living with my girlfriend and her boyfriend, I partied often, and I started blacking out more and causing my friends to be very unhappy with me. I was falling apart, but I couldn't stop myself.

One night I stayed over at the apartment of the boyfriend of one of the girls I hung around with. We partied that night and just chilled out. I rested there and in the morning headed back home. When I got to the house, my friend and two other friends of hers beat me up. I was still hung over, so they obviously won the fight. They thought I had slept with my girlfriend's boyfriend. My best friend kicked me out of her house.

I now had no place to live and a car that didn't run.

I slept in my car for a week and cleaned myself up at gas stations and other places that had restrooms. I was homeless and had burned all my bridges in one way or another. My tips from work had to go to buy gas for the car so I could keep it running all night to stay warm. I found out about Mrs. Pool who rented rooms for people who had nowhere else to go. She was a sweet, older widow with a big, two-story home with three bedrooms upstairs and a big bathroom. I only stayed a short time as my drinking and drugs would take ahold of my life. I had no one to call a friend now. It was just me out for me. I saw Danny again now that he was in the Air Force. And I even signed up to join the Air Force at one point, but I needed my high school diploma or my GED. I still wasn't ready to go back to school, so that plan ended quickly.

I eventually applied for and got a third-shift job at a mental institution. I learned to work with a lot of people who had mental disorders of all sorts. Things like mental retardation, schizophrenia, Down syndrome, and multiple personalities were common at this place. Some things I saw here reminded me somewhat of what I had once been like. I would cry at times, wondering why these people were so misplaced and why their families weren't there for them. My selfish-ness left quickly as I began to work here, and a new purpose for my life took shape.

I really enjoyed taking care of people. I helped get everyone up in the morning. Some laughed as we got them up, some cried, some grew angry, and some just couldn't respond at all. Every day was a new day full of surprises.

However, I was still not taking care of my own life. I continued to drink and do drugs, get into unhealthy relationships, and party with people I hardly knew.

On New Year's Eve my plans were to party, sleep, and then go to work. However, icy rain froze the locks of the car I had borrowed from a friend. I simply couldn't be late anymore, as I had already used up my "forgiveness" time with this job. I called work and said I would be late because the locks on the car had frozen. My excuse was the truth but it didn't matter. I lost my job. I hated to leave Mrs. Pool's place and she was also sad that I was leaving, but without a job and no money I went on the road again.

This gave me reason to drink again. I drove to where Mom lived. She suggested I go to Florida and stay with Dad. He paid for a plane ticket for me, and the next morning I headed out on Greyhound to Chicago where I caught a flight to Orlando, Florida.

I was starting over again – a new place, new people, and a chance to change. Dad and I danced together, drank together, and played pool and shuffleboard. I wanted to get back to school, to stop drink-ing so much, and to take more responsibility for my life. I enrolled in a GED program, which I hoped would help me finally accomplish what I wanted in life for a career.

Then I met a nice-looking man in the neighborhood who had a Camaro. His name was Robert. I had good intentions for completing my education, but I found it difficult to concentrate on school when I knew I could be partying with Robert. He worked the day shift so the nights were our time together.

A couple of months later Robert and I talked about having chil-dren. Since I had been told years ago that I'd never have children because of all the drugs I did and what they had done to my body, I went to a fertility clinic. I needed to know if that was still the case. I was crushed when the doctor told me what he did, but I still never gave up hope. I wanted to have ten children, but I would settle for one.

The doctor told me there was a fifty-fifty chance I could have kids. That was better than no chance at all. During this time, however, I acknowledged God again for the first time in many years. I decided it would be His will as to whether I would have a child, but I desper-ately wanted it to be His will. I had wanted to have a baby since the age of thirteen.

Somehow God had heard me. I was pregnant! Nothing else mat-tered in the whole world now; I was going to have a baby. Right away I knew I couldn't drink or do drugs. It sure would be a long nine months without those things.

Robert and I got married. Mom came down for the wedding and my sister joined the ceremony as my maid of honor. Dad didn't want to come to the wedding, even though he did send over a keg of beer which I couldn't even drink because I was pregnant. A terrible storm brought wind and rain on the day of our wedding and by evening it turned into a hurricane over Cocoa Beach.

Not long into the marriage, we realized we were not very com-patible. Since I couldn't drink or do drugs with Robert while I was pregnant, we didn't have much in common, except that we had a baby on the way. We would fight and make up, and then fight and make up again and on and on and on.

Nevertheless, I eventually delivered a baby boy with blue eyes and a bald head. He was everything I ever wanted and a joy to my heart. My son was my dream, my heart's desire, and my everything – the missing piece of who I was. God had given me the most precious gift ever. I enjoyed being a mother and learned every day how much of a gift it was.

Having this baby was something Robert and I cherished together. In spite of all our troubles, we were strong together because of this baby. Robert was a proud father and our new son, Josh, looked just like him. But Robert still went out drinking with his friends regu-larly. Then my drinking started again. I only had a glass of beer or wine, not enough to harm anything. But all of our friends drank, so before too long I hired a babysitter for Josh so I could join my friends to drink as well.

Then I started back into doing drugs. Pretty soon we couldn't afford where we were living because of the money we wasted on alcohol and drugs. We could barely afford diapers for Josh. When he was five months old, he got sick, and Robert and I fought about taking him to the hospital. Josh was barely breathing, his nose and mouth filled with mucus.

The hospital admitted him right away and started an IV in his little hand. It was the most awful night of my life. Since the doctors weren't sure what Josh's problem was, I couldn't stay in the room with him that night. I felt totally helpless as a mom. I couldn't fix things, and I couldn't take him home with me. They put him in a tent with a vaporizer and mist that helped a bit. They gave him lots of shots.

Every day got harder for me as I watched him in that tent. The doctors only let him out of it to be bathed, changed, and fed. I had been working at a strip club as a cocktail waitress, which quickly turned into the partying capital of my world.

I escaped into drugs and alcohol and found myself dancing with the other dancers at the club and meeting all types of strange men. I ended up being unfaithful to Robert and fell into a pit of selfishness. It took a little over a month before the doctors were able to find a magic drug that worked for Josh and made it possible for him to come home.

But being at home now meant living at my mother-in-law's because we didn't have our own place yet. I hadn't been saving money toward getting another place because I was using the money I earned for drugs and alcohol. Josh still had to be in a mist tent at home and no one was allowed to smoke around him at all. The doctors had deter-mined he had a severe sinus infection and was possibly allergic to smoke. I would do whatever I had to do to get him healthy again, so I did not smoke in the house or in the car.

Robert and I finally found another place to live, but again, it was with someone else, which made our marriage even more difficult. I just wanted a real marriage where Robert and I would be content and happy with each other and our son. I tried to stop drinking and doing drugs. It stuck for about a month, but I quickly returned to my old routine. I got so discouraged with my inability to quit drinking and doing drugs that I wanted to die. Only my love for Josh kept me alive.

I got a job working at Epcot and thought my life would surely get better. I put Josh into daycare. I wanted to better myself and figured by working at the biggest company in Florida and really enjoying it, my life would be better. It was a new beginning for me. However, before long I met people at Epcot who liked to go out after work. I promised myself I would have only a few drinks. That way I could still be a responsible mother and wife. But I failed terribly.

One day a girl I worked with in the dishwashing area kissed me. I had probably been flirting around a bit, so I got what I was looking for, even if I didn't know it. This girl and I spent time together with my son, and I was starting to feel like a real mom again, like I had always dreamed of being.

One night when I worked late and was overdue in picking up my son, I found she had gone to a movie with another girl from work. I didn't like that. She and I talked about my being upset with her going out with another girlfriend. Then we started talking about God. She bought me a Bible and marked her favorite verse in it from 1 John. We pondered together whether it was okay with God to be in a relationship with a woman. I hadn't given it much thought, and told her it didn't matter as long as you were happy.

One night after drinking I went out with Dad at his request, and when we got home he hit on me like he had done so many times in years past. I told him this behavior wasn't acceptable anymore and that it would be the last time he ever did that to me.

The next day Dad called me at work. "Your grandma is in my driveway."

I didn't believe him. Grandma hadn't come to visit me since I moved to Florida more than two years before. "Put her on the phone," I said. Sure enough, she had really come to see me and her new grand-baby, whom she had only seen in pictures.

I was excited to see Grandma and changed my plans to accommodate her visit. I decided we were going to go out together. I had to call Robert, as we were now separated and he had visitation rights. Unfortunately, this was his first visitation time and now I had to call him and ask if he could bring Josh to meet my grandma. Gram had never met Robert, so I figured she needed to meet him for the first time, too.

We all got together so Grandma could meet Josh and Robert, and I realized I still felt something for Robert. Grandma asked us to give our marriage another try and encouraged us to try to make it work. For Grandma, we decided to give it another try. When she left, Robert and I began our life together once again.

But neither one of us had really changed. We got back into doing cocaine and let drugs take over. I lost another job when Josh became ill and was not able to be with other children for at least a week. I had no more time off from work, so I found myself without a job and at home again.

When Josh got well again, I went back to a job I had enjoyed the most – being a CNA. I was good at it and found I had a special compassion for the elderly. This job was close to my home and provided the possibility of going back to school at some point.

But could I stay sober? Could I stay clean? Could I just do the right things? I wanted to be able to say no more drugs, no more alcohol, no more sex with strangers, no more this, no more that. But I couldn't. I wasn't strong enough. Where could I turn? There was no one to help me.

With Robert and I back together again, one of us always started the other back into drugs. I'd take LSD and not know how I got to places. After so many years of alcohol abuse and doing drugs, I couldn't remember what it was like to be sober anymore.

Robert and I worked with another cocaine dealer and his girlfriend who had a son Josh's age. We took turns watching each other's kids when it was time to do business. But things got out of hand when the boyfriend and I had an affair. We did cocaine together, and I soon learned how to cook it, which led me down an even more dangerous road and further from any chance of recovery.

We got together on many occasions.

I began doing more and more drugs to the point where I wasn't able to make a profit anymore from drug dealing because I was doing too many drugs myself. I couldn't sleep. I was paranoid. All I thought about was getting my next hit. I stayed home to sell drugs and wanted to teach others how to do the same so I would get free hits. I couldn't eat. I couldn't sleep. I tried to drink but would get violently sick. I was drastically losing weight and my muscles grew weak.

I was still trying to work at the nursing home, but found myself going out at lunch to take a hit. One night I began to bleed and, for some reason, I knew I was pregnant, even though the chances of getting pregnant again were slim. But if I was pregnant this time, the baby wasn't my husband's. But I couldn't stop the drugs. Finally, I decided to talk to God one day when I needed to just rest.

I prayed, *If you can hear me, God, please hear me. I am probably pregnant. I have all the signs. If you can hear me, God, I am asking that you take from me this gift of life. I don't deserve to have another life to care for. I am sick. I need help, but I know it is too late. I've poisoned a precious life. I am so selfish. I didn't think I would get pregnant. I can't stop. I don't know how.*

The next day I was in the emergency room.

I didn't want to die. I had a beautiful little two-year-old boy, and he was everything to me. Now I had a baby inside me. I wanted to be a good mom, but I was hooked on smoking crack, and my marriage was based on lies and abuse, including mental abuse.

Not only did I miscarry, but I was still pregnant. Turns out I had twins. This was a very emotional time in my life, and I made the decision to never be pregnant again. I didn't deserve such a, so I pleaded with the doctors to remove my tubes. Before the decision was made, they found I was also pregnant in a tube, and if a specialist had not been brought in at my request, I would not be here today.

The doctor on duty wanted me to go home and call my OB/GYN, but my sister-in-law came in and told them I wasn't going anywhere and, of course, I agreed. The pain was severe. When they finally took me into the surgery room STAT, my tube exploded. When I awoke from surgery, I was assured I would never be pregnant again. They had removed my one healthy tube. Sadness overwhelmed me.

My follow-up visit with the doctor concluded with these words: "I don't know what you are doing, but whatever it is, I give you two weeks or no more than a month to live." My weight loss was at about ten pounds per week, and now I was at seventy-five pounds. It was as if I was disintegrating.

I knew God must be out there somewhere. My final decision was to leave, get out, and run. I was always running from things and circumstances. Once again I ran. I called my family, and they were great in giving me money and on the road I went.

STARTING OVER

I headed to Illinois where my mother resided, but her idea was for me to stop in and see my mother-in-law in North Carolina. God was guiding the ride from Florida to North Carolina all the way, and His plan was in the works. I made that drive with a drink in one hand, my cocaine in the other, and my son on my lap half the time. When I finally arrived at my mother-in-law's (she was a new Christian herself), everyone was waiting for me with arms open wide. I experienced a warmth I didn't know before. On the first part of the trip I had managed to lose money and was broke enough that I couldn't travel any farther.

My sister-in-law and her husband were there. She gave me a hug, told me she loved me and was glad we were there.. But now something had changed about her. She didn't drink anymore and she told me she had dedicated her sobriety to God and to her new Savior, Jesus Christ. She gave Him all the glory.

When they hugged me, I got a sense of peace I had never felt before. The hugs seemed to pour life back into me. I hadn't seen Josh so happy with his family before. I knew, then, I was in the right place at the right time.

Something changed inside of me while I was with them all. I didn't do any drugs. I didn't have a drink. I didn't even think about these things while I was there. Sunday came and I was excited to join them in going to church even though I believed I deserved to die instead. I had lost sight of so many things in life, and by now I was just plain tired of running away.

As I watched my little boy go into the church with me, his smile melted my heart. I had never really noticed his sweet nature and his smile until that day. My selfishness and destructive behavior had blinded me.

At church everyone made us feel welcome, as if they had known us forever. I don't recall what the pastor said that day, nor do I remember the songs we sang. What I do remember, however, was crying fountains of tears as I accepted Jesus into my heart and asked Him to forgive all of my sins. I asked Him to take care of me and told Him I was tired of trying to do it on my own. I wanted to live for Him. I asked for healing in my body from all of the destructive things I had done. I put my face in my hands, knelt down, and cried until I couldn't cry anymore. Soon I found myself surrounded by people praying for me, agreeing with me in my prayers, and just being there with me. I felt I was being cleansed.

While I had prayed many times as a child, this time was different. I really meant it when I asked God to save me, and I had never had an encounter with Him as I did this day. When we were done praying we began singing *Victory in Jesus,* raising our hands high into the air, and praising God for all He was worth. I knew the victory was won. The battle was in the hands of Jesus now, and I didn't want to go back to where I had been before. I didn't want any drugs; I didn't want alcohol; and I didn't want to leave this place.

When we left church that morning, I was exhausted and went back to my mother-in-law's to rest. I was eager to go back to church again that evening for another church service. I wanted more of God, and I had NEVER felt such a peace as I did that day. I was truly free.

I never experienced a withdrawal from drugs, and I didn't suffer the things I could have. I was ready to change. I had already started by throwing out all the drugs and dumping all the alcohol I had stashed. I didn't hesitate. I knew Jesus was in my heart and that He had healed my body. He had removed the desire for drugs or alcohol.

I started loving my son in a way I hadn't ever done before. I told him everything was going to be okay now because mommy was going to be there for him from now on. Jesus had forgiven me, and I even forgave myself. My physical appetite was back, as was my appetite for knowing everything about Jesus. My mother-in-law gave me a Bible in which she inscribed her favorite verse, which also became mine, Romans 8:28: *And we know that God causes everything to work together for the good of those who love God and are called according to his purpose for them.*

I called my mom to tell her the great news. She was very pleased. I began reading the Bible every day and attending church whenever I could. I didn't always understand everything, but I wanted to keep learning.

I read about marriage and how God had a plan to mend my own marriage. Also I remember finding the answer to the question of what God thinks of two women together. The answer was that it was sin and unacceptable to God. I wrote to my friend to let her know what I had found out about this, but I never received a letter back from her. I figured she didn't want to hear that what she was doing was wrong.

I started thinking about returning to work and going back to school. My mother-in-law graciously allowed me and Josh to stay with her until I was able to find and maintain a place of our own. Before long I was working at Pizza Hut, and my in-laws willingly took care of Josh while I worked. I started taking a night class to complete my high school diploma. Having quit school in the ninth grade, I had a lot of work ahead of me.

Night school was great. The teacher was good, and there were plenty of people to help me understand what I was learning, including my family. I had never liked school before, but really enjoyed attending night classes. My sister-in-law ended up joining me in class two nights a week, so that made it even more enjoyable.

Everything seemed to be going well for me. I had a job. I was going to school to better myself. I had a second chance to be a good mother to Josh. However, the one thing still missing was Robert, so I began praying for him. I didn't know what would happen to our marriage, but I did know I wanted God to help us become everything good again. I wasn't sure if he would want to come to North Carolina and live, but I was not going back to Florida to live, if I could help it. If Robert were to move to where I was living, it would take God to change his mind. I wanted him to know I had changed, and I could do what was right and follow through on making us work again.

I decided it was time to go back to Florida and get my stuff. Heading back to Florida and facing all the temptations I hadn't had to deal with since being in North Carolina and giving my life to Jesus would be a real test. But I thought I could handle anything now and not go backwards. I was strong enough. I planned to read God's Word every day. Along with that, I would pray every day and didn't think anything could go wrong.

I was learning everything all over again now that I was a new per-son. I was learning the right way to talk, walk, act, and dress. I was excited about seeing Robert again and figured if he saw the change in me – as a new person, a better person, a different person – that would win him back. We would be better together and be really happy for the rest of our lives. With my Bible in hand and God on my side, that would be enough to make our marriage work again.

I was so excited thinking about getting there that I found myself driving faster and faster until I heard a noise in the engine. I pulled over and opened the steaming hood. It had overheated. I waited a few minutes until it cooled and got in, but barely managed to drive to the next exit and find an auto shop. I prayed and asked God for help. I only had an out-of-state check with me, which the auto shop wouldn't accept.

I managed to get the car going again and thought if I could at least get to a U-Haul, I could rent a truck and leave the car there until I returned to pick it up once it was fixed. When I got to U-Haul, a man who was a Christian helped me. He let me hang around there, even though I couldn't afford to rent a truck and I couldn't do anything about my car. I would have to leave it there until I could pick it up later.

I called my mother-in-law and also my other sister-in-law who lived in Gainesville with her husband. She agreed to come pick me up. My mother-in-law had called Robert, and he was going to pick me up in Gainesville and take me back to his mom's in North Carolina.

When my sister-in-law arrived, she took me to her apartment. She and her husband were newlyweds and I felt like an intruder in their small apartment. When Robert arrived the next morning, he had come on his motorcycle, so I was only able to take with me what I could fit in a duffle bag on the bike. We rode until evening and stopped at a hotel for the night.

Our time together wasn't as happy as I had hoped. I figured we could just start fresh right away and things would head down a better road. But there was too much bad stuff between us for that to happen, at least right away. But why couldn't he just forgive me right away as I had already forgiven him?

When we arrived at my mother-in-law's, everyone met us and hugged us. Josh ran to both of us, and we both wrapped our arms around him as if we had always been a loving family. I enjoyed every moment we were all together and hoped and prayed for the best.

I still had to get my things up here from Florida. The decision was made for me to take a bus to Florida. I needed to call my dad because I couldn't do this without him. I would have to store some things at Dad's place.

When I got to Florida, Dad picked me up at the bus stop and took me to my house. Once I started gathering my belongings, I realized how much stuff I had. Dad and I went out to eat the night we arrived, and he asked me about this new life of mine that didn't allow me to have a drink with him. He had seen how bad I looked when I left Florida and was glad to see I was looking more alive now, even though he wasn't convinced Jesus was the reason for it.

While I collected my things, I met up with some old friends. I managed to stay sober with them, for which I was patting myself on the back. But all of a sudden a girl in this group made a pass at me. I was in shock, and yet it brought back old feelings and desires. I wanted to put the past behind me and not be tempted again in this area at all. I wanted to focus on my marriage.

I started going through all the stuff in my house, but it was taking too long, I was running out of time and getting weaker in my will each moment. I should have been strong enough to say no to a drink and no to smoking and especially no to sex, but I didn't feel strong now. I had gone to church while I was in Florida but struggled with feelings of being unworthy of forgiveness.

I had crossed the line again and, in my mind and with a lack of willpower, was no better than I had been before. I felt I really hadn't changed. But I knew I had to go forward with Jesus no matter what. I had to get out of Florida immediately and didn't feel I could stay another day. Nothing I owned, or that Robert and I owned together, was worth keeping for all that I had already gained with Jesus.

I called Dad and asked if he would help me get on the next bus out and if I could leave some of my stuff with him. I'd let someone else have the rest. I wouldn't miss anything except some pictures I had planned on taking with me. I pretty much left our house full of stuff. It contained all Robert and I had worked for together, and now it was gone.

Robert had decided to stay in North Carolina since he wasn't working in Florida anyway. So we stayed with his mother who became like a mother to me, like someone I had always wanted my own mother to be.

The ride back to North Carolina took a couple of days but gave me time to pray and read the Bible. It was a time for me to renew my relationship with God. I just had to believe God was still hearing me when I prayed.

At the last stop before reaching my mother-in-law's, I did get a chance to talk to a girl on the bus about Jesus and shared with her about reading the Bible. She was cleaning up some of her own messes in her life and was going through some changes.

Once I settled in at my mother-in-law's, I didn't miss going to church at all. I would go Sunday mornings, Sunday evenings, Wednes-day evenings, and to every get-together for fellowship that I could.

Meanwhile I had received a call from U-Haul. One of their trucks had gone out of gear and rolled into my car, making it undrivable and totaling it. So not only would I not have to pay to get my car fixed from the initial problem, U-Haul would also pay for it to be towed to where I was. With this extra money we didn't have to pay out, Robert and I were able to afford some acreage up the mountain from where my mother-in-law lived. We got a camper to live in until we were able to purchase a home. God took care of our needs to keep us together as a family and begin again.

We began working on building our home. Robert traded in his motorcycle for a horse for Josh. I had always wanted a horse, too. In fact, I had always wanted to live the country life – have a garden, grow my own veggies and potatoes. And not long after this Robert came home one day with some pigs, rabbits, chickens, ducks, and even a goat to milk. I was more than busy enough with my job, with night school, and with taking care of all the animals. Robert traded some wood for a tiller so I could get my garden going. He had found a regular job, but spent time after work with some new friends drink-ing and doing drugs when he could get a hold of them. I chose not to be involved in these outings so I would not be tempted to head down that road again.

Meanwhile, I kept hoping and praying Robert would change and let God be his guide. I thought he actually got saved one Sunday after Josh had prayed for him, but he soon found other things more important to him than going to church.

In the summer of 1988, I took a test to graduate from night school and failed by only a couple of questions and was about to give up. My mom and dad decided to come for my graduation ceremony, so I took the test one last time. How could I tell them I hadn't passed? I failed again, but they came anyway and I had a good visit with them. Mom saw me as a different person and that I was finally happy after so many years. I had quit smoking on Josh's birthday that year. I had simply turned my desire for smoking over to God, and He took it away.

In November of 1988, I learned I had indeed passed my high school equivalency test and earned my diploma. They had made a mistake in counting my credits.

With renewed excitement, I applied to nursing school but found there was a two-year wait to get in. I had been working as a nursing assistant for some time but wanted to complete school so I could be more than just an assistant.

Robert kept coming home with more and more animals for me to take care of. And what upset me most was he was not being the man of God I had hoped and prayed for. Robert really hadn't changed.

I started to feel like I didn't want to put up with this anymore. Maybe if we went on a vacation it would help things, so we prepared to go visit Mom in Illinois for Christmas. Robert was working at a car dealership and making pretty good money. He had to dress nice for work every day, and he looked good to me. But I reminded myself that his outward appearance was what I went after the first time we met.

When we got to Illinois, my stepsister and her husband invited us out to the bar where they usually went for karaoke and dancing. That sounded good to me since I had felt pretty cooped up living in the mountains. I figured one night couldn't hurt. Mom advised against it but realized she couldn't tell me what to do. I wasn't too concerned about it, and besides, Robert wanted to go out and I was trying to keep him happy.

When we got to the bar I told myself I wasn't going to drink, but I sure wanted to just have one drink. You see, I didn't have a problem with drinking; it was drugs that I almost died from. I had vowed to never touch cocaine again, but just being at the bar opened the door to compromise.

We headed back to our home in the mountains after Christmas. I stopped going to church when we got back because Robert said it was better for me to stay home with him.

Robert and I were having credit problems. When I called one day to see about paying our debts, the woman I talked with turned out to be the wife of the man I had had an affair with in Florida, but both of whom were also our friends. They had moved to Tennessee. I told Robert about this and we made plans to go see them.

After we visited them, they decided to come pay us a visit. They were happy for me and how my life had turned around. We started visiting each other's homes more often.

Robert had taken a temporary job at the dealership in another town. At first I thought this would be a good thing because he would be able to make more money. I would still visit our friends in Tennessee, sometimes taking Josh with me and sometimes staying overnight. The wife and I always had the boys' days planned when we were together. We even took a trip together to Illinois where her mother lived not far from mine.

We went to the bars a few times together where I would drink, but soon I would have more than my limit and get sick. When the husband and I happened to be alone together at their house, he would make advances at me. I always said no, but the lustful feelings were still with me even though I thought they had disappeared long ago. Eventually I ended up giving in to them.

In the middle of all of this, my old friend Danny called and left a message. He was still in the Air Force and had been married, had a kid, and was now divorced. He was coming through our area and thought it would be nice to meet up with me and meet Josh and Robert. Robert didn't know much about my past life, as I didn't talk about it much with him. But I had told him about Danny and that we were just good friends. I was excited to see Danny because we could just talk so well together, something I couldn't do with Robert.

Danny came and stayed overnight. We all went horseback riding one day. The visit was short, but it was good to see him again. I got his phone number and address, as he was now living in Maine. He realized my marriage to Robert was not the best, but I tried not to say anything to him about Robert.

I had not been living the way I should have been, and I couldn't forgive myself for that. I tried to, but I'd just end up staying up late and having a drink. Then I started smoking again and hanging out with my husband and doing whatever he did and going wherever he went. Then the fights intensified the more we drank together.

My sister-in-law came up to our house one Sunday to plead with me to return to church. She asked me just to come back this one Sun-day. I started crying. "I'm not coming back," I told her. I had done so much I could never go back. I believed the Holy Spirit was upset with me, so I hardened my heart and I told her I was going to do what I wanted to do from now on. Even though I heard the Spirit's still, small voice inside of me telling me *Don't do it, don't walk away, don't give up,* I told her not to ask me to go to church again.

My sister-in-law brought my Bible back to me on another day because I had left it at church the last time I had gone. I accepted it from her but kept it out of sight in my home most of the time.

I knew how much God had changed me when He saved me. He had cleansed me instantly, but I had failed Him miserably. I thought I was strong enough to face my past and not give in to the tempta-tions anymore, but at the same time I was thoroughly enjoying all the attention I was getting from my ex-drug-dealer friend in Tennessee.

We found times to be alone, until one time we were caught out in the open, mostly because we had been drinking and then he was driving. It was embarrassing and it could have meant jail for both of us. I was scared. The Scripture verse came to my mind about all secrets being brought into the open, and that was surely the case now, but I never told Robert about it.

Another secret. Another betrayal. One more night out with Robert changed everything at home. We got into another fight, and it got physical. We each wanted to have the last word, but he won this time. I went to my sister-in-law's down the road from us, taking Josh with me.

My sister-in-law told me to give Robert another chance. Even though what he had done was not right, he was still my husband. But I was tired of hearing that from so many people. He wanted me home with him and didn't like my going to church. He said I had a goody-goody attitude. But I knew there was nothing goody-goody about me anymore. I was as cold as ice. Even though he wanted to try to work this out between us again, I did not. I didn't see anything left to work out. I was tired of taking care of all of his stuff and never being appreciated for it.

About this time my other brother-in-law's wife called to ask if I could come for a visit. They lived in Georgia and were going through a divorce. I was going to take Josh with me, and she had the whole weekend planned out for us: a babysitter for Josh and her kids, a place for us to party, and I would get to meet her new boyfriend and his roommate John.

This time I really partied. I was too self-conscious to dance unless I had a drink or two first. John liked me a lot upon first meeting me and I really enjoyed his company. He was nice and treated me with respect and kindness. He was much older than I was. I made it clear there was no way we could be more than just friends as I was still married.

Danny still called and tried to convince me we should be together because I was not being treated well by Robert. He said he could take the place of Robert for me. His words felt so right to me, but he was so far away. It made me wonder.

I told Robert I was going to give him two years to change, but he wanted me to change instead. He wanted me to go back to being the old person I was before I got saved, the person he liked better. So I went back to being that old person, but I also became cold to his needs.

I thought I should have just told him about the affair with the husband of our good friends, since I hadn't shown any interest lately in going to visit them. He must have known something was going on, but he never said so, and neither did I.

I was still determined to leave Robert and go to my mom's. Danny wanted me to come straight to Maine; my ex-sister-in-law said I could stay with her; and John said I could move in with him. My friend in Tennessee didn't want me to go, but instead wanted me to work things out with Robert. She didn't know, and I didn't have the heart to tell her, I was leaving to get away from her husband also.

I had everything figured out. I got directions from Mom to her place. She already knew I wasn't going to give Robert another chance to hit me. My mother was sympathetic to this, as my real father had regularly abused her before she managed to get away from him.

The only love I retained was for my son who was my life. I would never hurt him. I did not want him to be raised in this hate. No mat-ter what, I would always protect Josh, my pride and joy. I felt I would die if I ever lost him.

The plan was to leave as soon as I picked Josh up from school; I would be packed and ready to go. I wasn't going to stop anywhere until I got to Mom's.

As Josh and I headed out, a country song came on the radio that talked about *these chains are gone.* I suddenly felt relief. I was out at last and headed to Mom's. I knew things wouldn't be the same at Mom's. She had given her life to Jesus, and I thought this time we would actually get along. I had seen a new Mom, a Mom who might really care about me.

Once I got to Illinois, I went to see a lawyer to start divorce proceed-ings, only to cancel them a little while later. I wasn't ready, so I waited.

I got Josh enrolled in school and found a job at Chuck E. Cheese's. For years I hadn't wanted to come back here because I had such ter-rible memories of living and growing up here. I was ashamed of who I had become. But I had learned about forgiveness, and it was time now to put into use what I had learned to make a better life for myself.

It wasn't long before Josh and I had a place to call our own. Mom said I couldn't stay with her, if I planned on drinking or staying out at the bars. Nor could I use her to be a babysitter to do anything like that either. I started going back to church soon, but my heart just wasn't really there.

Robert called many times the first couple of months. I made myself so sick. Every time he called I couldn't keep food down. I just wanted him to leave me alone.

Before long, however, I decided it was time for me to take a trip – to Maine or to Georgia. I wasn't sure where my final destination would be anymore because Mom and her husband were moving to Arkansas. Some issues had come up between Mom's husband and his ex-wife that caused him to quit his job of twenty years.

I couldn't leave, however, until school ended for Josh, who had gotten the chicken pox. Dad was also coming for a visit, as well as my sister. When my sister arrived, we all went out one night, and Sis decided to stay longer than Dad or I wanted, so I drove her car home. The next day she called and informed me she was getting married to a guy she met the night before. She was convinced he was the one for her. She didn't know where she was but would find out, ask the guy's name, and then call me back. I guess she had learned what I had always lived by: to do whatever you felt like doing.

While on the phone with Robert one night, I began talking about returning and going to work in Georgia. But later I wondered if I should go to Maine to see Danny instead. Robert wanted to see Josh before I made any decision, and I really wasn't ready to let go of Robert. I had always loved him. We just couldn't live together. Our conversations since I left Georgia were always bitter. It had become a war for us as to who had the most power in parenting Josh.

Somehow we managed to agree to Josh spending time with Robert no matter what. I had been kept from knowing my real dad, and I didn't want that for Josh. My child never knowing his father would not be acceptable.

I decided to make a trip to Georgia just as a vacation. I didn't feel like I belonged in Illinois and thought a vacation would give me a chance to decide what I really wanted to do.

So Josh and I went to Georgia. We stayed with my ex-sister-in-law again, who was still friends with Robert's brother. She and I had developed a girls'-night-out relationship when I visited her before, along with her new boyfriend and his roommate John. John had recently divorced and owned a very nice home with enough room for my sister-in-law's two girls, Josh, and me. While I was there we enjoyed going out to eat, shopping, and having cocktails.

I felt pretty pampered by John. He was full of good energy and stayed plenty active even though he was considerably older than me. In general, I enjoyed the company of older people, since usually they carried on interesting conversations. John was no exception. We laughed together, and he always treated me with respect. He put my feelings and needs ahead of anyone else's, and treated Josh and my sister-in-law's children well. I loved the sound as they laughed a lot together, too. He ran the dishwasher, made reservations for us, bought me flowers, made dinner, and served dinner by candlelight with or without company.

I made the decision to move back to Georgia, and my new girl-friend decided to take some time off from her job to go back to Illinois to help me prepare for the move. John had offered to let me stay at his house once I moved back. Robert was excited because Josh was going to stay with him while I was in the process of moving. My girlfriend's daughters stayed with someone else on our way up to Illinois, so we borrowed her ex-husband's truck and headed out for our next adventure.

Mom came to visit me while we were packing up in Illinois. I was a mess when she arrived. I had been drinking most of the time since I left Georgia. Mom didn't mince her words. "I don't want you to continue drinking," she said. "It's getting way out of hand."

Tears stung my eyes. I knew she wanted to say even more to me than she did, but finally she just said, "I love you, and I can't live your life for you, but I will be praying for you." *Praying for me.* Worry showed on Mom's face, but I also saw her disappointment in my behavior.

Mom was probably wondering what I would do next. Where would I run to? Who would I hide from? What would it take for me to call on Jesus again?

Once Mom moved to Arkansas, I focused on packing up my stuff. I sold what I could so I wouldn't have as much to store.

My girlfriend and I picked up her girls on the drive back down to Georgia and then we headed to her place. John offered to let me put the things I brought with me in his garage, until I decided what I was going to do.

I needed to find another job in Georgia. John owned his own business and suggested I help him with the small stuff there with the possibility of doing more later, if I wanted to. I wanted to find something regular and part-time because I had been on vacation and needed to replenish the savings I had.

My friends and I started having cocktails every evening and get-ting together for lunch some days. I found myself becoming addicted to brandy. This new "drug" wasn't cheap, and quickly became my evening-after-dinner drink. In no time, I was drinking a bottle a night and talked on the phone until all hours of the night. A lot of this phone time was with Danny, whom I considered my one last friend. He was the one I had stayed in contact with for so many years of my "adventuresome" life.

While I was in a new place with new friends, I was still making the same bad choices and committing the same sins as I had before, with the exception of doing cocaine. I had vowed to stay away from it and managed to keep that vow. I still thought I could quit alcohol anytime I wanted.

I decided I would go back to church. John and I went to church together, but it wasn't good. John was Methodist and the church we went to was huge. I wasn't sure why I was going there. The only thing I felt whenever we went was shame and guilt.

John wasn't the best at keeping up with his own financial obligations, and finally his house was foreclosed on and we had to move out. I went out that night and decided I was not going to go back until I had figured out a new plan for my life.

By now I had learned who the real John was. Not only was he a jealous man, he also wanted to control my every move. Robert had given me so much room to be free and to do whatever I wanted. I wasn't sure what it would take to get me away from John now. Money? A person to help me? A new place to go?

What did open up for me was an apartment in a different dis-trict of Georgia, which was closer to Robert, who had moved off the mountain in North Carolina in order to find work.

Now that I lived closer to Robert, I could visit him at his work and take Josh to see him as often as possible. But he had no need for me now.

I eventually connected with John again. He persuaded me to come back into his life and promised to let me be whoever I wanted to be. I gave in. He helped me find a lawyer to have some simple divorce papers drawn up. His objective was to marry me after my divorce from Robert was finalized.

The papers were sent and the divorce was denied, until we agreed on everything, which we did except for visitation rights regarding Josh. I had assumed I would let Robert see Josh whenever he wanted to, and that was good enough. But child support also became an issue, which I didn't want to receive from Robert, and I was also required to have a phone with me at all times so Robert could always contact me about Josh wherever I was. I let him have our property since I was able to have custody of Josh.

It was bittersweet when the judge asked if this was all we wanted when the final papers were drawn up. I admitted to the judge there was nothing between us anymore worth reconciling, as we had tried all the recommended avenues of fixing things between us. I conceded. It was official now. I would never have to worry about Robert taking Josh away from me even after all the threats he had made.

Even after the divorce, however, I struggled with who I was and what I had done to Josh and to Robert. John, on the other hand, was way too happy for me. After the divorce was over, I felt like I wanted to sleep, not celebrate. But John insisted I needed to bounce back and enjoy the new adventure ahead of me.

I became consumed with what I wanted. One night John and I went out with his girls and my Josh to a party with several other people. After a few drinks, John wanted to leave, but the girls and Josh were having fun with some other children. John and I were playing cards with the adults and I was winning. So there was no way I was going to leave at that point. One of the guys across the table from us kept looking at me as if he was interested. John didn't like that. At first I wasn't looking back at the guy with any interest, but I figured since he wasn't shy about it, I would join in on the flirtation. I liked a good game of jealousy. But John didn't play like this and finally got upset enough that he left the party. I usually drove myself to parties in case things like this happened, but tonight I hadn't. I had trusted John not to leave me and Josh in someone else's house without transportation, and this time he had done exactly that.

I waited and waited for John to return, but he didn't. I even paged him, asking him to return. This guy and I played all the games that night, including sex, until I knew I had to get Josh up from sleep-ing so we could leave. I just couldn't stay there anymore. We started walking back home in the middle of the night, in a not-so-good part of town. I took a chance to trust a truck driver who gave us a ride to a place close to home.

Once again, I decided I needed to cut back on my drinking because I was putting my son in dangerous situations. I never wanted to hurt him or let anyone else hurt him, and yet here I was doing exactly that by my actions and lack of self-control.

John and I did work things out, and we decided we would do other things together besides drinking and partying. We went fish-ing and to the underground mall and didn't drink when we went out. I decided I wanted to go back to work full-time and also wanted to go back to school.

I signed up for college and got a job at T.J. Maxx. I had always wanted to work retail and now I was finally able to and became the best employee at the service desk. I felt things were starting to come together for me again. I looked into a computer programming course, because entrance into nursing school was backed up for at least a year. My mom had suggested I go to college for something that would be a moneymaker. The first quarter I made Cs in all my classes except for business math where I managed to get an A/B. But I went home from classes every day with a headache. I knew I really wanted to be in nursing school, so I tried another option to head in that direc-tion, but my request for entrance into this program was denied. I was stuck where I was. School and work seemed to leave very little time for Josh, so I reduced my hours to part-time at T.J. Maxx even though I loved working there.

I looked forward to my days off and our weekends together. I allowed Josh to visit his dad often and sometimes would drive an hour just for Robert to see him for an hour.

John had some friends in the mountains of Georgia, and we would sometimes go there. They had a pond on their property where we could fish and go paddle boating. They also had a pool table in their house, and I gained a sense of self-esteem by often beating the others at pool.

I thought I was doing pretty well, so I felt I deserved a drink every so often. Besides, I had more fun going out with friends when I drank. John and I took a weekend off together one time and went to a place where no one knew us. We danced and enjoyed dinner and he asked me to marry him. That deserved a drink as well, in my mind.

So there I was again, back to the same old me. What was I think-ing? That I could just have one drink? Who was I kidding? Every so often I would miss a day of school in trying to keep up with classes and would resort to a drink to be able to stay awake. Then I was awake all night and in the morning, it would be time to take Josh to school. The long days and nights were starting to catch up to me again and no one could help me. I couldn't stop. I kept trying and I couldn't do it. What would it take?

I started to feel smothered by John. I would go to school, head to work, and then come straight home. He figured out how long it would take me to get home. If I was late by even five minutes he would start accusing me of messing around or of stopping in to see someone. Sometimes he was even waiting in the parking lot of my work with Josh, until I would finish for the day. I started to get upset with his being jealous of my co-workers or of me even speaking to certain people.

One night I had had enough. I packed a suitcase for Josh and decided to meet up with my ex-sister-in-law and her new boyfriend who were heading out to the lake for the whole day. I had taken the day off and had just gotten paid, so I had some money to be able to pitch in to go waterskiing.

Josh and I talked on the way to my ex-sister-is-law's place. I asked him how things were going at the house with John while I was working. I also asked about his school friends and his teachers and if there was anything I needed to know to help him out. I listened as he spoke of school first, saying he wasn't happy with one of the teachers who was hard on him. I assured him I would go in and talk with the teacher.

He started crying as he talked about John being harsh with him at home. Josh was eight years old and it sounded like he was being treated like a dog. When John didn't want him around, Josh said he would kick him all the way to his room and tell him not to come out until his mother got home. At that point I knew it was good that we had made plans to be on the lake and away from John that day.

The relationship John and I had was only headed into more problems. Summer break from school was about to start so I had to make some different arrangements. I needed to keep my job, but I could change some things with school if need be. I didn't want John hurt-ing my precious son anymore.

During this time I had managed to get a disorderly conduct charge leveled against me. I had run from a situation with Josh and had put him in danger. Robert called the police and they found me hiding with Josh in the woods. That cost me a night in jail and some com-munity service.

Another time when I got drunk, I decided to go back and set some things straight with John. This was not a good plan at the time. As I headed down the interstate, I was doing 85 mph with the car radio blaring music. The next thing I knew flashing lights filled my rearview mirror as a cop followed me. I was speeding, and I had beer bottles all over the floor of my car. It took two officers to assist me to their car. The tow truck came to take my car, and I headed to jail for DUI.

I called Mom collect from the jail. We talked only briefly, but long enough for her to tell me she wasn't going to bail me out of jail. "You need to get help." She ended the conversation saying, "I love you, and I'll be praying for you."

I didn't think God was listening to me anymore. I believed because I had walked away from God that I was not allowed back. My sins were many, and now this jail time just added to them. I was grateful I didn't have Josh with me this time. He was safe with his dad.

Since this was my first offense, I was released on my own recognizance but had to see the judge later that month. John came to pick me up. I hadn't had any sleep and was drained emotionally. We went and got my car later that day, and even though I lost my license for six months, we were able to get the car back with the help of a friend. The judge had taken away my license for six months except for work and school. He also ordered an assessment for me, required me to go to AA, and made me pay a large fine. Some friends said I got off easy, but I sure didn't see it that way. Who were they kidding? I lost my license and was on probation.

PART 2
HITTING BOTTOM

Dear Mom,

First I want to apologize for whatever it was I said on the answering machine. I was drunk and I just know that I called. I have really done it this time, just messed little Joshua's life all up. Just maybe he will be okay. I am so embarrassed for my improper actions the other night. I had gotten very, very drunk and found myself sitting in jail one last time. I just am not a good drinker and every time I drink, I just make things so bad for everyone, especially those who love me. I am scraped up all over my body and can't move my hands very well. I did not want to live anymore, so I took some pills I had hoped would kill me. Of course, they did not and I am glad.

Today I told John I would be staying home as I have a lot to think about.

I just got through praying and reading the Bible. I feel a lot better. Now to stick with it. I have no place else to turn and am tired of hurting everyone.

When I went to jail no one knew where I was except you, and I didn't know if I may have ruined everything we had together. I pray for all to find in their heart to forgive me. I am an alcoholic and I have asked God to help me.

I am a nervous wreck. I just can't do anything right. I have made so many mistakes, and I do blame all of this on my drinking. Now I can never, ever pick up another drink again. I may have lost Joshua forever. He is with his father, and now this may cause me to lose him. Maybe in time I will get him back. Robert met Josh and me at the end of the road. I was hiding with Joshua in the woods when Robert got there, and he brought two police cars with him. Then he took Joshua from me, and they took me to jail for public drunkenness.

Oh, Mom, what have I done? I can't change what I have said or done. I consider myself in deep depression and just wanting peace so bad.

November 1991

I felt I had hit bottom and called Danny. He had just bought a truck and was excited about coming to get Josh and me. First, however, I needed permission from the probation officer, and I needed a plan from Danny to get me started and have my fine paid in full. I thanked Danny for trying to save me from my own destruction, for paying my fine, and for being my friend even when I wasn't a very good friend to him.

As Danny left Maine and headed down to Georgia to get Josh and me, I discreetly packed all my things and got ready to go. I had to tell Robert and he made sure I had a phone with me so he could contact Josh when he wanted to. When Danny arrived, Robert asked him to take care of us and to make sure he could see Josh when he wanted to. Danny told Robert he was planning to marry me, but being mar-ried again was the furthest thing from my mind.

Danny let me have my own room in his house in Maine. I needed some solitude and a quiet place to try to heal and look at my life differently. Danny went back to work. His son was about the same age as Josh, so Josh had a new friend nearby.

Danny paid his bills. He made sure food was in the house, and he bought me smokes and beer so I could stay home and drink. I couldn't drive my car because of a transmission problem, but it was a small town and everything was within walking distance. It had everything I needed, but it also had at least one person who reminded me of another place I have lived. It seemed at times as if I were traveling in a circle.

As each place reminded me of another, I once again found myself returning to old habits. I drank more and more as the disappoint-ments of life caught up with me again. Depression overwhelmed me along with a lack of self-worth. Drinking served to cover up my brokenness. I totally hit bottom again.

I was tormented with thoughts of how I could have fixed things – all the things I should have done and did not do.

November 29, 1991

I sat in Maine with a beer in hand and life running in repeated circles. Decisions confused me. Turbulent feelings of love and regrets for mistakes clashed within me. I couldn't get what I truly desired from life. For the first time I actually realized I was the most confused person I'd ever met. Why? When? And for how long? These were questions I couldn't answer. I second-guessed myself many times, wondering if I was doing the right thing. Is i*t too late for happiness? What, what, what can I do? I* had prayed and cried and still I had no sense of direction. I knew I was hindering my life, and just couldn't believe someone could love me anymore.

I wanted another man for one thing, and one thing only. I couldn't believe I would shatter my happiness for that one feeling, but I did. Now what could I do? Readjusting was the hardest thing I had to do. Being hurt was the only life I really and truly knew. I wanted that call from John, hoping he would say he didn't love me, although I knew he really did. But I also knew his love was fading and would be gone soon. Bad as it sounded, I couldn't go on knowing the hurt never mended.

I didn't want to cry all the time, but I couldn't stop the pain. At times I wished I could just go back to Georgia. At the same time I knew Joshua would not be happy, and I would have to give him up. No way.

I blamed John for this pain because of him not loving my son like he said he would and should have. I cursed myself. Day in and day out the pain consumed me.

My trust in men was gone, vanished. Could I ever believe a man again? What would it take to find a man who was true to his word? I wanted a man to love me for me, a man to respect me, a man to confide in me, a man to trust me, and a man whom I could trust, a man of God.

Danny was my best friend. I could tell him anything. One day I told him about my troubles from the very beginning. I told him how I had been violated at the age of five, and then again at age seven, and again at age eleven, by three different people. As I relived it in my mind, the tears came like buckets. Danny embraced me as he listened, and I continued on to the age of fourteen. I told him about my fight to escape from home. Danny grew angry that someone could hurt a child like I had been hurt. He wondered why I had held onto this for so long without getting help. I told him I believed I needed more women around me who would understand. He called some new friends of mine for that help.

December 2, 1991

Since we moved from Georgia to Limestone, Maine, in the middle of the school year, Joshua's first day in his new school was December 2. He seemed like he'd be all right. I met his teacher and she seemed very nice. I called John just to see how he was doing. He decided it would be best if we did not contact each other anymore.

John had been a part of my life for two years. There was a lot of pain in those years but also a lot of good and happy times. I left him and struggled with some regret for my actions, although I did know it would happen someday. I really still loved him a lot, but we had stopped talking about Joshua and how he needed happiness as much as anyone else. Although a part of my life was unhappy with John, I really wanted us to be married. Robert, Joshua's dad, had not even called since we left Georgia, and Joshua hadn't even mentioned Robert – that was pretty bad.

I remembered when I left Robert in 1988. I never thought I could go on in life. It seemed like I would die with all the pain. Now it was hard to let go of John. He had just been so good to me and during the good times had showed Joshua so much love. *But I must not for-get the pain we caused each other.* I needed to look at the new life I had as a start fresh and to believe God had a reason for all that had happened in my life.

December 3, 1991

Joshua was very happy in his new school. He already had four friends. I needed to get a job. Sitting at home was fine but not ideal. Working could help keep my mind off things. Writing things down began to help me, but I wished it was Friday so I could drink and not worry about getting up early. I hated getting up early and being alone all day.

The kids in Maine were very well behaved, unlike any I'd seen before. That was good for Joshua; he needed friends. All kids needed friends. I believed he would have had a problem with that if we had stayed with John. As I pondered this, I thought about having a beer and seeing how things went. What I really would have liked was to go down to the bar, but I didn't want to get a reputation as the town drunk or anything.

My thoughts drifted to marriage. I wondered what it would be like to be married again. The thought scared me because of all I had been through. *If I ever do get married again, I just want it to be God's will, not mine. I* prayed about finding a good church, and that I wouldn't be a drinker anymore. Right then I was still trying to adjust. Joshua had done well.

December 5, 1991

The move was hard on me. I struggled to find balance and mental clarity. I went into it with a defensive attitude. My mind was confused I couldn't even begin to live. That song played on the radio again: *When a Man Loves A Woman.* John and I shared precious moments with that song.

It was time for me to decide what I was going to do. I hated decisions, especially because I make all the wrong ones. I needed counseling or something. I had to do something. All good things come in time. I just didn't know how long it would be till the good part of me would come out.

I loved Joshua so very much, but I didn't love myself anymore. Because I didn't love myself, I couldn't accept that anyone could love me. I had to dig deep and find an answer to this charade in my life before I flipped out, or I wouldn't even be good for Joshua. I wondered if all the pain was worth it.

The hard truth was I didn't want to love anymore. It hurt too bad, cut like a knife, and took all my energy to get rid of everything. My drinking grew worse. I had to get control again and find myself.

It didn't work with John because of Joshua and him not getting along. It turned my love for them into hurt. I couldn't split myself in half. All I ever wanted to do was to have security, love, and happi-ness, and all of that was there at the end of our relationship. I could not stand the fact that the man I loved could not love my son in the same way as I did.

If I went back, would things be different like John said or would it all happen again? I wondered if John really loved me enough to love Joshua the way he needed. On the other side of it, would Joshua allow his bitter memories to pass and give it a chance for a new start? I just wished I had the answers to all of this. I didn't want to make another mistake.

December 8, 1991

I skipped writing in my journal for a couple of days. Mostly I just wanted to not say anything in writing and then maybe my mind would rest, but I still worried about making a wrong decision. I wanted to be back with John. I thought that would make me completely happy.

With Christmas coming, I got a tree, and it is very pretty. I went to a tree farm to pick it out, and had a sleigh ride pulled by two beau-tiful horses. It was very cold. Frostbitten feet were enough pain for the day. Also got a haircut, but then lost all energy. I didn't feel like doing much of anything except going to sleep.

Since Danny had a son of his own, he understood how important Josh was to me. After sharing with him about my past and how impor tant Josh was to me, he decided we needed to go to church together, a new church he had found similar to a Catholic church. I promised I would give it a try with him.

I went to church with him; however, I burst into tears as soon as I entered the building and ran back to the truck where I sat and cried.

When Danny and I got back to the house I decided I needed closure. I hadn't closed the door with John. Since I left him, he has stayed in contact with me, calling and asking for another chance, and promising things would be better. I wanted to believe him. I wanted a new life with someone to love me just for me, but that life was not to be with John.

As much as I tried to be good, I fell back into my old ways. I man-aged to get involved with drinking with some women who had feel-ings for other women. One night I had been a tease the whole night, knowing all along what could happen. Shortly after this, I met another woman and there seemed to be a spark of interest between us when I realized she wasn't seeing anyone.

I shared all of this with John. He said he still wanted to work things out between us, if I would just come back. We could get past all of these little things that had gotten in the way of our relationship.

December 10, 1991

My life was such a rollercoaster. I spoke with Mom on the phone. We prayed. I felt better and cried a lot throughout the day and just let all of it out. I didn't want to make a wrong decision and regret it at all.

I grabbed my Bible and prayed from my heart. I didn't know what would become of it. Basically I was scared of the outcome. I bawled like a little baby who needed their mom. It didn't make me feel any better, and I decided to sit down and talk to Joshua. It was something I had put off and should have done long ago. The talk didn't really-clear anything up. The only sense I made of it was that Josh hated John because he locked me out and called the police on me. It was my fault this all happened.

Danny and I talked about everything, including my seemingly new attraction to women, something I hadn't shared with him before. I hadn't ever really wanted to tell anyone else this.

I decided to go see John for closure one way or the other. Danny reassured me he would take care of Josh, so I was comfortable in not taking Josh with me. I made a flight reservation for Georgia. My mind was at ease about facing John, whether we worked things out or not.

December 20, 1991

I took a plane to see John for eight days. The flight was out of Presque Isle, Maine, on a small plane, which made me nervous. We hit some turbulence early in the flight, and I prayed and asked God to let us land safely, reminding God that Josh needed his mom. It was only the God of the universe who could guide us safely through the rough flight.

I had a layover in Boston and decided to have a few drinks. I met some people at the bar who also had layovers so we joined in conversing with one another. I wasn't shy as long as I had a drink in my hand. We got to talking and laughing over drinks, and I missed my flight out of Boston. I had to reschedule it, call John and Danny and tell them what happened, and then returned to the bar. My new "friends" became concerned about my safety because I was drunk enough to be slurring my words. I started to cry again.

Nevertheless, I finally made it to Georgia where John met me. He had made arrangements for us to go to Pigeon Forge and Gatlinburg, Tennessee, and spend our time together there. We drank together, went out and had wonderful dinners together, shopped, and rested. We hadn't changed in our desire for each other, but the more we talked, the more I realized we really didn't have much in common anymore. My love for Josh was still a barrier for John, and his words didn't sound sincere when he talked about us getting back together.

I hadn't prayed before I moved to Georgia. God allowed me to go but hurdles were always in my way. I thought about the times I actually wanted to move into my own place with Joshua, but still have John come over. I never had the guts to leave or to be away from John. I liked being with him but his jealousy really shut up my true feel-ings. I loved him and probably always will, but in my heart I know it is time to move on with my life.

As I gave John a final good-bye, I felt a sense of relief. I left things without saying I would return but only that we should remain friends, if possible. I really didn't know if I just needed John to be with me or what my intentions were for going all the way down to Georgia. I loved him deeply but not enough to be with him forever. But then again I couldn't imagine being at ease with just myself.

The trip home to Maine was less eventful. This time there were no layovers so I stayed sober. I missed Josh a lot and couldn't wait to hold him and tell him how much I loved him.

Danny was happy I decided to stay with him, and I was happy to hear only good reports from Josh about his time with Danny while I was gone.

The day after I returned home, I really felt good. It was so nice just to be alone with Joshua while I took my time getting things done. I felt comfortable. That scared me a little bit. I hadn't felt like I had a real home in a long time, well, actually since I moved from my trailer in Illinois.

I just want to be happy, but I wanted it to be God's will not mine. My way of doing things had only put my heart into jeopardy and always ended in more pain when things didn't work out.

Did God put Danny back in my life for me or is this something I am doing 'cause I want to? I need answers, and God is the only one that knows what is right for me. I had almost said "yes" to marrying Danny, but I wanted it to be for the right reasons. I do want to settle down, to be a wife again, and a good mom.

December 22, 1991

As Christmas approached, my thoughts really took hold of my emotions and feelings. In my journal I wrote:

I would rather be dead than have these feelings. I feel like I've been driven to hell and back. Why do I have to put myself through this? Why is it I am always living the crybaby life?

What is wrong with me? I just know I haven't acted like this before. I have a major problem and I just cannot deal with it. If I totally let go, I will be all new, and then again be hurt. I just can't bring myself to enjoy anyone other than John, but I do desire companionship with a girlfriend or just someone to go shopping with.

Christmas is only a couple of days away and I will do anything for Joshua to at least be happy. I really don't care if I get anything. Never expect anything and then you never get hurt by what you don't receive.

I guess my drinking is out of hand again. Does it come with the changes of life? Is it going to take another one and a half years before I quit or will I ever consider it again?

Decisions are hard to make and I refuse to make anymore as of now. I feel so drained and confused still, even though I did get up for church this morning. I really wanted to go. This was very differ-ent for me.

December 31, 1991

On the Thursday night before New Year's I went out to the only bar in town. I was in an uneasy mood. The fact was I was out to get drunk and I succeeded. I played darts and did a lousy job of it. The bartender, Glenda, cut me off because I was driving. I started to get offended, but instead, I just let it go. My friend Lorrie, being the only sober person in the bar, agreed to drive the truck home with me. So the bar closed and we left. When we arrived at her house we both went in. In the morning, I woke up in her bed with her.

Later John called. He had always said I could talk to him about anything, and I told him about what had happened with Lorrie. He said if that was what I wanted, then it was all over with us.

His reaction shocked me. I said, "No, John. I can't let that happen. I love you too much."

"I'll talk to you later," he said and hung up.

I broke. I went crazy screaming, crying, and yelling. I really did not know how stupid I might be.

Then with the new year came a new direction. On New Year's Eve Danny asked me to marry him. And Priscilla called me to say she missed me because she was at a party and I wasn't there.

I said "yes" to Danny's proposal and we set a wedding date. We'd get married on my son's birthday. The new friends I'd made in Maine were happy for me. Even Priscilla called and told Danny to take care of me. She said I was special to her and that she loved me.

January 1, 1992

The following day I sat there thinking about all the decisions I needed to make. I still felt unsure about many things. One thing I knew for sure: I didn't want a woman to be a lover of mine or to continue that kind of relationship.

Right then I just needed friends. I needed comfort and reassur-ance, but no more than that.

I knew the Lord was working in my life and doing a lot through the people around me. On the first day of the new year I received a call from a woman named Cindy. She was a sponsor for AA. She said, "I've had your number for two days but was afraid to call." I invited her to come over, "but just don't talk about my drinking or AA," I said to her. I needed a friend. So she did come over and we talked a lot. She was a very nice person who had been a drinker just like me. She had just celebrated her one-year anniversary without a drink. She seemed to be very happy with herself and her life.

Lorrie called while Cindy was still at the house. I asked her to bring some beer over that I had left at her place. When I hung up, I felt a little guilty with Cindy sitting there. After she left, Lorrie came over, but she did not bring the beer for me. I was a bit shocked. Instead of going to buy some I made a mixed drink even though I don't care for mixed drinks at all. At least this way, I knew I wouldn't drink much.

Cindy called to see if I changed my mind about going to the meet-ing, but stubborn me, I just wasn't going yet. I dumped the drink out. I don't know why; it tasted okay. Just didn't want it for some reason.

January 1992

Priscilla came up to Maine to help with fixing my car, since she is a mechanic. She had told Danny she wanted to have me go with her to New Hampshire to pick up some things from her former girlfriend. She also told Danny she loved me again. When Danny told me about this I said, "It's nothing serious; she was just saying that because that's the way she is. She just loves everyone, you know?" I hadn't given much thought to living that kind of life with Priscilla anyway, since I was now in the process of marrying my so-called high school sweetheart.

So my trip with Priscilla to New Hampshire was set to take place a week before my wedding to Danny. Josh had overheard the conversation between Danny and Priscilla in the garage earlier and said, "I don't want you to go away, Mommy."

"What do you mean? I'm only going to New Hampshire for a couple of days and then I'll be back." I told him he was going to be in a safe place at Priscilla's daughter's house and that he could talk to me anytime he wanted. "I'll call you while I'm gone."

Josh said, "No, Mommy. When you get married to Danny, he said he's going to send you away." Later, once I had dropped Josh off and was on the road with Priscilla, I asked her about this conversation Josh said he overheard between her and Danny. She looked at me and said, "I thought you said you wanted to get help with your drinking."

Inside I was furious with Danny, thinking he was going to force me into a treatment place. He wanted me as his wife, but was it only so that he could put me away? I mentally replayed my conversation with Josh about this. I had to do something.

No one was going to lock me up or put me in a place I didn't deserve to be in. I thought of Danny leaving me locked up somewhere and the thought of not being able to see my son. Danny hadn't said a word about this to me. The more I thought about his plan, the more upset I became with him. Suddenly, just overnight, Danny became my enemy.

After Priscilla and I arrived in New Hampshire, I spent one whole night talking with John, Robert, Danny, my dad, and my mom, on the phone. Weeks before, at Danny's insistence, I had told my mom about the abuse I had experienced as a child. Mom was shocked. I didn't feel any better inside after telling her; it just made me feel like I needed a drink.

Those days I needed a drink to calm down, a drink to help me tell the truth, a drink to play pool, a drink to talk, a drink to cry, a drink to laugh, a drink to drive, a drink to do just about everything.

With everything going on with Danny I made up my mind. I'd had it with men. This plan of his was the final straw. After all these years, my trust in him was now broken.

While still in New Hampshire with Priscilla, I called Josh's babysitter and asked her to take Josh to a safe place and not to allow anyone to know where he was. I called Danny and told him our wedding was off, and I would not be back at his place ever again.

Here I was starting over again with a new life. I vowed to never let a man hurt me again. I vowed to never allow my son to be affected by a man again. I vowed to never marry a man again. I'd had enough of what men stood for – deceit, lies, and betrayal.

I met more of Priscilla's friends. They seemed to take a liking to me. I felt like I belonged with them, and I enjoyed Priscilla's company. She never asked me to do anything I didn't want to do, she never put down Josh, and she never said a bad word about me. She was a special person who had also been abused and taken advantage of like me, and she was funny and fun to be around.

I was determined things were going to change. I would run my life from now on. No man would ever get close enough to hurt me. No man would convince me to sleep with him. No man would be by my side. No way would I allow a man to hurt my son. The more I didn't have to see men in my life, the easier it would be. I really wanted nothing to do with men because all they had ever managed to do was hurt me in every possible way. I had given years of my life away believing I would find the right man, but it had never happened.

Danny and I parted as friends but with a brokenness between us we had not experienced before. Danny wanted to give me security,

but for him that meant control, and I only wanted someone to love me for me.

Priscilla made room at her place for me and Josh, which she was already sharing with her best friend and daughter. She had a small trailer with a room built on. While she was a wonderful person inside and out, she was a woman and so was I. Was I ready to compromise all I had ever been taught and all I knew about right and wrong? Had my life gotten to the point that there was no hope for a God-given relationship?

January 26, 1992

> *Marilynne, if you really want a friend to talk with and be honest with, I'm here. But if you don't want a true friend who loves and cares about what you're really going through and cares about Joshua's wellbeing, I'll understand!*

> *You have a problem and you do need to get help. Whether or not you choose to get that help is still up to you. The game you have been playing for such a long time needs to come to a close. Your actions are hurting someone else who won't be able to heal very easily. That person is the one you love the most, Joshua. The other night you said to leave Joshua out of it. Well, I can't and neither should you! I love you, but I have grown too close to Joshua to see him go through the life you're presently leading.*

> *Stopping drinking is only the first step to recovery. You need to go to psychoanalysis. Your mother tried to get you to go when you were 16. Robert tried to get you to go. The state of Georgia tried to get you to go to Alcoholics Anonymous. You've fought it every step of the way. Why? You've lied to Robert many times and to*

John. You have lied to me on how many occasions? I don't want to count. You told Robert you were working; that was a lie. You said you were going to stop drinking after Christmas, and then the first of January. You've lied to yourself and to others too many times. When are you going to realize you have a bigger problem than just alcohol and get the help you need?

Why did you come up here with me? Be honest with yourself first and then with me! Was it because you took too much from Robert and John? I'm sorry you want to throw away what we could have, but maybe the love in this relationship is one-sided: me giving and you taking. Question: How long before you discover it's you that you've been running away from, and how much more are you going to put yourself through?

You said I was a fake. Well, that did hurt, because you know as well as I do I'm your truest friend. I'll tell you what you need to hear, not what you want me to say. If honesty is fake, then I guess in your eyes I am a fake. But you know in reality I'm not!

I hope you don't take what is said in this letter wrong, but that you take it to heart so you know I'm a true friend, extending a helping hand. Reach out and take my hand, if you want to get help. I'll be there always until you don't need that holding hand. Please don't take a defensive attitude. First look into yourself and be honest with yourself, and then get mad at me.

With Love Always,

Danny

March 24, 1992

Danny and I got engaged in January. At first I was sure of my deci-sion. The only thing was, I was marrying him for all the wrong rea-sons. Security just didn't seem to be enough of a reason. Love him? Yes, in a very different way than man and wife. More like a brother or a security blanket I had held onto for so many years, wondering if we could make a marriage work after being just friends for so long.

I was ready for marriage. Just one thing: I was still in love with Robert and also John. I just could not shake those strong feelings.

But this time the marriage was called off. It relieved me as the pressure dropped off. I still felt very uneasy living where I was. In the meantime I had decided to leave and go back to Georgia to marry John. I had become so addicted to him it seemed the right thing to do.

I hated the idea of leaving Maine. By this time I had developed new friends and was able to be myself and not worry who liked me or not. At this point, Lorrie and I were not even speaking to one another. That was fine because Lorrie's feelings were more intimate than I wanted them to be. Priscilla, a very special person to me, and Becky, a friend of hers, were coming over a lot. At first when they would call, I was a bit concerned since Priscilla had said she loved me. I took it as a friend kind of love and let it stay that way.

Summer 1992

One night I talked with my ex-mother-in-law and described to her my life of sin. "I just can't change." She boldly told me both Robert and I needed God. Robert and I had recently talked about getting back together again, but we just ended up yelling at each other on the phone. I shared all of this with his mother. Again she said, "You both need God."

I decided not to call her again, because she had said nothing to make me feel any better. She doesn't agree with me, and I simply refuse to call people again who don't agree with me.

I spent a lot of time calling my friends in all the states I had lived in, rambling on and on with them on the phone for all hours of the night. I told them how I was mistreated all my life, and I asked over and over again, "What did I do to deserve such a life?" All of this only served to pull me further away from God. I was hoping they would make me feel better, but they never did, and I kept refusing to go to the only One who could. I still thought I was important to my friends, because they continued to listen to me. What I really wanted was someone to love me for me.

I was bold in letting men know I was with a woman and in telling them "no." I still joined them in their partying, but I finally felt respected by men, even when I said no to their advances. It even felt good to say no to them.

I was sure I must be doing the right thing, because everything seemed to be working out. I was working, and Priscilla was not working because her back wasn't the best. I started to find humor in things that once made me cry. I began to think there was hope for me in pursuing my dream of being a nurse. I wanted to be a good mother to Josh, but being a wife again was the furthest thing from my mind.

Then I was laid off from work and couldn't find another job. Food stamps and insurance supported me and Josh. Priscilla and I decided to move to Florida, and I let Josh spend the summer with Robert in Georgia.

Dad sent me money so Priscilla and I would have enough for food and gas on the trip south. We sold all we could of our stuff and the rest we fit into our cars.

My car began to overheat on the trip; Priscilla told me via the CB to turn the heat on full blast in the car. She said it was necessary to save my engine. With the heater turned on full blast, the tempera-ture went back down to normal, but I had to do this several times during the trip.

We arrived in Georgia to drop Josh off where it was ninety-five degrees, but Dad was waiting for us in Florida, and we still had more than six hours to drive, so I didn't stay long with Robert.

When we got to Florida, we went straight to the pub where Dad was waiting for us. I could tell the barmaid was the same as Priscilla and me. When her girlfriend came in later, they both bought us a drink.

While Dad accepted Priscilla, I could tell he wasn't pleased with our relationship. The next day Priscilla and I both headed out to look for jobs. We knew we couldn't stay in Dad's house for too long. We appreciated his kindness to us, and that he never said anything bad to us while we were there.

Dad had a renter living in his house whose car was having prob-lems. The renter let Priscilla work on his car, and he paid her to fix it. We needed the money so that worked out well.

July 10, 1992

> *Danny, the way you spoke in the last letter, I really never thought I would hear from you again. This letter is a much more positive one.*

> *Since I have not written or spoken to you in a while, I have had a lot of changes in my life. I am trying to get my life into order and everything keeps coming back to me.*

> *Joshua has been with Robert for 1-1/2 weeks now. He will be coming home Monday. I sure do miss him when he's gone, although I need that space for a while sometimes. Joshua asked about you the other day, and I just said you were fine. I also told him we would be staying right where we are until whenever.*

> *I'll have to pass on Illinois for a lot of reasons: no money; and school requires everyday attendance. They use your atten-dance as a grade; if you miss too many days your grade goes down. Miss ten days and they kick you out of school. I really wish I could go. But I guess you just think this is another excuse. Well, it isn't.*

August 1992

One night after being out late drinking, when Priscilla and I got back to the house Dad actually hit on Priscilla and tried to get her to sleep with him. I couldn't believe he would do such a thing. On another night, shortly after this, when we got home late from the bar, there was a woman sitting in the living room. I shouted to Dad, "You couldn't get Priscilla so you found another woman?"

I have never been so embarrassed. It was my own mother. Apparently Dad flew her to Florida to try and talk some sense into me about my lifestyle and to get me to change my mind.

After the initial shock of seeing Mom, I realized that in the few years I hadn't seen her she had changed enough that I didn't even recognize her anymore. But I remembered she had said she was going to be here. I was so drunk I had forgotten I sent her a letter before I left Maine telling her I was heading to Florida. In that letter, I invited her to come down and see me, if she wanted.

The next day Mom talked with Priscilla and me, separately. She said to me, "You know I won't and can't live your life for you, nor can I tell you what to do." She asked me if I was happy, and I said "Yes."

Then she said, "Well, I like Priscilla. She has a good personality, and she really cares for you. I will say this. Could you two just remain friends and nothing more?"

I said, "No. This is what it is, and we are together."

She responded with, "You know it isn't right," and then said again, "I can't live your life for you nor will I tell you what to do, except I do love you and I always will, no matter what you decide to do."

So my dad was upset with me because I had left Josh with Robert, and now my mom was upset with me because of the lifestyle I had chosen. With things as they were, she decided there was no reason for her to stick around. Oh well. My mind was made up and there was no turning back.

Dad made me an offer. He said he had been looking for houses for me and Josh and found a nice one. If I liked it, he would buy it for me and pay all the costs of upkeep so his grandson could have a home of his own. The kicker was that Priscilla had to go back to where she belonged, in New Hampshire. He even offered to pay her way to get back up there. I suddenly realized he was serious. He would do whatever it took to separate us.

Priscilla and I decided to pack as much of our stuff into her car as we could and put the rest in storage. I planned to leave with her the next day. My bags were packed with what I could carry; we were ready to go. Dad asked if I was going somewhere.

I said, "You know, Dad. I love you, but I can't stay here with you. I'm going with Priscilla. It would never work with me here, and it isn't right to send her on her way like this, so I'm not going to."

Needless to say, Dad was angry. Very angry. So angry, he dis-owned me.

We headed for New Hampshire where Priscilla had already lined up jobs for us and an apartment. Josh would stay with Robert. I made arrangements to pick him up later. Josh had his turtle with him and was content with that. But soon after I got to New Hampshire, I received a phone call from Josh. He wanted to stay with his dad for the whole school year. I didn't like the idea, but I couldn't find a rea-son for not letting him stay either. I agreed as long as he promised to keep his grades up.

A week after school started, however, I got another call from Josh. He was crying and told me he had hurt his knee weeks ago but couldn't tell me about it then, because his dad said he was a wimp. I packed in record time; we borrowed some money and headed to Georgia. I was angry with Robert for not seeking medical attention for Josh, and I was shocked at his way of handling the situation.

Once we picked up Josh, we headed right back home to New Hamp-shire. I hoped Josh would like our new home, or at least the home we were living in temporarily while we waited for a three-bedroom apartment to open up. Once we got home, we took Josh to the doctor, who put him in a cast from his thigh to his foot. His ligaments had torn and would have caused a shortening of his leg due to the surgery necessary to repair it if we hadn't gotten him to the hospital when we did. I vowed to never let Josh be away from me again.

Priscilla was supportive as I continued to make decisions about our new life together in New Hampshire. One night Josh got up and saw something he shouldn't have between Priscilla and me that gave away the true nature of our relationship with each other. He was so upset he packed up his things that night and moved to the shed on our porch. I followed him out and sat down to talk with him.

He had been hoping his dad and I would get back together, and I told him that wasn't going to happen. I reassured him he would always be my precious boy, my pride and joy. But from his point of view, I had been lying to him all this time. By the time our conversation was finally done, he was okay with knowing I had decided not to have any other man take his dad's place. We didn't discuss that evening again.

Fall 1992

One day Mom called and I told her about being invited to go with a friend of mine, Gee Gee, to Florida. Mom said I should stay with Dad when I got there, even though I told Mom what Dad said to me before I left Florida the last time. Because of Mom's gentle insistence, I got brave enough to call Dad and make the necessary arrangements to have him meet up with me where I would be staying with Gee Gee and the special-needs people she took care of.

When we got to Florida, Dad met me at Gee Gee's, and he and I drove to the storage area to get my car from where it had been sit-ting since I moved to New Hampshire. It needed a new battery, after having sat for so long, and once again I didn't have the money to pay for it. Without me asking, Dad offered to get a battery and he paid to put gas in it, too. He asked me to meet him later on at the bar where he would be. I agreed.

A couple of days later I went visiting some old friends of Priscilla's and mine at a bar we frequented. When I went to leave and put the car in reverse, it refused to work even though the transmission on the car wasn't that old. Again, Dad offered to pay to have it fixed. I was so grateful.

I didn't know if Mom had been talking with Dad over the last few months to soften his heart toward me again or not, but I was grateful to him for helping me out of another jam. He cared about Josh, and he knew I would take care of Josh. In order to do that I needed my car once I got back to New Hampshire. I finally headed back to New Hampshire, later than planned, but with a car that worked enough to get me there. I was so happy to be home and to see my son and Priscilla.

Spring 1993

When spring arrived, my mom and sister decided to come for a visit. And, to my surprise, Dad decided to visit as well. They were coming for my birthday so it added to the celebration of being together. Dad stayed at a hotel over a bar about two blocks from our house and Mom and Sis stayed with us. It was a good visit which gave my sister time to spend with Josh. They even made dinner for all of us one evening in our small kitchen.

It was a short visit, but we were all glad to see each other. My sister didn't question my lifestyle while she was there, nor did she give an opinion on it one way or the other. She did ask Josh his opinion, but I already knew he was happy with the way life was going for him, so it was no big deal.

Spring came and went and so did summer, and Priscilla and I had no jobs. Once again, we had to decide if we were going to stay there or move elsewhere to try to find work. Priscilla's brother was mov-ing to Wisconsin, and he and his wife and kids stopped by for a visit on their way. They invited us to come out there, if we wanted to find work or to just come for a visit.

Once again, we decided to pack up our things and move. We sold all we had in order to by gas for the car, and we made a box to fit on top of the car to hold all the things we were going to bring with us, mostly things for Josh. Once again I left a place I had called home, a place where people made me feel welcome and who were the best of friends to party with.

Even with all this, I felt something was always missing in my life. I wanted the white picket fence and big house and lots of children running around and laughing. I was missing the peace of God.

As we drove down the road on another adventure, in our move to Wisconsin, we decided to visit Niagara Falls. It was July 4. We had little money except to get gas, but we did get to see this beautiful spot and take some pictures. Then we were on our way to Chicago where my sister lived, and to her boyfriend's house, which was about an hour from her place.

He had a nice house in a ritzy neighborhood and was a quiet guy who didn't seem too excited about our visit. Our beater car really stood out in his driveway. With our homemade car-top carrier, all we needed was a rocking chair on top of the car. My sister, on the other hand, had a cute but small apartment she shared with another girl. We felt much more welcomed in this much tinier place and enjoyed our short stay there.

The next morning my sister headed to her work, and we headed out for the last leg of our trip, another four hours to reach my mom's place where I had grown up. Mom and her husband had moved back from Arkansas, and he was able to return to his former job of twenty years. I loved my mom and wanted to be near her. I liked that we could talk more and got along better now than we ever did. I was enjoying this "new" mom of mine. She was just so different than before; she didn't get angry anymore.

When school did not work out well for Josh and Priscilla and I needed better jobs, we told Mom we had decided to make our way farther north in Wisconsin where Priscilla's brother lived. It was another five and a half hours away. We had to get a loan from Mom to make it that far. She was okay with our decision and graciously helped us out.

We set out for Wisconsin, into cow country. We arrived in the small town where Priscilla's brother lived. They had agreed to let us stay with them until we got established with jobs and our own place. Everyone was glad to see us. Josh already knew her brother's children, so we all kind of had instant family.

Priscilla and I settled in one more time, in another small town. This town had a couple of bars, and they didn't have a closing time. I only drank once in a while, because we were still on a very tight budget. Since Priscilla's brother was in alcohol recovery, we respected that and didn't drink at his house. Instead, we walked to the local bar where we would meet up with more people to shoot pool or share pitchers of beer. Somehow I always managed to go somewhere with just enough money for one drink and ended up staying until the bar closed down.

It was time for us to find jobs, however. We drove up to Barron, Wisconsin, where Priscilla's brother and sister-in-law had interviews lined up for us. The interviews went well, and we finally got jobs. Priscilla met the owner of a hotel in the town where we were living who rented rooms out by the day, week, or month. He graciously gave us a room to rent for a month on credit. The room was small, just a hotel room, but it had what we needed to make it a home. We found someone to check on Josh each day, feed him dinner, and help him with his homework while Priscilla and I were at work.

We ended up staying at the hotel until October 1993 when we moved to a nice two-bedroom house. We settled into our new place and set things up for someone to watch Josh since Priscilla and I were working the night shift. With those hours, I didn't see Josh much except on the weekends, but we were working on saving money so, hopefully, one day soon we would be able to buy a house and not put Josh through any more moves.

Thanksgiving came and it was a chance to enjoy time with new friends, good food, and reunite with our families. Everything was looking up for us except that inside I still felt I was missing some-thing. As we sat down to pray over the Thanksgiving Day meal and do our ritual of saying what we were thankful for, we began with, *Thank you, God, for our new home, our jobs, and especially for family and friends.* It made me think of my real father. I wondered where he was and who was with him on this special day. I didn't even know if he was still alive. My friends suggested that since I knew his name I should call Information in the town where I thought he currently lived and see if I could get a hold of him.

I found his number. My hand trembled as I dialed it. I wasn't sure I was ready for conversation, if he actually answered the phone. "Hello," a man's voice answered.

"Is this Don who married Sharon?"

Before I could tell him who I was, he said, "Marilynne, is that you? I've been waiting a long time to hear from you."

We talked for a while that evening as my friends listened in. I was thankful he was still alive. I asked him to forgive me for treating him with such disrespect. He said he probably deserved worse than that.

That opened the door to a relationship. From then on we talked almost every evening after I got off work. Finally we decided it was time for a visit. I wanted to visit Mom as well, so we decided I would stop at his house to see him and then continue on to Mom's.

I learned that in all my growing-up years, my dad lived less than an hour away from me and in the same town where I used to visit Grandma. It amazed me I never ran into him while walking about in that small town and that no one had told me he lived there.

When we finally met up, the visit wasn't anything like what I had imagined it would be the year I got saved. I had wanted to meet up with him then so I could talk to him about God. I wanted him to be saved and forgiven so he would stop drinking. Instead, our visit was like going to a party. We got together for drinks and to talk about the past and things we had missed over the years. As I walked in the door he greeted me from his bed in the living room. He had a degenerative disorder of the discs in his back. The doctors had determined there was nothing they could do for him – not even surgery – so his drinks and his pain pills were his only relief.

A part of me right then just wanted to pray for his healing. But I didn't. I thought, *Who are you to offer prayer to God for your father?* I looked at the drink in my hand. I was a hypocrite. So I didn't pray. Instead, we just talked for most of the night. I wanted to know the truth as to whether he had done the wrongs to Mom and me that oth-ers had said he did. Was he man enough now to admit his wrongs? I felt I had to ask him the hard questions now that I was with him, but I didn't know how he would respond.

I learned family secrets far worse than I ever imagined. Dad's inappropriateness with me came from his own tormented past. His own father had asked him at a young age to sleep with his mother, and then with other women. His family was a drinking family, so Dad learned early on how to drink. He also followed in his father's foot-steps of beating whomever was nearby in his anger and drunkenness.

As I headed to the door to leave, I was grateful I had gotten to meet my dad and to talk at length with him. He asked me to tell Mom he was sorry for all the terrible things he had done to her and to me. I felt sorry for him. The following morning, I headed out to Mom's.

One day, about two months later, I got a phone call before head-ing out for work. It was Dad's sister. She said Dad had passed away that day. "But he said to tell you he loved you and to thank you for the last couple of months."

I fell to my knees and cried uncontrollably. There was more I had wanted to say to my dad and now the opportunity was gone. I never did tell him what God could do for him. I should have told him. Why didn't I? As I tried to remember his last words to me, it struck me that maybe he had waited to die until we had seen each other again. I had only a couple of months to talk with him or see him, but was so glad I had called him on that Thanksgiving Day.

When Mom found out about his death I could almost see her relax a bit, knowing he would never be able to hurt her again. I shared in her sadness and disappointment that he was the way he was. And now it was over. There was no funeral service. All I had left of him was his obituary and some papers showing he had been licensed as a barber.

At last, I felt it was time to put the past behind me, but the more I tried, the more I drank. My grieving process consisted of consum-ing alcohol and cigarettes. Sadness lingered that he was gone and I had not finished talking to him. I never got to ask him what could or would have helped him to change.

Spring 1994

My whole life seemed to be a series of ups and downs, and either way I drank. I'd drink to get rid of one hurt and smoke to get rid of another. I was a complete mess. Inwardly, I knew I had to pull it together, and soon, before I lost any happiness I still had. If I didn't, I would go off the deep end. Maybe Danny was right all along. He had said I was manic-depressive. I thought, Maybe I needed pills or something. But then my precious son would say, "Mommy, I love you," as I held him on my lap. It helped me focus on what was important for him and for me – a new home, a job, and our relationship.

Spring came as I anticipated a visit from my mom for my birthday and for Easter. The dad I had known for most of my life, the one who lived in Florida, was also coming for a visit. He would join up with Mom on her way to see me so they would arrive together. Mom went with Josh to my uncle's place the day before Easter, and Dad and I celebrated that night at the local bar.

We stayed late at the bar playing games and drinking, and then came home for a few nightcaps before bed. Everyone else who had come home with us fell asleep, but Dad and I stayed awake and drank and laughed some more. I got up to go to the bathroom and stumbled and fell into the tub. I called to Dad for help and he came in and pulled me out. While I was drunk I had the courage to tell Dad that Priscilla and I planned to commit to each other in "marriage."

The next morning, I couldn't remember how he reacted or what he said, since we were both drunk. It was Easter Sunday. Mom came back with Josh so we could celebrate the day together. She asked that we all stay sober, which we did, and we enjoyed a nice dinner with the friends who had stayed overnight with us.

Shortly after Dad and Mom left, Priscilla and I got "married" with a few friends along as witnesses. Josh was even pleased to take part in the event.

Many people I knew expected me to change my mind about doing this. When I called them, after it was over, I expected to hear congratulations. Instead I got lectured about how what I was doing wasn't right and that I was outside of the plan God intended. Mom said she was not happy about the decision, but said she still loved me and acknowledged I was her daughter.

Summer 1994

Once summer arrived and the end of the school year, we got to spend more time with Josh. We planned a trip to New Hampshire to pick up some of the things we had left stored there. Dad wanted Josh to spend some time with him in Florida so we flew him down there.

Priscilla and I worked a lot of overtime in order to save up enough money to eventually buy our own home here in Wisconsin and to be able to take the trip to New Hampshire. We worked hard, but we were happy. Everything seemed to be going right for me. There was no room for me to doubt the decisions I had made, but in my heart I knew Mom was right about the relationship between Priscilla and me. But for the first time in a long time everything seemed to be right, and I didn't want to change anything.

We headed to Maine and to New Hampshire, seeing old friends and celebrating our new commitment to each other in both places.

When we got back to Wisconsin we found a house, well, actually a two-bedroom trailer we wanted to buy, and we headed to the bank for financing. They said, "You haven't been at your place of employ-ment long enough," and denied our application. Priscilla always had a way of talking to people to get what she wanted. She found a woman at our work who was able to help us purchase the home.

The next day we went to the home to meet with the owners. Things worked out as far as financing went, and we were soon to be the own-ers of a two-bedroom trailer located close to work for both of us and not far from the new school Josh would attend in the fall.

We finally felt settled. Now that we were actually going to own our own home we felt established. Josh would have the opportunity to make new friends but would still be close to the friends he had already made. I vowed at this point not to move again until after he graduated, no matter what. I wanted him to enjoy the rest of his school days in one place. We went to football, baseball, and basketball games with him, as well as to wrestling matches and a few school plays he was involved in.

I should have been happy, but I found myself binge drinking again. It happened at times when I wasn't feeling content. I put on a good front most of the time with my friends at the bars. But at times Danny's accurate assessment of my manic-depressive state came out and others saw it occasionally. I was good at manipulating people, too.

I started to hate my life and the relationship I was in with Priscilla. I had never felt so far away from God.

I was drinking my way to the grave. I knew I couldn't go on like this anymore. I was scaring myself into the loony bin, feeling like I was having a breakdown. I wanted to stop but all I did was drink more and harder stuff.

I needed help desperately. I couldn't help myself. But how was I going to get the help I needed?

One morning I dumped all my drinks down the drain and told myself I wouldn't drink hard stuff anymore. This was after I had already been to treatment after getting a DUI following a night on the town. Getting a second DUI was a reality check for me. I had really messed up everything. When I went to treatment I made a vow to stop drinking. I really, really did want to change. Being in treatment wasn't just a front like it was for some of the other people I met in the group.

After a couple of days in detox I started feeling better. My outlook on life changed. I was ready to head in a new direction. Unlike the others I met there, I wasn't really an alcoholic; I just let my drinking get out of control once in a while.

I stuck with my vow not to drink the hard stuff, but I couldn't get the same effect and the same high with just a beer. So it didn't take long before all my bad behaviors resurfaced. I binged again, some-times staying up for twelve to twenty-four hours – all day and all night – until I had to go to work.

Even with all this going on, I didn't consider myself a bad person. I still managed to handle all of my responsibilities at home and at work. I still had fun doing the types of things most families did together. In my way of thinking, true alcoholics didn't take their responsibilities or families seriously. Since I did, I figured I must not be an alcoholic.

1995

I finally went back to work in the nursing field after quitting my job. I had spent years at my job while my name was on a list waiting for an opening on a day shift. I had been promised it would happen at some point, but it never came. After hours and hours of overtime resulting in painful hands from the type of work I was doing, I just quit my job without notice. I had found another job in a nursing home, so I hadn't quit without something else waiting in the wings.

It had been years since I had worked as a CNA, but I never for-got how to care for others. This job gave me no time to be selfish. It was a time to get away from me-me-me all the time, like I was used to doing with my friends on the phone. I was focused on others to make sure these elderly people were given all the help they needed and to show them how special each one of them was. I knew I was right where I needed to be.

At the same time I started this new job, one of my friends made a bet with me that I couldn't make it three months without a drink. The challenge was on, and I focused hard on trying to win this bet. I was going to show her and everyone else that I didn't have a drink-ing problem.

Mom called one day and said she was headed to Arkansas and wanted to know if I could join her. Over the years I had taken several trips with Mom to Arkansas to see Grandma. On the way down to Grandma's, Mom and I talked a lot. It was much different than when I was younger. She didn't yell at me anymore. She only listened. I felt a healing process going on between us.

We talked a lot about Josh and about Grandma, and Mom shared with me her husband's problem with alcohol. After our weekends together, she would always pray for me. Grandma, too, always prayed for me and told me she knew God was protecting me.

I was living totally against God. I couldn't live with who I was, and I didn't even like myself most of the time. I felt locked in a place I couldn't escape from.

What would I do without a drink? Where would I go? Who would I see and hang out with? About all I had to do now was work. I didn't drink while working, so this would work out perfectly for me, or so I thought. I would put more hours in so I had less time to be with friends who would be drinking.

It was the longest three months of my life, and I could hardly wait to get back on track drinking again. I won the bet, but made up for lost time right away.

I didn't seem to have a conscience when I drank. It was my excuse for reckless behavior or a risky lifestyle. Once again I felt like running, but there was no place left for me to hide and no other place I could run to that would work for me. I was sick and tired of being sick and tired, but my patterns never changed. I kept going to parties, staying in the bars until closing time, and drinking more and more. I was in and out of the doctor's office due to the physical problems caused by drinking. I would be off work for a day or two to recuperate just so I could feel well enough to go back to my job and hopefully keep it.

1996

One day I fell at work on a water-covered floor. I hurt my back, knee, and shoulder pretty badly and had to take a leave from work to heal. Now at home I didn't have to worry about how much I drank, because I wasn't concerned with being sober enough to go to work.

One night I got into an argument with my son. He was trying to keep me from driving, because I had been drinking. I took off any-way, feeling like the whole world had come to an end because I had argued with Josh. I was so upset about it I wanted to die. I drove down a familiar country road and headed for a telephone pole, intending to end my misery. Instead the car died and stopped just about a foot in front of the pole. At first I thought, I can't even do this right! Then I thought there must have been angels surrounding me, because when I tried to start the car, it started right up. God must have been looking out for me.

The incident didn't stop me from drinking, however. And yet it made me think again about God and made me recognize what seemed

His obvious work in my life. The portions of the Bible I had learned years before were always in the back of my mind. But my heart stayed hardened. I didn't believe I could return to God because I had told Him to leave me alone. I also believed I had broken just about all of God's laws and that I was doomed seven times over.

I had written down Scripture verses about drunkenness, but had sent them to Robert, not kept them for myself. Could those verses have been warnings I refused to heed? Instead, I used them to judge someone else, pointing out the speck in his eye without seeing the log in my own.

I was guilty of all the things I told others not to do. I found myself in the throes of my own deception and thought surely I was going to die in a worse way than my real father, because I felt I was worse than he had ever been. I felt like his sins were becoming my sins, but I was taking them even further. If only someone could help me.

In the midst of all of this, I still felt as if God was watching over me, even though I wasn't living for Him. I was sure I had done way too much to ever be accepted back into His realm. I was a mess, and I didn't know how to turn myself around.

November 10, 1996

By November my inner battle continued to rage. This entry from my journal reflects just how tortured my thinking was:

I just got finished typing two letters and now I'm going to write how I feel besides. The battle with my inner self is crazy. I've asked so many times why can't I just let go? Oh, why? Everyday something changes. I wish I knew the future. I really do not understand why I can't let go. I do hope someday I can say, "Why did I wait so long?" Although at this time I can't see the answers.

Today we went to church. Mom called this morning and I just was more than ready to get going. But now I am having a beer and that is probably so wrong, but I don't want to deal with the wrong part of it all. I figure it could be worse, but it's just a few beers, and there I go again. It's what I want to do. See? I can't even allow one day to say, "Okay, Lord." This is terrible and I can't help it, honestly! I wonder if I shall ever understand.

Summer 1998

I liked my job. I had been there four years and still challenged the system for time off because I hadn't gotten any better with my sup-posedly "controlled" drinking. I did set boundaries for myself. I would only have a few drinks and eat some and make sure I went to bed and got up refreshed for work. At the start I had begged to get this job since I had failed the drug test when I first applied. They gave me another chance, and I made up my mind not to do drugs and to really give this job all I had.

After four years, however, I experienced another setback. It forced me to refocus on still another new start to my life and another direction. I had been canning some green beans at home and when I placed the hot jar in cold water it exploded. Boiling water from the jar and tiny shards of glass went into my face and arms. Josh was at a friend's house nearby and heard me scream inside the house.

I ran to the tub and frantically splashed cold water on my face. Priscilla wet a towel to help me, and we headed to the emergency room. The drive seemed to take forever. When we got there the doc-tors checked my eyes, as I hadn't opened them since the explosion. They were afraid I had gotten glass in them, but I didn't. "Thank you, Jesus," I said.

The local hospital couldn't do anything else for me, so I was driven in an ambulance to a hospital burn unit in Minnesota. Priscilla fol-lowed the ambulance in her car. I had no idea how bad off I was. When they found out I was allergic to narcotics, they gave me another drug in hopes of relieving the pain.

My face was cleaned and wrapped like a mummy and I could only use a straw to eat and drink. But I was lucky. I could have been in a lot worse shape. Someone called Mom, Grandma, and also my sister, who was going to fly from Chicago to see me. No one could do anything for me, and I could do nothing for myself – except pray. No one knew what I would look like once the bandages were removed or how badly I would scar. All the while I couldn't believe I had been so stupid as to let this happen – and I wasn't even drinking at the time! It seemed inevitable. Every time I tried to quit something bad, something happened that gave me another reason to drink.

They kept me in the hospital for two days. They removed one bandage from my eyes. For the first time I was able to see the burns on my arm. It would heal and maybe have only a few scars.

When the time came to remove the rest of the bandages from my face, I looked in the mirror with my mom by my side. She said, "You're still as pretty as you have always been."

But that's not what I saw. I saw a scarred-for-life person. My eyes filled with tears. I was just happy my eyes were not damaged and I could see. As I began to heal after leaving the hospital, I started to focus on a new job and a new life. I decided not to just give up on life as I so often felt like doing, but rather to put everything I could into a new life.

My new job was different from any job I had ever had. I really enjoyed what I did, and the pace of it picked up the longer I was there. However, as I was there longer and longer, working in the cold with knives, I developed carpal tunnel syndrome and ended up having surgery to fix it.

January 13, 1999

I sat at the table having my usual morning coffee – missing the cigarette, and reading the twelve-step book given to me by my counselor. Every time I read the word "alcoholic" tears fell from my eyes. I wasn't sure if it was the word or because I knew I was a victim of this hor-rible affliction.

Questions ran through my mind like, *Why does it have to be this way for me?* I felt hurt and angry at the same time, but I also felt bet-ter without drinking. With everything I liked doing or thought of doing, alcohol was there. The temptation was very strong. I feared summer activities, which always included alcohol.

I had my first taste of alcohol before I could even say my first words. Without my mother's knowledge, my baby bottle had been filled with my real father's favorite drink. I was eleven years old before I learned about the hidden secrets of my mother's past, which played a great role in my future. At that time I had no idea how much of a role it had already played. Now to find out I was actually born an alcoholic. As disturbing as it may sound, it was worse for me that I had learned a way to live without dying from this disease.

March 2, 2000

The battle goes on. Someday I'll be fine with God, and drinking won't be the issue. There was a time when God, my son, and my husband were more important to me, until the day drinking once again began to be the only way to get my husband's attention. I feared quitting and not being able to make him happy. He'd rather me drink than stop, so we were not meant to be together forever!

However, he quit ten years later, and I went on for who knows how many more years. It left me with unanswered questions. Josh was my reason to be good, but I couldn't even do that right. Everything I did or I said was wrong. I just didn't feel like myself.

I was lost in confusion. Lost without knowing who really, really cared or not. Right then nothing much mattered – today, tomorrow, or yesterday.

2002

Priscilla and I started looking for property to buy. We put money down on a place, but didn't really think anything more about it, since I was out on medical leave and hadn't applied for any kind of loan to buy property. After hunting season was over, we received a call that the property was ours. We took Mom and a few friends out to the property to celebrate. Mom wasn't too happy I wanted to stay in Wisconsin.

The property was in a beautiful spot in the country, surrounded by trees, wildlife, and a lake. We walked around all 6.8 acres and talked about putting up a home on the hill. As we walked the acreage we came upon more swamps than I realized were on the property when we contemplated buying it. As beautiful as this place was, I didn't know why I had bought it. I didn't even feel I deserved anything this nice. I thought, *I am trying to replace the property Robert and I had owned in North Carolina.*

Six months later Priscilla and I were looking at buying a double-wide as a temporary home until we could have a house built. I asked the banker what it would cost to have a house built on the property, and he said he would have no problem giving us a loan for $100,000. I thought he was out of his mind. There is no way we could afford that.

We finally made a decision; we both became co-signers on a loan to purchase a double-wide home, as well as dig a well and installed septic, a driveway, and electricity. This was to give us a place to live until we could have a real house built on top of the walk-out base-ment we dug.

During the summer of 2002, as the home was being built, we began camping on the private road to our house. We hired some guys to cut the trees down to make room for our driveway and to mark the land for the place where the home would be built. I continued to drink more but was also working more overtime.

All of a sudden Priscilla lost her job. How were we going to pay for this house now? She received no reason for her dismissal. She had worked there for four years and never missed a day. Then the company got a new owner. Priscilla suspected it was discrimination on the part of the owner in letting her go, but she had no proof. However, it didn't take long before she found another job, and everything continued as planned with the building of our new home.

The house was delivered in two pieces and set on the foundation of a walkout basement. A convoy of trucks arrived filled with all of our belongings, and we celebrated by having some friends over for drinks. The house was beautiful with three bedrooms and two bath-rooms. Some would call our place a mansion, but to me it was a just a special place to call home. It was the fulfillment of a dream.

I had always shared whatever home I lived in with my friends, but with our new home I almost sensed a feeling of envy or jealousy on the part of those who visited. Or maybe it was me who had changed. Had I gotten a big head because of this big house? I hoped not.

Even with this newly fulfilled dream, my drinking got worse. Since we now lived too far from our friends, we often had them over to our house for parties. I also started going out again after work and didn't come home right away. I began to feel lonely being so far away from my friends. I had a phone so I could always call them, and I always kept a bottle close to keep me company. And yet, something was always missing.

So once again I started looking for something to help me feel bet-ter. Nothing I was currently doing worked. I started hanging out in town with the people I knew did drugs. *Why not do it too?* I wondered.

Also in 2002, Josh was set to graduate, and Robert and his new wife were going to join us for the celebration. I felt as happy as I did the first day I held him in my arms as a newborn. I didn't feel I had much to do with this accomplishment or with all he had achieved over the years, yet somehow he gave credit to all of us who stood beside him on graduation day. I was so proud of him. He had asked me not to drink until the graduation was over, and I didn't. That day was worth every sober minute.

October 3, 2003

On October 3, 2003, I had been in sobriety for eight days going on nine. When I started drinking, at first it was for fun and only on weekends. Then it was every other day and especially weekends. Then all of a sudden I found myself staying up through one day and continuing to drink into the following day. My drinking was getting out of control, but I didn't stop. I developed crying spells and a sympathy attitude.

While one part of my being was crying out, the other part stayed true to my drinking. The struggle included stress, depression, anxi-ety, and unsure thoughts of suicide, all while in the process of get-ting settled in a new house and the responsibilities that came with it. With my job on the line and my body breaking down, I found myself turning to drinking even more.

I went through bouts of anger, which were manifested in many different ways. Good friends meant nothing. I used family members to cradle upon during my drinking episodes. I was no longer myself, and I couldn't seem to find who I was or what nature of a person I should be, or could be.

I experienced many blackouts. First not remembering what I had said or for that matter what any person had said to me. Confusion took over my mind. I started feeling paranoid that everyone was talking about me. Nothing being said was good, but I didn't care. I would just have a drink and soon I was back to myself, whoever that seemed to be at the time.

I told everyone I was going to explode and didn't know what kind of outcome would transpire. After a day's work and a few write-ups, which consisted of verbal and written warnings about my attendance, I had only two days left to miss and a three-day suspension looming. I found myself in the bottle for one and a half days. I had also been suffering from neck surgery and back problems. I felt I was being picked on at work and was being punished for trying to get better.

I could not stop crying and I couldn't stop drinking. Nothing mattered anymore. I had hit the deep end of life. With my job hanging by a thread, my body dealing with continuous pain, and my mind tortured with anxiety and stress, depression became a great concern to me.

The fact I didn't care about my friends surprised me. I had pushed away two of my best friends who left without me at a bar. What was next?

October 5, 2003

By October 5, I had been sober for eleven days. I started considering spiritual needs. Some things were coming together with the house, while some were not. Josh no longer lived with us, so Priscilla and I were alone at home. It sure was different. We've always had Josh or someone around. This change was certainly hard to get used to. Being alone at home, I hoped to get a lot of things done.

October 6, 2003

The following day, Priscilla and I attended First United Pentecostal Church in a nearby town. This was exactly what I needed. It brought back the presence of the Lord. However, my legs wouldn't move when they invited people to go forward for prayer. I didn't know why I was holding back. Uncontrollable tears fell from my eyes, but I just stayed in my seat. I wondered if anyone knew how badly I needed prayer! Then the sermon began and, lo and behold, it was from Romans. I heard:

> *So God abandoned them to do whatever shameful things their hearts desired. As a result, they did vile and degrading things with each other's bodies ... That is why God abandoned them to their shameful desires. Even the women turned against the natural way to have sex and instead indulged in sex with each other (Romans 1:24, 26).*

86

Those verses made me realize how I had let go of God and turned to the worldly life. I felt as though the judgment was on. I sat in church and tried to act as if everything was all right. I felt a hardness over my heart, and now I was in a pickle. I needed to decide what to do next.

Trust in the Lord with all thine heart. A sense of being helpless ran over me. The battle was on and I was sure by letting go I would not win. It was as if I were sitting on a fence trying to figure out which side to lift which leg over to. I planned to return to church that evening, even though all I was feeling was guilt. I wondered if anyone knew Priscilla and I were partners. If they did, would I be looked at in a different way? I decided not to go; however, part of me still wanted to go because I knew I needed the Lord's help with all things. For I can do everything through Christ, who gives me strength (Philippians 4:13).

Today was the twelfth day since I had been sober. One day at a time, sweet Jesus. That was all I asked, and it became my new "awake prayer" and my new beginning for the strength I desired. I knew I was a long way from total recovery. I feared I was only in remission and someday I might fall back. I sure hope I am wrong.

October 7, 2003

October 7 marked thirteen days without a beer, and with it came a better understanding of alcoholism. I read the little red book, which explained the twelve-step program in detail. So far most of the steps I have let happen in a fashion only God could help me to know. I didn't realize I was doing any of the steps, until I read them. I could see God has been leading me all the way.

At the same time, I was also dealing with anger and resentment because I could never pick up another drink. I had to admit I was an alcoholic. I was beside myself. I cried real tears and wanted to let it all go, except part of me was afraid of failing. I must let it all go to the Lord above, in order to be free of this disease in my mind and body. A power greater than myself was at hand, and I knew I should let him work on every part of me. God could take away all things holding me to worldly thoughts and actions.

The aches and pains in my body were reminders of alcoholism. I hurt and nothing was helping. I used to drink to ease the pain. People say don't look back; it's time to look forward. But this day and every day I must look back to remember what a drink would do to me.

October 8, 2003

October 8 marked my fourteen days of sobriety. The day before was difficult. I really wanted a drink, but instead I got some nonalcoholic beer, which satisfied my craving. I became angry again because I couldn't have a drink like other people. I had an appointment with the AA counselor and didn't know how it would go. I decided I would try to go to church that night.

When Priscilla arrived home from work she seemed to be doing a little better. I was having a hard time being close to her and wasn't sure why. I guessed I really was a different person compared with my drinking person.

October 9, 2003

> *Today Shell Lake has an AA meeting. I will proceed to make it today. I do realize my weakness of human self is at hand and so this means my entire future is at stake. I will have to stay strong to be able to see how Priscilla and I will be.*

> *Thelma called. It seems as if there is a different way we talk with one another since I told them to move out. If I hadn't told them to move, I would not have made the first step to stop drinking.*

October 10, 2003

I made it to the AA meeting in Shell Lake. A lot of people there were in recovery for many years, while some, like me, were there for the first time. We spoke on humility. I admitted for the first time ever in a group that I was and am an alcoholic and that I had sixteen days of sobriety.

I woke in the morning feeling nervous. Today was my luncheon for being at my job for five years. I was nervous because I'd been out of work off and on since June when I returned after surgery. A per-son I disliked, who also had the power to hire and fire, would also be attending the luncheon. My anger had been tested with him in the past, and now he's had the ammunition he needed to fire me at any time.

When Priscilla arrived home from work, we would leave for Mom's. Mom was always there for me, and I was grateful for all she has done for me.

I now had sixteen days of sobriety. At times it seemed easier, then other times it seemed impossible, but here I was hanging in there day by day. The test of change: The things I had done while drinking I have been doing without it and it seemed strange.

October 11, 2003

I reached seventeen days of sobriety. I found joking around about going to the bar and such helped me through yesterday off and on. I headed to my AA meeting and was amazed as I listened to the people's stories and how the system worked, and how God has done such work in all of us. I began to feel as though I belonged there.

God seemed to be working through me. I talked to one man who was in relapse again after six years of off-and-on sobriety. My advice to him was to cry, and cry as long and as many days as it would take. I knew this was what I needed, but I didn't know if this would be beneficial for him. I've come to an understanding that God knows why every tear falls and I believe he picks them up and starts his movement. Anyway,

I know I probably shouldn't be giving advice, but I sure felt it was my place in that situation.

October 13, 2003

I went to church twice Sunday, once at Mom's church and then at the nursing home with Grandma. Both lessons were good ones for me. The first one was on the lost son-lost sheep (Luke 15). I really related to this for I know the Lord let me go my own way and now, thank God, he is there for when I returned to him. Most people don't forgive, but I am grateful we have a God that does, no matter what we've done.

Eighteen days of sobriety had passed. Day by day it seemed to get better.

October 14, 2003

I had read some of the AA book and also my *Our Daily Bread* guide. It talked about self-centeredness, fear, security, and how the Lord has us to shine our light for him, and how if we allow him to take fear and selfishness away we can show our light and that he gives to us freely of his will.

I would just have to let him take all of this away and let him instill in me what it is he wants for me in my future of sobriety. Letting go was hard, but it needed to be my only way to stay free of alcohol.

I had reached twenty days of sobriety and was starting to feel bet-ter. The anger of not being able to drink had lessened. At times my mind slipped away; but that's when I asked God to help me once again.

October 15, 2003

I went to the park and saw Robin, whom I hadn't seen or talked with for months. We didn't have much to say to one another, which was unusual. Maybe it was just showing I had changed. It was probably a good thing that most of my drinking friends had been fading away for quite some time. This made everything much easier for me to deal with my drinking problem.

Twenty-one days of sobriety and it was only the beginning of this new life.

October 16, 2003

On my 21st day of sobriety I felt very worried about our finances. With me not working and Priscilla doing her best, we were just broke. With so many demands on us for bills to be paid, I hoped something would happen for the good and that we could at least get caught up.

October 19, 2003

Day 25 of sobriety fell on a Sunday. We planned to attend church that morning. Lord knows I needed all his strength that day and every day. Friday I was close to a fall, when I went to the store and bought some nonalcoholic beer. That craving for the taste of beer was so strong. I sure missed the satisfaction of a genuine buzz. Finally, when I felt pretty full I realized I didn't want it anymore. And no after-effects!

Who am I and what will I be? How will I be? When will the joy and happy nature be natural?

October 20, 2003

We went to church yesterday, and I enjoyed both Sunday school and the service. I needed both lessons very much. The first one was about asking God for a vision so we can stay focused on his works. The other included renewal of mind and body and letting Jesus lead us to our futures.

How can we afford to turn from Jesus? We don't have time to walk away from God. Yesterday was my time to kneel before Jesus and ask him back into my life, heart, and soul. We can't afford not to walk with Jesus. I knew by walking away years ago it threatened the gift of the Holy Spirit I was so freely given. From this point on, I planned to pray for his presence daily. All I had seen until now, in a sense, was me tugging on the bottom of his robe and him looking down at me. I needed to feel the victory of reassurance that he had forgiven me of all things.

With his help, I would be okay. I couldn't do anything right on my own. I knew today or yesterday – every day – I needed to get on my knees and continue to ask for God's presence. I was unhappy most all the time – wanting back what I had lost, but wanting what I wanted at the same time. I needed to let go of myself. I needed the presence of God. God was providing the strength and courage I needed. Without him, I would be drinking again. He was teaching me it was not easy to live with self and how important it was to let his will be done. Self was what set me back for all these years.

selfishness

self-pity

self-endurance

self-satisfaction

self-understanding

I want, I want, I want

me, me, me

Now it was time to let go but only if I really meant it. I had always been independent. It would take a lot of prayer and acceptance to let go. I used to say, what's one more day to drink? And, I'll stop tomor-row. Now I prayed that if the Lord saw fit for me to have all I desired of his presence, I would not take it lightly. They say you don't miss what you never had. Well, in my case, I had a special Spirit and I missed that. Obedience.

October 21, 2003

I reached day 27 of sobriety and was having a hard time trusting all things would work out with God, if I just let go and trusted him to fix all that was needed in me. I knew if I cared about Jesus and had the confidence in him by faith, I would trust in his power to keep me in his hope of being a new person. So that day I held faith in God as I trusted his power to save me and renew what he saw fit for my future.

October 22, 2003

I felt the need for spiritual music. Praise unto Jesus. I could feel him working with me. I gave thanks to the Lord for I knew, now, that he was working with me. I had gone to a meeting yesterday and the topic was promises. I didn't have much to say, but I listened carefully. God's promise for us was that he would never leave or forsake us. I was standing on the faith of belief that this was so true.

Today by the grace of God I was alive. I believed he had a purpose for my life. I surely would be ready when he led me to my works and a vision to know what it was I must do.

Twenty-eight days of sobriety and it seemed not so much a battle today. I thanked Jesus for giving me another chance for his love. The burdens I'd been carrying didn't seem so heavy as before.

I must never forget how much confusion and depression, stress, and so on were in my past. For a great many years, while it was easy to fall back into the world, it was not as easy to fall back into safe arms.

I really didn't experience any real happiness in my worldly ways. Alcohol was what I lived life on. "Cope" was a word in the sermon yesterday, and today I understood: I had to cope with what I had created and someday all would be better. I was learning to cope with situations normally a drink would cure. I had never been good under pressure. It seemed I always ran to a way out or just ran away.

October 23, 2003

I was thinking back on all the times I drove while intoxicated. The Lord, I believed in my heart, had given me another chance. I knew this was it, and I prayed he would not leave me and that he would give me strength and courage every day for his will and not my own.

October 26, 2003

Learning to have fun in sobriety was a must for me. I needed the support of all the AA members and was the kind of person who needed fun things to do. In my drinking days I was always the planner for activities and food, places to go, and so on. The thing was I also made sure there was enough beer, too. Now there was no beer but all else remained the same. It was a good feeling when people joined me in a sober time of fun, even though I knew some people would be dis-tant from me because I didn't drink anymore. These people were the ones who only cared about their own drinking. I was once that kind of person. I'd say, "What? No beer? Well, then I'm not going there!"

October 27, 2003

I went to church and Sunday school and enjoyed both lessons. They had to do with words we utter aloud to others, and how careful we should be in what we say. As we all know, words cannot be taken back and sometimes cannot be forgiven. To be more like Jesus – that is what Christians are about. Then, now, and forever we should continue in prayer. Pray to have all his riches in glory.

At church, I went up for prayer. I knew the Lord was blessing me in some kind of way. However, I still felt as if I was in a fog of spirituality. I would just keep on going to church and AA. Whatever it took, forever. I would continue to seek the Lord and strive for his knowledge and his peace. From past experience I knew the Lord could do all things.

October 28, 2003

On day 34 of sobriety I felt a bit of fear. Fear that I would probably fail again. I rebuked this attack on my mind as I knew it was not of God. I would continue in prayer. One day at a time, sweet Jesus. Give to me strength and courage.

October 29, 2003

I have to remember today that God has done all things with his power. To take my life back in his hands, I must realize he is in control, not I! How do I know any step in this new life is of God and not of self?

November 16, 2003

Fifty-four days of sobriety! I never thought I would make it past two days. I didn't do it alone, but with the help of God, AA, and sober friends. I was looking forward to church. I needed the presence of God and felt a bit slack on his moving in my life.

November 23, 2003

I was excited. I had made it to sixty-two days sober and I was finally starting to feel better. I was learning to let go and let God do for me what I could not do for myself. The search for God's will in my life was also a one-day-at-a-time issue.

November 28, 2003

Yesterday was Thanksgiving Day and my first holiday in years without a drink. I felt lost for a while, but then I realized I'd be okay. Thanks to the Lord. Without God, I would have been drinking. Sometimes – most times, I can't really tell if he's with me. However, I knew he was working with everything around me and in me.

I still hungered for that victory and joy. I figured I must be hold-ing back on certain circumstances in life with the fear of letting go without knowing the outcome.

I knew the Lord worked in mysterious ways. I was very thankful he listened to my cries.

November 30, 2003

There sure was a lot of talk out there from past friends. I got to the point where I didn't trust any of them. I had never felt so distant from everyone. A lot of trust had been broken and over things that didn't even make sense to me.

No matter how you've helped people out, they tend to only think of the worst things you've done, not the good. This was very hurtful and unbelievable. It made me all the more thankful to have a church to attend and an AA group where I could express myself. Without these two important places, I would be drinking again.

At least my family was supportive. God had helped me in a num-ber of ways and for this I was grateful. I knew with God on my side I couldn't go wrong. I prayed I would always remember what I had become and the difference God had made in my life. My past life was something to learn from and not to return to.

December 26, 2003

Blessing. This was the topic presented at AA on Christmas Eve and what an appropriate one. I have had so many blessings. My health, which was getting better, a warm place to sleep, and food in my tummy. It was a real blessing to know God had given his Son so we could live everlasting. It was a blessing I still had a job, and without the Lord this would not have been the case.

My sister made it here on the 24th. It sure did feel good to have a Christmas together with no one drinking. I didn't miss drinking as much as I first did. I found a way to be in the in-crowd without giv-ing in to it. I would call that a blessing since my way to fit in before was to join in.

February 4, 2004

Four months into sobriety and a lot has gone on. I feel much better, now. On February 4, my sister and I visited the Walt Disney Resort. While it had been some time since I had desired a drink, today was one of those days. Through God's strength I overcame and now peace has returned.

February 9, 2004

We made a trip to Dad's for his birthday. His birthday party was good with quite a few people stopping in and some staying the night. Kinda like home for me in a way. I thought I would clean Dad's house as a birthday gift. This kept me away from alcohol for a time. Deb-bie tended bar while I cleaned and later played a few games of darts.

Later in the day I took her spot tending bar and by then I was sur-rounded by people who had consumed enough alcohol to be obnox-ious. As I listened to them talking, arguing, and such, I realized how much I didn't miss any of those conversations.

Dad and I thought alike about certain things, just as Debbie and I were so different at times. I was grateful I was not the person I had been four and a half months ago. If the old me had come for a visit, this time with Dad would have been one of fighting or arguing, and this day with him would have been shot.

February 29, 2004

I arrived back home from Florida. It was cold here. I had made it without a drink now for five months. A few times I was tempted, but that faded. Thank God.

Thursday I went over to Lorrie's. She told me she has let the Lord into her heart. I was shocked, but very happy for her and prayed for God to lead her in all the right directions.

Krista, Lorries girlfriend, is Catholic like Priscilla,. They have different ways of praising, praying, and confessing. Only God knows the road for them. All I could do was pray they do what God would have them to do.

Lorrie was also in that conviction stage, and it isn't easy to know the right thing to do. I haven't been to AA, but I knew I needed to get there this week. If for no other reason, I needed the fellowship. I have no friends except Lorrie and Krista and that is even fading.

March 7, 2004

I had a scary dream last week. My birthday was very close, with a month to go. In my dream I had a party and gave in and drank my used-to-be-favorite drink. People were there whom I hadn't seen in a long time. In the dream, I made several phone calls. My old self was surely back except this time I didn't remember anything spoken of, only that I drank and now couldn't stop.

Thank God it was only a dream. I believed it was a warning sign. My conscience was letting me know I was becoming weak. I hadn't attended an AA meeting in over a month. It was time to put the first step of AA into action. The fact was my AA group of friends was needed every day, not just the first day. That's the way it would always be. Together, we thank God for a second chance.

So on Friday I attended my used-to-be-usual meeting and was so glad I did. I knew I had a sponsor but had never really taken advan-tage of that fact. At one point this woman wasn't ready or comfortable being a sponsor, but eventually she had asked me again if I wanted a sponsor, and I said "yes." I had someone to talk to anytime about anything, and this for me was the time.

My sponsor said, "It's time for you to get more involved and take responsibility." So now, on Friday nights, I would be in charge of the meeting. A commitment for me like this was scary. No excuses. I had to be there for other people going through what I had been through. This would be a blessing; a way to help others on their road to recovery, and it would help me keep my sobriety. Without that, I was a drunk.

March 14, 2004

I was called into the supervisor's office at work and prayed all the way there. "Lord, I can't take any more bad things." I was to the point where I hated going into his office. Another review. I had already had one, and it wasn't good. I expected this one wouldn't be either.

Well, he went back to 2002 again. All I could think was, *Does it ever end?* I was told my review was going to be in October of this year. I was upset. That meant no raise again for another year. I was so disappointed I took a half day off and went to pick up Lorrie. It wasn't until I began telling Lorrie about my day that I realized God had something to do with this. I started looking at the review as a fresh start, a clean slate.

Nothing bad was on my report from that day forward. All the write-ups were removed. My attendance became clear of problems; with another review I had a chance of a higher raise than it would have been. God had renewed my thinking. I was now saying it was a blessing, a new chance, a new beginning. So I went to my AA meet-ing and was asked to be speaker later in March. I never have been a person to talk in front of people unless I had been drinking.

A new beginning, yes indeed. I told them I had to pray about it. I just let it go. Then I asked Lorrie and Priscilla what they thought. After talking with them I figured it was a time for giving my testi-mony and guessed I was probably ready, so I said I would. If God be with me, no one can be against me.

I took over the Friday night meetings. That week there were only four people there. I was glad there weren't a lot of people, but my confidence grew and I thought I'd be ready the next week for more. *Thy will be done, not mine.*

June 4, 2004

As I was going on nine months without a drink, I was shocked I'd made it that far even with God. I still had the meetings on Friday night, and my Uncle David had bought me a daily devotional book. The gift surprised me and made me happy.

I certainly enjoyed God's place for me in his church. I almost hated to leave and go somewhere else. I'd gotten used to God's power and moving Spirit. I craved the presence of the Holy Spirit every day and every chance I got.

With Jesus helping me through the battle, I prayed one day at a time that he would grant me peace. I still struggled with some issues regarding God's will but together we were working it out.

This Sunday I would attend Mom's church. It would be different. I prayed for the Spirit to have his way. I'd gotten to where I could hardly sit still at our services. I was so thankful I didn't have to hold the Spirit of God down, but rather was free to rejoice and be glad in it.

July 3, 2004

On June 26, I received my nine-month medallion from AA for being sober. Temptation still came once in a while, mostly on Fridays after work. I understood why. It made sense to have to fight the hardest on that day, the day that used to mark the beginning of no end.

I thanked God every day for my sobriety and asked each day for another.

For the first time in this new life, however, last Sunday I didn't want to attend church. It was a good thing I didn't give in to that temptation. The message was about change. Homosexuality. And how mankind tries to change the Word of God to fit his needs and wants.

I needed to hear that message, but at the same time I didn't. I would just keep going to hear the Word of God and some day all his answers would be clear for me. We were making some decisions on some very important issues, and I believed God had the final decision.

I was looking at a program where I could bring patients into our home to care for them. It was a twenty-four-hour-a-day job. It paid well, and while that was important, the most important thing was to have the right person. I wanted to take in foster children eventually. We would have to see how it worked with one person first.

Josh finally got up here from North Carolina yesterday morning. I couldn't believe he has a mohawk. I didn't really care about his hair, though. I was just thankful he wasn't in trouble or doing drugs. I was blessed with a good son. The Lord had been really good to me.

I had two gardens going, and they looked good. We had cleared more land, and everything was starting to look good around the house. I learned there was a time to relax and sit back and enjoy accomplishment. I thought about when God made the heavens and earth and on the seventh day he rested. And it took me how long to do what I had done? He's an awesome God.

Sunday I would have Josh with me at church. First time since he was very little, especially in a Pentecostal church, and I was thankful.

August 13, 2004

We have been told about caring for people with disabilities in the home. So since this is something I've always wanted to do, and Pris-cilla too, what an opportunity to use this house for a good purpose. God is really working for the good in my life.

Joshua was here to visit and it was a good visit, too.

I decided a couple of weeks ago that I would not continue the Friday night AA meetings, since I really needed to go fishing and relax after work instead of go-go-go all the day and night long. I felt pretty strong with the Lord. At least I am open to him and pray to give my all. I have a lot to learn.

I have decided to get more reading in. There are times when I get this good routine going and it's working for reading my devotions and my Bible and for praying, and then all of a sudden I change and break the routine. All of these should be greater than they are. I've decided I need a special place just for Jesus and me. No distractions. I like the water on the boat in the lake. But that won't work for winter, so I really need the place soon. I think getting the basement going might give me a Jesus-and-me place.

Since I last wrote, Thelma was saved and the Spirit was really moving. Lorrie was also there. Josh attended church with us and for me it was great.

Our application was accepted and we passed for the caregiving job. Tonight would be our first night as official caregivers. Vickie was a special young lady. We were blessed to be trusted with her care.

August 15, 2004

Heading to church this morning. We have Vickie to get ready and all is going well. I have probably stepped on some toes this morning suggesting we not smoke on the way to church. Well, I just can't see smelling like smoke today, even though I probably do.

I must not be judgmental and I find this hard lately. Lor-rie and Thelma both know the Word enough now to do the right thing, but I must remember where I've been and not to be judging what is right for them. With all this, I must concentrate on my relationship with God and know that I am right with him. Am I?

In three days it will be eleven months since my last drink. One thing is for sure; I only got this far with God's help, not mine.

Lately I have faded away from the AA group, finding a lot of language I'd rather not hear. I'll have to pray about this 'cause I think I still need the support there as well as church.

August 29, 2004

I had a trying week of work, and I wanted to drink. My arm was healing from when I hit it on a steel part of a frame press earlier, but I couldn't use it much. I hated this. I wanted to drink badly, but my eleven months of sobriety stopped me from doing that.

I had done some things I couldn't even imagine I would do. It made me wonder where I stood with God. The lukewarm thing had become my issue.

I had missed going to AA meetings for three weeks. Finally yesterday I went. After everyone spoke, it was my turn. I realized I wasn't alone with the "I don't care" feelings and attitude. It was a good thing I went. The meeting dealt with the first step: that I am powerless over alcohol and my life would be unmanageable if I were to drink again.

I couldn't believe how God worked, even if I didn't want to acknowledge him. I had been in a fog, had let myself down. Now I had to get back up. Today we would go to church and then head to Shawano for a revival. Maybe I would feel something. I didn't want to go back to drinking, and now I was feeling very tried about other things. I sure needed prayer!

August 30, 2004

Following Sunday school, I went to the revival yesterday. I felt as though I needed healing in every part of my being, especially spiritual. God touched me and I actually felt some peace. I started wondering about another thing, too. Was I baptized properly? Did I need to renew this to be sure?

Yesterday morning before we left church the pastor spoke with me for a few moments. From what he said, I feared he knew about the battle I was fighting, and that I could not do it without Scripture and the help of counseling. A reality check! God was at that moment working in his people.

It had been a while back when the pastor had asked to speak with me about receiving the Holy Ghost. At that time I feared we would speak of much more – things I wasn't ready to talk about. So that conversation never took place.

This time was the right time. I needed help with this relationship, and I needed to humbly ask for it by losing my pride. It was time to stop hiding and to come out in the open. The need to be let free was still at hand. I was supposed to be letting go of those old habits and be new.

September 2, 2004

I was not sure if the Lord Jesus heard me regarding my arm heal-ing. Or maybe he has. I wasn't giving up. I wanted more of the Lord. Tested and failed. Yes, I was human, but did that give me an excuse to do wrong? I could answer that, but the thing was I didn't like the answer much at all.

I sat back wondering if God had forgiven me of my sins! How would I know? The closer I thought I was, the more it seemed I allowed something to take back my peace and joy.

This was a month, too, in which I had cried to God often, and he had answered me in his way by not allowing temptation to take over. In twenty-two days I would be sober one year!

September 6, 2004

Yesterday I went and saw Grandma and got to spend some time alone with her. I asked her if she went to church and she said, "Yes." Then I asked her what the preacher talked about.

"Salvation," she said.

I thought it would be good to read to her from my daily devotional for the day. Never would believe it would also be on salvation: John 3:16. I felt the need to say a prayer with her. God answers prayers. I let her know God was and is a sure part of my life.

Part 3
The Turning Point

Only in God is there true victory and true freedom. Only in his Word can we find peace and security. Only after a turning point in our lives can we know God and the blessings he has for us. Like Saul on the road to Damascus, I reached a turning point and God led me out of the darkness.

September 16, 2004

Even though I had been in recovery for a year, it was still a struggle. AA worked for some of it but not for the spirituality part of it. My uncle who was a minister had recommended I read the Recovery Bible. I had asked for it for my birthday and received it as a gift from my mom. I started reading it every day, and it opened my eyes to the deceptions in my life. I was still in life situations where I didn't know how to go the right way and the Recovery Bible started showing me the way. Each step revealed a situation in my own life. God showed me this through people he used in the Bible. At first it didn't all make sense, but gradually, step by step, I started to see where my own life was. It was a transition for me. I started reading the Recovery Bible every day, and it opened my eyes to the deceptions in my life and offered encouragement. I've shared my journal entries and the les-sons I learned in hopes they will help others.

Step One (AA): No-win situations. Genesis 16:1–15. It's a double bind. To please one is to disappoint another. Self-deception: Powerlessness over dependencies. After victory, feeling emotionally and physically spent. Must not go back into failure and become discouraged. Surely we will fail. I need God, and it is God who has given to me the strength I have needed not to be a slave to my addictions. I am like Samson. God gave him a power to overcome his enemies. Likewise he has also given to me power to overcome alcohol and now I need the Lord's strength to overcome all things. I realize from past failure that the minute I take my eyes off Jesus I am sure to fail.

Humble beginnings: 2 Kings 5:1–15. Naaman, a man with leprosy, was told by a man of God, Elisha, to wash himself seven times and he specified where. If Naaman had not listened to the exact instruc-tions, he surely would not have been healed as promised. This was true in my life. Had I not thrown my hands up to God and with faith believed there was a God who could heal all things, my destruction would be final. The Lord God has answered the cry of my heart. And like leprosy, so are my dependencies. As I obey the Lord in all things, recovery happens.

Hope amidst suffering: Job 6:2–13. Grieving is necessary to be humble before God. I must suffer the loss of my addictions, gather hope, and by faith believe God will do for me what he sees fit in his time.

Watching for those who don't believe in my recovery. I believe only in God and his will for my life. I'm going on a year of having this grieving experience. Beer was my best friend. Losing that friend and having a hope in God that I could and would be able to live with-out this sort of friend is a day-by-day process. I was consumed by its power and was defeated by its outcome. It's a self-inflicted desire to have something so strong in my life. Humility in all things is my only way to recovery.

September 17, 2004

Like little children. Mark 10:13–16. Have the faith of a child. Jesus said, *"Verily I say unto you, Whosoever shall not receive the kingdom of God as a little child, he shall not enter therein"* (KJV).

As a child it seemed I was crying out all the time. Not exactly sure what anyone would do to help me. No one could help me with my efforts, and at a young age my problems were now only mine – no one could be trusted with the information I held.

It seems God was there for me. I remember I looked forward to Bible camps and was at peace while I was away. The attention I needed was there. However, I still had to return home. At an older age, my way to get someone I could trust enough to listen to me was to run away. When that didn't work, the reality and problems I carried were only mine. No one could possibly believe such a story. So I think I relied on my own understanding and not that of my elders or God. No one helped before, so I believed no one could help me then.

Leaving all of that behind. Promising to raise my own child with understanding no matter what he was to say.

I learned how to have different personalities. One was the girl who was good and pleasing in the places where no threat existed. The second one was the girl who did wrong and found more trouble than she needed.

Still the battles of good and evil were present in most of my young life and then I faced the same in adulthood.

Obedience and discipline were never part of my life. Somehow I learned not to obey and, instead, got an attitude of doing things my way no matter what. I take that back. I was disciplined much but found it to be unjust. I did obey in most things and that at a young age was the problem. Obey your father.

Now in life I still have two fathers: one heavenly and one not. This time I am learning a new trust for my heavenly Father and a new forgiveness for my earthly father.

I think because I lost trust in my father at a young age, I am hav-ing problems believing in the Lord. It says to trust in the Lord with all thine heart. I have faith and I have to hold onto that. I believe I can trust my Father in heaven who will supply all my needs accord-ing to his riches in glory.

September 18, 2004

A time to choose. Acts 9:1–9. The Scriptures talk about Saul who wanted to destroy the believers of God. Saul was blinded for three days and went without food and drink. Then Jesus spoke to Ananias and told him to find Saul so he would see again, for Jesus was to use Saul as an instrument to save the Gentiles. Instantly he was filled with the Holy Spirit and regained his sight.

It's September. Almost a year ago I needed to choose to live or die, and by dying I would surely be alone with my bottle. I knew what I needed to do, and wasn't sure where it all would end up. One thing is for sure. I needed to make a decision to either drink or not to, and in order not to, I knew nothing but Jesus himself could help with my disease. One day I threw up my hands and cried out for help. I knew this might change my entire life, but my cry was real, yet my own desires were as well.

I explained to many of my friends that they probably wouldn't like me or want to be around me after this transformation took place. I think they feared what I might do if something else was to go wrong. I knew somehow I was on the road to self-destruction.

That day did come. I lost it and remember it not. To drink or not to drink was the option. The time had come to choose which way to go.

My prayers started with, Help me, Lord Jesus. Then he did. He gave me the courage to enter into detox – an important first day of recovery. Today I think of the ways I was led into this life with Jesus.

I need to take one day at a time with Jesus – every day. The choice is mine, but the end decision will always be his.

I don't believe I choose friends. I believe God puts them there and removes them if need be. I must accept whatever his decision will be. The fact is, I surely had no control over self and still don't, if it wasn't for Jesus.

September 21, 2004

<u>Step Two (AA): Persistent seeking. Job 14:1–6. How frail is humanity. How short is life and how full of trouble.</u> In my first months of recovery, some questions would not have made sense, except that trouble was always my problem. When I had to accept that I could no longer drink, I suppose I said to God, "Why can't I be like those who can put it down?" In fact, I still ask that question but now real-ize I am of God and he surely cannot be in the nature of me when I drink. I cried out many times for God to help me and cleanse me. One day at a time, sweet Jesus.

At the rate I was going, I was surely going to die before my time. Now I am grateful to God that he has renewed my mind. Even though my human nature tries to get in the way, I continue to seek God. I am still a babe in Christ. I got up to walk by myself and failed yet again, not by drinking but by other natures of sin I can no longer live among. Today I continue seeking wisdom and knowledge, and I need much peace and joy.

My heart is in awe. I'm still seeking God, and yesterday I believe I got an answer: Just don't quit. Today is realizing how short life is and how full of trouble. Job 14. That's just it. We don't know how long we have or even how much we will endure while here on earth.

I had a talk with Thelma yesterday, and I pray the words I said were flowing from the Lord. She commented on how strong I am. I had to let her know this is of God, because I am the weakest without him. My strength comes from Jesus, and she can have that, too.

The paradox of powerlessness. Second Corinthians 4:7–10. Don't quit. I must continue going back to church and keep learning. However, there are many things I still don't want to hear.

> *Those who indulge in sexual sin, or who worship idols, or commit adultery, or are male prostitutes, or practice homo-sexuality, or are thieves, or greedy people, or drunkards, or are abusive, or cheat people – none of these will inherit the Kingdom of God (1 Corinthians 6:9–10).*

When my past resulted in a number of all the things listed above in some way or another, my life was doomed. By God's grace, he has let me back into his righteousness. I have failed in a few ways by own my desires and have come short of the glory of God. The peace within me did leave for a time. I will not give up. I must continue to listen to God, even though my human nature failed again.

I have faith God can take away my sinful ways. I also believe there is a time for everything. I have a fear of knowing. The more I know, the more I am concerned for my life with God. We know right from wrong and still do the wrong.

Oh, where do I stand? Once again I'm at the feet of Jesus asking for forgiveness. Now I need to ask for strength not to fall into diverse places. God doesn't just erase our sinful behaviors. Now I'm realizing it is not only being addicted to drinking, but in all things ungodly I have to look up always to not fall down.

Jesus obeyed God in all things and looked to God for answers. Jesus was God, but he still lived in a world as we do today. He looked up for answers instead of leaning on his own understanding. Like with Adam and Eve, God made them both and it came down to obey-ing, not questioning what the plan is, and believing God knows all things before we do.

Today I understand God has answered many of my cries and will be there for all of them. Seek ye first.

September 23, 2004

I've given in to Priscilla, and I just don't know where my life is headed. Am I damned? 'Cause if I am damned I should just give up on everything and go back to a year ago.

If I still have a chance, I don't want to miss out on that either. I am surely in a bad situation for myself and surely pray and hope to understand.

Am I living a lie? Will I not be saved? Am I? What is my purpose here? And how does a person change just like that? Am I supposed to change and be weak or am I weak because I never really changed?

Sometimes I have this feeling I was and have been cheating Pris-cilla out of a good life relationship. Something she could have forever, not just for a time.

Have I cheated myself and her from a wonderful plan God may have? Where and how can I get those answers? Surely I need spiritual guidance. I also need God, Jesus Christ. If I keep messing up, where will I be? Will God help me and forgive me for all I continue to do? The battle of right from wrong.

September 24, 2004

One Year Sobriety. Grandiose thinking. Daniel 4:19–33. Grandiose means showy or pompous, not really magnificent, but trying to seem imposing or impressive.

The warning to the king was to change his sinning and break from his wicked ways. He did not, and one day boasting of how good he was and of what he had, an hour later he lost it all and was not to return to human society until he honored and recognized the most high God.

The king was gone from his palace long enough that his hair was as long as eagles' feathers and his fingernails were like those of birds' claws. When sanity returned to him, he praised God and honored him, saying, God's rule is everlasting and his kingdom is eternal. God will remove our sufferings when we have learned the lessons he wants to teach us.

Since I started drinking back in 1989, I didn't want anything to do with quitting. I lied to myself and denied I had a problem with drinking. This denial went on for years, and the outcome of those years included DUIs, going to jail, disorderly conduct charges, being out of money, going to court, losing my driver's license, a divorce, and on and on.

In 1996, I truly knew I needed help, but I didn't want to give up everything forever. So needless to say I went back to the bottle. I had to hit bottom before my stubborn self would begin to change. I had to admit all things were completely out of my control.

In 2003, after a night like many other nights, I realized I always drank when I couldn't deal with situations or really didn't want to deal with them. I had to hit rock bottom before I could understand a new beginning. In tears, I threw up my hands to God with all my heart. I knew this time I really wanted God back in my life, and I would do whatever it took. I had a beer in my hand, holding it up to God and pleading with him: How will I be able to let go of the one thing I love so much in this life?

One day at a time. Because I was drinking I couldn't imagine these words, but somehow I believe God comforted me by letting me know he'd be there for me. Still today, one day at a time, sweet Jesus, is the best way to start and finish a day. I believe with all my heart he will help me, if I let him in. I didn't stop drinking instantly, but there was a sort of peace when I didn't have to be alone with this.

Hi. My name is Priscilla and I have seen Marilynne through her program and now it's been one year with her sobriety. Marilynne, I want to let you know I could not be any more proud of you than I am right now. At times you've struggled, but you made it.

And on behalf of your family, they are very proud of you, too, and know you will continue to strive to remain sober now and forever.

So I am giving you this medallion in honor of your one year and every time you look at it, you'll be reminded of how far you've come.

September 25, 2004

Internal bondage. Mark 5:1–13. All that is needed is faith, believing Jesus Christ can do all things. As I read about the insane man in this Scripture, I was kind of the same in my addictions. I lost all concept of life, not caring if I lived or died, acting crazy, and doing things I would not do now. Jesus healed a woman who only touched his robe by faith. He brought back a little girl from death and told them not to say a word. Him telling them not to say anything; I don't understand.

I believe in Jesus and all he can do. But I still think about things I think he can't do or maybe it's just I haven't asked for forgiveness from him to be able to do these things.

I yelled out to Jesus and now I am trying to follow his words. I still have feelings to do what I want, and I slip back into my sinful nature only for a time. Sometimes I am sorry and other times I am not. I feel myself slipping away to a place that is not good.

I still have internal bondage of disobedience to the written laws. Surely I have to let go and let God. The thought of slipping back scares me, for I understand the many consequences.

My belief is there, but my strength is weak. Still I hold on to the belief that God, Jesus Christ, can do all things.

September 28, 2004

Healing faith. Luke 8:43–48. The woman in this story believed if she could just touch the robe of Jesus she would be healed from a hemorrhage no doctor could heal. Her faith resulted in complete healing.

This reminds me of going into detox and how one doctor was in charge of me, but I needed more help than that. I left detox with faith believing God would help me. My cries were continuous and my belief was strong. Every time I felt like drinking I would cry to Jesus. I realize now that I was grieving a loss, and it was all for the good. The glory be to God. God has taught me much. One thing is to look to him when I cannot do things by myself and have faith in him for all things.

I have begun a new year in sobriety. Earlier today I went to an AA meeting. The topic was "dry drunk." That is at least part, if not all, of what has been wrong with me lately. My attitude was like it was when I would use excuses to drink. The only difference was I didn't give in to my wants and excuses; instead I asked God to help. But the times I haven't asked is when trouble came in. This slight problem I really need to work on with God.

I start to clean up and don't want to talk to anyone and especially not God. Even though I feel trouble pressing in, I close my mind and heart, thinking if I don't feel anything, then I can't get in trouble for anything.

Well, I was being deceived. I need to let go of whatever the situation is, ask for help with this attitude, and pray it's not too late for forgiveness.

September 29, 2004

Restoration. Luke 15:11–24. This is the story of the lost son. I can relate to this story because the son left the good life, went into the world, and found all the bad ways to live. He was lost, spent everything he had, and then he became humble and sorry. His pride and disobedience taught him a lesson in life. His father opened his heart and arms to him with love and compassion. The son asked forgiveness for sinning against heaven and his dad. It did not matter to the father what his son had done wrong, but only that he was home asking for forgiveness.

I went out into the world away from God and did all I knew was wrong. I shut the door on all good things and decided to do what-ever my heart desired. I was gone for fourteen years. In those years, a couple of times I tried to go back to God, but somehow I didn't get there. I wasn't sincere. God and the church had open arms for me. The longing for goodness was restored in me just as it was in the lost son. God has granted me a second chance in life to live for him in his kingdom, and I must always remember the grass isn't greener on the other side.

Goals:

• Continue studies in the Steps program.

• Start walking again.

• Keep the house in order.

• Start reading the books on homosexuality.

God is trying to get through to me. Maybe if I go walking he'll have time to get across to me what I need from him. I am especially scared of going to the Cher concert alone with Thelma. This doesn't feel right. *God help me in all I do. Every day guide me in the right direction, I pray.* I really would rather spend my time going to revival for God.

My feelings of helplessness were bad yesterday, and I slept most of the day away. I'm more than ready to open up to God. I truly have to be concerned for where I stand with him. This is certainly a time in my life where God will have to come first and be a part of my every decision.

Evil is already trying to overwhelm me, and now I'll have to find a way with God's help. Lean not unto your own understanding.

September 30, 2004

Coming to believe. Romans 1:18–20. God's anger at sin. A question was asked of me the other day. If God made all things, then who made

God? Where did God come from? My answer is that we are just to believe in him that he exists and not to question it. Also, there is nowhere in the Bible where it says where he came from.

In this Scripture it seems to me it angered God when people could not just believe in him even though they had seen the great things he had done.

This reminds me of not believing God was and is greater than any addiction I have had. As long as I keep my eyes on Jesus and believe all things are possible, I will be fine.

God has put the knowledge to know him in our hearts but has left the decision up to us whether we follow him or not.

God has done for me what no man, doctor, or psychiatrist could do. God has taken away my desire to drink for today and has caused me to believe him always.

A verse comes to mind about how we know God but yet still look for other things to replace him because our faith disappears. And they began to think up foolish ideas of what God was like. As a result, their minds became dark and confused (Romans 1:21).

Romans 1:24: *So God abandoned them to do whatever shameful things their hearts desired. As a result, they did vile and degrading things with each other's bodies.*

I am that sinful person who God has let go to do what I wanted. I carry the burden of all the wrong I've done, and I now look to God for help.

Romans 2:4: *Don't you see how wonderfully kind, tolerant, and patient God is with you? Does this mean nothing to you? Can't you see that his kindness is intended to turn you from your sin?*

Sometimes I feel like I am sitting on a fence and might fall to the wrong side and that I won't be able to lift my leg back over. I pray to

God I don't fall short of knowing all he has for me to know. I truly have sinned in many ways and am not boasting in any of my sins.

Prayer, thanksgiving, praise, and worship. God's will is to be there when we ask him and to mean it when we ask. He knows our heart even in the womb, and I'm thankful he does know me. It is better for me to let him help me in all I desire of him.

Fourteen years ago I walked away from God and into sin. I pray I will always look up and that this does not happen again.

How long does it take? My commitment to Christ and to the process of change. When I quit drinking a year ago, I knew I would face the difficult decision of my relationship with Priscilla. From day one back in church, I knew the way I was living wasn't of God's will. However, at that time I felt pressed to take one thing one day at a time with God's help.

It's been a struggle to know who I am without a drink in my hand, let alone face losing the person I cared deeply for and committed my life so freely to. Our relationship changed once I quit drinking, and it wasn't the same for me anymore being sober. I've felt my spirit move backward instead of ahead where I need to be. I need to keep reading this book and praying to God for mercy to help me.

I finally have asked God to forgive me for what I have done and pleaded with him for help, even though I knew a long time ago it would come to this.

At church last week the preaching was on separation, and then today the AA meeting was on choices. How many more hints do I need? I know what we have to do, and today I started moving things into separate rooms. I continue to pray for God's will and his strength in giving to me the courage I need.

October 1, 2004

Hope in faith. Hebrews 11:1–10. Believing and having faith as a mustard seed comes to mind. This was about as much faith as I had at first when I raised my hands to Jesus. Today I have faith Jesus will do all things, maybe not in my time but surely in God the Father's.

Today I have faith God is going to lead me in an abundant life with him. I have come to realize how important it is to listen to instruction. God is working with me. I just wasn't obeying him, and my faith weakened. I pray God will strengthen me with the courage I need to follow his instruction.

I believe God can work through me and change my heart. I have faith knowing his will and that it will be done. God has given me his instructions to follow, and I believe with all my heart he is leading my path daily. Through faith I have started the step of separation with Priscilla and me. I didn't want this to happen, but then I felt the joy and peace God had given to me disappearing. I've asked God, What am I to do? What is it you want from me?

The stories and readings I've been doing lately have all reminded me I was looking in other directions. But now, in seeking Jesus first, my eyes and my heart have begun to open back up. This verse just popped out at me: Hebrews 12:5–6: *My child, don't make light of the LORD's discipline, and don't give up when he corrects you. For the LORD disciplines those he loves, and he punishes each one he accepts as his child.*

I believe this with all my heart. One weekend recently me, Pris-cilla, and two others went to the casino. We had some free money to spend, but by the time we left that money was gone. I felt bad and said this is as bad as drinking. I get started and I don't want to quit.

Well, Sunday came around and I went to church. Just like that the pastor's wife says, Christians don't gamble. I thought to myself, *How did she know?* God had just spoken through her directly into my heart. I don't even buy a lottery ticket anymore. Yes, I got my discipline for that day. First I lose money, and then I was told I can't be in those places anymore.

When I was young I remember I looked at women and thought how I could make them happy. I was always excited to meet people who were in a homosexual relationship. In fact, I looked up to them and wanted just what they had: the look, the talk, everything. I even looked at people walking down the streets and could almost be sure who was and who wasn't gay.

One day I was called a lesbian. The fear of being beaten to death made me deny it, so later I started hanging around with guys older than me to save my reputation. But as I grew older I found myself missing something men couldn't give me.

There was a time when I was really serious about a guy. He went to the church my aunt and uncle attended. It was different when I was around him. He liked me, but not to have sex with. We talked and went to church together, and during the summer I would see him. I was at ease with him and didn't desire sex. We talked about lots of things. The only time sex was brought up was when he said if we were to be together long enough to be married. This was good. Then I went home after summer and again the old person in me came back.

October 5, 2004

Step Three (AA): Trusting God. Numbers 23:18–26. Balaam was given a message by the Lord to go back and tell Balak, *Rise up, Balak, and listen! Hear me, son of Zippor. God is not a man, so he does not lie. He is not human, so he does not change his mind. Has he ever spoken and failed to act? Has he ever promised and not carried it through?... But Balaam replied to Balak, "Didn't I tell you that I can do only what the LORD tells me?"*

> *It is better to take refuge in the LORD than to trust in people (Psalm 118:8). For God has said, "I will never fail you. I will never abandon you"* (Hebrews 13:5).

This past week and a half has been a time of listening to and trust-ing in God. I believe God is helping me in this decision of separating rooms with Priscilla. I have cleaned out closets and moved things around, but I actually questioned this decision. With my sobriety and all God has done for me in this year, I didn't have peace with God about this relationship with Priscilla. We've shared fourteen years of our lives, and every time we got close again I would lose my touch with God. Finally it was time to let go of the fear and trust in God to do this. Trusting anyone with my life other than myself has been difficult for me.

I have been dreaming of my past. When I wake up I'm not sure what the dreams mean. Today with this lesson I believe God is letting me know he is going to fix the hurt I endured as a child and give me a peace I've never had.

From my childhood until now I learned not to trust, but now I finally trust in God with all my heart. No person could or can fix my heart, but I believe God can and will.

I do have this question: If God knows the hearts and desires of man, why was I not protected by God as a child? I pray someday I can understand what the purpose was and is in my new life with Christ Jesus. I do believe God can change things if we ask. I am an example of this in many ways.

October 6, 2004

Free to choose. Deuteronomy 30:15–20. We have been offered by God a choice that only we can make between life and death. Life in Jesus Christ or death by not letting God be in our lives.

> *But if your heart turns away and you refuse to listen ... then I warn you now that you will certainly be destroyed* (Deuteronomy 30:17–18).

This is a serious choice for me to make, and I thank God for not giving up on me. I truly believe God knows our hearts, and I believe he knows how far we will go with our addictions. When we can't take it anymore, we have a choice to live or die.

I came to an end and really was close to death. I was even considering taking my own life. Instead of giving up, however, I lifted my hands to him for help. I didn't care anymore about the life I was living, but hoped for a chance to receive his help.

I always remembered the special feeling I had when God moved in my heart. I could not have that back again without choosing God to be in my life. There were certain things I didn't want to give up, but I needed to choose one way or the other.

Today I am blessed to be able to say I am saved and that God has all parts of my life. Each day I learn something new. He is a gentle God who teaches me only what I need at the time. I've prayed for his will in my life, and today I remember the freedom he has given me to make choices. I choose not to drink and with God's support I won't.

October 7, 2004

Giving up control. Psalm 61:1–8. *Don't be drunk with wine, because that will ruin your life. Instead, be filled with the Holy Spirit* (Ephe-sians 5:18).

> *O God, listen to my cry! Hear my prayer! From the ends of the earth, I cry to you for help when my heart is overwhelmed* (Psalm 61:1–2).

Not long ago I cried out to the Lord to help me with my life, to give me the courage to do what he wanted me to do. I was overwhelmed with the thought of obedience and had to ask God with the little faith I had to hear me and help me. I was still holding on to past ideas. The danger with that was failure and self-destruction. We can get into that comfort zone of sobriety so easily, and then not work on the rest of the dreaded things we need to do.

As a very independent person, it is hard for me to let God have all control of my life. However, I have learned where relying on my own understanding has gotten me.

I like to listen to music and most of my day is spent listening to gospel music. I need to completely focus on God. For fourteen years of my relationship with Priscilla I have not been in control of my life. I have to let go now and let God lead me in all decisions. If I do things my way, I would return to what would end up killing me in time. I must not wait another minute to pursue God's righteousness.

I do not know the future, but he does, and I truly believe he will do his work, if we ask. I seek his knowledge and wisdom daily, and most of all the courage to go through what he may ask of me.

The only time in my life I was bold with character was when I drank. So even more now, I need God's courage because without him I have none.

Psalm 62:7: *My victory and honor come from God alone. He is my refuge, a rock where no enemy can reach me.*

I just got done reading all my devotionals for today and my mind is full. The Lord has been working with me daily, and I need it. Today is the day Priscilla and I finalize the rooms. She will be in her own as will I. After all these years together it doesn't seem possible to live in this way. In all my life my saying goes: things always have a reason for happening the way they do. In this case, I need God. His will for me is to not be with anyone right now. Hopefully that won't mean never. There is a lot the Lord and I need to work on and this will allow just that. His will, not mine. One sin leads to others. At least this is how my past has been. I don't just get into a little trouble; I go all out.

If I can do that with sinning, why not let God have his fair chance with me? I know in my heart he has a plan, a future, and it will be more abundant than the one I've done on my own. The past is the past, and I don't wish to shut the door on it. However, I sincerely want to learn from it.

My dreams are somewhat sacred. I had a warning sign, a red flag, not to go to the Cher concert with Thelma. She may not understand, but this flag tells me, if I want to go, I am putting myself in a non-controllable situation. Therefore, I am not going. There was a time I wouldn't listen to such a sign. However, that was then and this is now.

October 8, 2004

Redeeming the past. Isaiah 54:4–8. *Fear not; you will no longer live in shame … You will no longer remember the shame of your youth and the sorrows of widowhood. For your Creator will be your husband; the LORD of Heaven's Armies is his name! He is your Redeemer, the Holy One of Israel, the God of all the earth.*

My past years away from God turned my heart into stone as I walked away from just counsel and abandoned my spirit of hope, faith, love, and all that was needed for peace. Today's lesson is a great one to be learning and right on track for me. My dreams last night were of my past and the disgrace of all the wrong I have done. Today God has just answered the what, why, and how. That was fast. All I had to do was read his Word, and finally at the end of my morning devotions the answer hit home: we hand everything over to him, or, to rephrase that: I hand over to God every moment of disgrace, every tear I ever cried, every word I wish I could take back, all of my broken promises, loneliness, dreams that died, dashed hopes, broken relationships, my successes and failures, all of my yesterdays, and all of the scars they've left in my life. This is my prayer of mending and letting go to God.

My dreams are many but most confusing. My past with my ex-husband is in my dreams, but I don't understand what they mean. During our marriage my deceit and adulterous ways caused great unhappiness. I was looking for something then that still hasn't been found today. I'm not sure what these dreams are showing me other than the fact I've been with more than I care to count.

Finally, staying busy and getting things done are not a way to stay sober but a reward for achievement, to look at a job well done.

Isaiah 54:4 says to fear not. I no longer have to live with shame! When we give to God the past and our dreams of the past, he can make up for all we have lost. He can rid us of the shame and fill the empty places in our hearts. I understand now that I must give to God even my dreams of the past.

October 9, 2004

Submission and rest. Matthew 11:27–30. *My Father has entrusted everything to me. No one truly knows the Son except the Father, and no one truly knows the Father except the Son and those to whom the Son chooses to reveal him. Then Jesus said, "Come to me, all of you who are weary and carry heavy burdens, and I will give you rest."*

There certainly are times when the burden I try to carry on my own needs a rest. At the beginning of my worldly life I did not go to Jesus for help. Then, years later, I thought death was my only way out. Suddenly I realized only God the Father could take my pain away. I must never forget what God can do for me. I pray today that God will help me in every decision. My days of leaning unto my own self were times of destruction. Now only God can change what I have done. I've messed up a lot and need forgiveness on a daily basis with things that come to mind. I need to not only be forgiven but also to learn to continue in a life with God.

Awhile back I carried a heavy burden for my grandmother. I wanted to bring her home to live with me. I had everything planned and figured out, except it was what I wanted. I had to let this burden go to God and look for his will to be done. I saw what I will call a vision of Jesus holding onto my grandma and a sort of peace and joy grabbed my heart. Then a couple of weeks later a phone call came from Mom. She had spoken with my uncle, a minister. My answer from God came through, that if Gram was to get better, then by all means it was the perfect plan. But the consensus by the doctors and others involved was it would not be in Gram's best interest to live with me. I had to accept this as an answer from God. When I did, my burden became light and I rested in that.

Another burden way too heavy for me to carry was that of a homosexual relationship. I wanted God's will to be done. I am at ease waiting for the joy I know will come. God is an understanding God and he has the power to do all things. I've asked for guidance and strength and, of course, courage in this situation.

I did end up having the strength to change things and move my things from one room to another, and I had the courage to believe everything would be okay. God gave me the wisdom to know what I needed to do.

October 11, 2004

Discovering God. Acts 17:23–28: *He is the God who made the world and everything in it. Since he is Lord of heaven and earth, he doesn't live in man-made temples, and human hands can't serve his needs – for he has no needs. He himself gives life and breath to everything, and he satisfies every need.*

If the good news we preach is veiled from anyone, it is a sign they are perishing. *Satan, who is the god of this world, has blinded the minds of those who don't believe. They are unable to see the glorious light of the Good News. They don't understand this message about the glory of Christ, who is the exact likeness of God* (2 Corinthians 4:4).

God's promise: Jeremiah 29:13: *If you look for me wholeheartedly, you will find me.* When I lived in the world outside of God, I did not want to see or know what he could do. I just wanted to be selfish and live the way I wanted to live and be whoever I wanted to be. I found myself getting into drinking more and more and justifying all I did by saying the things of the world were mine to do with as I pleased.

For years I wanted gay marriage to be legalized so I would be right. Now that God has opened my eyes, I want totally the opposite and I think it is so wrong. The day we said our vows in front of other people, my son, and God, I justified it by the lies of the world, and now I will answer to that one day.

Blinded by Satan's lies, my life was in chaos, as I messed around with whomever I wanted to and didn't care about any of the conse-quences. One day, however, I got so miserable I knew this wasn't the way life should be.

Once in a while I would get some peace along with a flashback of when God was taking care of me. And of course I would pass that off since I had gone so far away from him I was blinded. I didn't believe God could or would forgive me for what I had done.

I sure missed the peace and joy God had given me so freely. I wanted it back. I needed to let go and let God have all of me no mat-ter what the outcome would be. One thing is for sure: today I'm at peace and God led me on this path of his courage and wisdom to know the difference. I am no more blinded by this world's deceit but am on a road to recovery that surely will be acceptable to the Lord Jesus Christ. If God be for me, who can be against me?

To God be the glory as I sit here reading morning devotions, realizing where God has brought me from and how the things of the world do not look pleasing to me any longer. I seek after God's will, the truth, and the light that is beyond anyone's imagination.

"Let go, let God" is my new start for each day as I seek after his wisdom and knowledge to be able to have the courage to walk in his likeness of righteousness. Yet I am made human. I must continue to seek God in all things I do.

God is real and if it were not so, I'd be drinking today. I don't have a desire to drink, and I feel a sort of peace about me. Although I feel like I need to do something, I'm not sure what.

We have a revival coming up next week. I really am looking for-ward to learning more. I'm anxious for what God's plan for my future is. Step by step he is leading me and I am trying to hear him day after day. Sometimes a message I hear or read doesn't make sense until later.

The service yesterday was, don't ask God if he's sure he knows what he's doing. God knows what's going to happen before we do.

Last week while moving some things out of my room and put-ting them into Priscilla's, I asked God, are you sure this is what I'm supposed to do? Then, sure enough, I got my answer. He would not have put the move in my heart so strong, if it wasn't what was right to do. One step at a time, just like one day at a time, sweet Jesus. Let go, let God.

Letting go of my life to God has been a hard thing to do, but with his constant reassurance of his words and teaching I find it easier to let him take care of things. My decisions and choices in the past have led to corruption, and now I must let God have all.

God, I want to know you. I want to love you and worship you. I want to be a woman who reflects your image. Cleanse me from everything that stands between you and me.

I have fears of making this decision of turning this and all things over to God.

- Friendship with Priscilla
- Closure completely
- Loss of home
- Her becoming involved with someone else
- Comfort
- Affection towards one another

October 12, 2004

Single-minded devotion. James 4:4–7. You adulterers! Don't you realize that friendship with the world makes you an enemy of God? I say it again: If you want to be a friend of the world, you make yourself an enemy of God ... But he gives us even more grace to stand against such evil desires. As the Scriptures say, "God opposes the proud but favors the humble." So humble yourselves before God. Resist the devil, and he will flee from you.

When growing up I can recall the nature of myself in wanting to do good and always ending up being bad. The battle continued as I grew older. When I would be with God's people I yearned to be like them. When I was away from them, I always seemed to find a place in worldly things. I was never satisfied by either one.

Today I yearn for God's presence daily that I may be drawn close to his power and strength. God created me with decisions only I could make. Today I want what he wants for me and to leave the world behind. I need to stay focused on the Lord and seek only knowledge and wisdom from him. Lean not unto my own understanding but in all things lean on God.

There was a time when I wanted what I wanted in this world and nothing else mattered. I would go to all lengths to get it. Today I want what God wants of me, and I will go to all lengths for good and not evil.

If I need to be focused only on God and not on worldly friends, then God will see this through, and I ask him to replace what isn't right with what is.

Remember, it is a sin to know what you ought to do and then not do it. Today this Scripture is a fine example of me. I need to get an alarm clock for Priscilla and do what is the right thing to do: the separation necessary to obey God completely.

October 13, 2004

Step Four (AA): We made a searching and fearless moral inventory of ourselves. Genesis 3:6–13. Coming out of hiding. Even in the beginning of time Adam and Eve decided to go against God's plan.

When they were found out they used excuses for what they had done wrong. Because of the serpent Eve took her eyes off God and failed him and gave in to her own desires.

Because of the great sin of Adam and Eve, we all come into this world as sinners, and as it was for them, we still have the right to make our own decisions. God had grace upon them to have them stay together to build a new life.

- Responsibilities

- Excuses

- Actions

From this past year's experience of living free from alcohol and drugs, I found times when an excuse for drinking would come to mind. It didn't matter what the excuse was. It could be as simple as it was a Friday. No matter the excuse, it was still my response that would bring about the outcome. I ask God for help in most all areas of my life now, and we still work on many.

God's plan is pretty direct. He says if you listen to what I have told you, then you will be okay. In his Word he says, follow my instruc-tions. I never wanted to listen to any authority years ago, and I have found the many reasons or excuses why. My actions led me down a trail of deception. Although I believed in God, I didn't at that time really think he could fix everything. I believe today in the power that is greater than any, and somehow I will be okay.

October 14, 2004

Facing the sadness. Nehemiah 8:7–10. Don't be dejected and sad, for the joy of the LORD is your strength.

There have been many days of crying and today it is a joy to be freed from the bondage of this world. Daily inventory of my life is based on the reading of God's Word, which is where I find out if there is anything I need to do or change.

At first the sadness of losing everything was overwhelming and almost took my joy of God away forever. I find today that God is my strength, and daily devotions are my learning process.

In the Scriptures it says the Law of the Lord was read, but the exciting part was the people understood the Law. This brings me to a time before I confessed my sins to God, when the words of the Bible really made no sense. Then when I let go and let God, I understood his Word. First the weeping; now the joy.

Today I am not sad to lose anything. I am thankful God cares for me enough to remove the things that cause me to fall back into the sins of my past life.

Having to face the wrongs of my life while drinking was very hard. Daily I would turn to Jesus and he eased my desires for the world. But I still had to confess to God and others my wrongs and take responsibility for my actions.

I cried at times and wasn't even sure why. But God surely knew the reason for every tear that fell. And by looking to God, I am sure he can help me in all areas of my life.

October 15, 2004

Confession. Nehemiah 9:1–3. *Those of Israelite descent separated themselves from all foreigners as they confessed their own sins and the sins of their ancestors.*

In the time of sobriety I've found God was daily working with me as I confessed all I had done wrong in the past, all I needed to be forgiven for. Sometimes I'd like to think I've covered it all, and then something else comes up that must go also.

Because of an adulterous act on my part I felt so much shame I thought I didn't need to be in church. My heart hardened and my marriage ended, and my drinking, smoking, and lesbian thoughts all started again. Back into the world I went, and all of these years later I still needed to ask forgiveness for adultery and not only that, but for everything added over the years.

I realize now how important it is to talk to God before making such harsh decisions. All I needed to do was confess my sins, ask for forgiveness, and follow God's plan. Instead I walked away and still had to answer to the thing I allowed to put me back into the world in the first place. I needed to own up to my own sins and truly be sorry for them.

I am truly sorry for ruining my marriage and raising my child in a way God did not intend. I feel the need to apologize to Robert for what I did, but it was so many years ago, I don't know. It might not be a good idea since he is remarried, and I am thankful he is now in church.

I have to write down what just happened. I went outside to tell the Lord I was sorry I ruined this marriage, and that I didn't want to be punished by not ever being married again. Then my phone rings and it was Don. I haven't spoken with him in over a year. He was my sidekick for a long time, but it can't be like that now. I told him I don't drink anymore and am trying to stay out of trouble. I'm going to go see him at 10:00 a.m. and I pray God guides my day. I will ask him if he would like to attend church with me. We'll see what happens.

October 16, 2004

Family influence. Nehemiah 9:34–38. But when all was going well, your people turned to sin again, and once more you let their enemy conquer them. Yet whenever your people cried to you again for help, you listened once more from heaven. In your wonderful mercy, you rescued them repeatedly.

I often wonder today what would be different if I had not been sexually abused. If I could have been a child and not been made into an adult at such an early part of life. In past sexual encounters I craved for someone to just love me. But that's just it: sex is what I got, not someone loving me for me. And even worse, those who fell into my needs were hurt. When someone began to love me without sex, I couldn't believe it was possible and pushed them away. Still to this day I have quite the problem in distinguishing the difference. In my mind, when you love someone sex usually is involved. I learned this as a child. Then it becomes lust. I am guilty because I tried not to allow any feelings to hold me in.

I cry to God again from my heart and wonder what I am to learn now. Where do I stand and what's next? How will I know if I'm doing the right things or not?

October 18, 2004

Finger pointing. Matthew 7:1–5. Do not judge others, and you will not be judged … And why worry about a speck in your friend's eye when you have a log in your own? This is the same as Adam and Eve blam-ing each other for the wrong they did.

Human nature has tended to be that way from the beginning, but we must take inventory and responsibility for our own actions. No one but me caused me to sin. I alone made the decisions, and I must say I rarely if ever made the right choices. So now I'm asking forgive-ness again and praying not for the temptation, that I might serve the Lord the way he meant for me in the beginning.

The same things I've talked about that aren't right I myself now have been caught up in. From now on to each their own decisions and I must trust in God to lead me down this road full of tempta-tions and lustful desires. I pray these will subside and holiness will be put into their place.

> on't waste what is holy on people who are unholy. Don't throw your pearls to pigs! They will trample the pearls, then turn and attack you. Keep on asking, and you will receive what you ask for. Keep on seeking, and you will find. Keep on knocking, and the door will be opened to you (Matthew 7:6–7).

As for today, I am thankful I went to church yesterday when I wasn't going to go. I'm grateful for the message that in God's house is where questions are answered. And even though I fail, God can help me, if I ask. Not sure how many times I will fail and have to repent. The important thing is not to give up on God. To remember even Jesus was tempted, and only he is free from sin.

October 19, 2004

Constructive sorrow. Second Corinthians 7:8–11. *You showed that you have done everything necessary to make things right.*

Sorrow – sadness or mental suffering caused by loss or trouble, regret.

In recovery, at first all I felt was sadness. I wanted to drink, and I knew only God could help me not to. I would cry often and sometimes I wasn't even sure why. I had hurt many people while drinking and wasn't sure how to make amends. I knew I needed to, and the time came so I could. There are others who I still can't have any conversa-tion with because they are still drinking; however, some day, if it is meant to be, it will happen.

Since the day I let go and decided to let God, my life has been much better. I do not desire a drink, and I am grateful I don't drink. If I was ever to do so again … I don't even want to think of where I would be.

Things have happened. Once again I've done wrong. I will con-tinue to go to God for his understanding. I require his wisdom for the courage to say no to everything sinful in this world. I will continue in his Word and will go to him even when self fails.

October 20, 2004

God's mercy. Revelation 20:11–15. No one will be able to hide. We all will answer: those from the grave and from earth on the day the Lord returns. This will be the second death. Those who refused God's mercy will be judged according to their works on earth. Anyone whose name is not recorded in the Book of Life will be thrown into the lake of fire.

Fearfully and honestly asking for forgiveness of sins and for God's mercy. I find myself continuing in a sinful nature and need forgive-ness daily. I am thankful for another chance to serve God and daily I need his help in all areas of my life. I ask today that my heart does not harden ever again.

Tonight revival starts at 7:00 p.m. I pray to be there and to learn also to let go of whatever is hindering my spirit. I must wait on the Lord for good things to come and stop messing with my future on this earth. I must only look towards the everlasting future with Christ and not be concerned with this one on earth. Jesus is coming soon and I need to be ready at all times for his return.

October 21, 2004

Step Five (AA): We admitted to God, to ourselves, and another human being the exact nature of our wrongs. Genesis 38:1–30. Overcoming denial.

> Jeremiah 17:9–10: *The human heart is the most deceitful of all things, and desperately wicked. Who really knows how bad it is? But I, the LORD, search all hearts and examine secret motives. I give all people their due rewards, according to what their actions deserve.*

Now I understand that we promise one thing and do another. I must be careful of what my plans are and not allow my thinking to become deceived – understanding God knows my secret thoughts.

Admitting all my wrongs is a hard thing. I have asked forgive-ness for most things I have done wrong, but I haven't gone to anyone admitting I have been in a lesbian relationship, nor have I talked with anyone of my recent sins. However, I have brought them to God. I am mostly ashamed that I can't even be true to myself.

My motives are wrong to even think God would want me to put myself into a sinful situation. I must admit I was wrong and let go of any lustful feelings or thinking of a future the way I want it to be.

October 22, 2004

Unending love. Hosea 11:8–11. How could God (or anyone) still love me? But God asks, Oh, how can I give you up…? *How can I let you go? How can I destroy you…? My heart is torn within me, and my compas-sion overflows…. for I am God and not a mere mortal. I am the Holy One living among you, and I will not come to destroy.*

> Romans 8:38: *And I am convinced that nothing can ever separate us from God's love. Neither death nor life, neither angels nor demons, neither our fears for today nor our worries about tomorrow – not even the powers of hell can separate us from God's love.*

After reading a bit on Hosea's wife, I feel like her: always falling back into my old ways even though I have had great things. When I was able to be back with my husband years ago, I still reverted to my old ways and committed the same sin of adultery. Even as I have a hard time forgiving myself of that sin, it hasn't changed the fact that in any and all relationships I have sinned in all ways. I could say, "I can't understand how God can forgive me when I still cannot forgive myself." I have a hard time with this endless love stuff. I really need to know how to truly love someone. Most of us, including myself, love this and love that, but unconditional love – where's the catch?

Jesus loved me and died for me. I will start there. God knew who I was before I was born. I need to continue in his Word to know who I am and where I am going. I have so much of my will and my wants inside me that it is so hard to be obedient, so I need more direction and courage to say no, when I surely know what is wrong.

Had some weird dreams lately. John from Georgia was in one, and so were a few of my ex-in-laws. It seems in some kind of way that my past is coming up at me. Years ago I drank so I didn't have to dream, or at least didn't remember my dreams, but today I want to know what they mean. Is there something I am supposed to be learning from them?

Priscilla doesn't do anything except work. I am not exactly sure what I am going through, except we are not together in my eyes. But in hers I think she believes I will change my mind and we will get back together. I feel that it is all up to me, and I pray that I just allow God to work in my life.

When I read the book about coming out of homosexuality, it says you should allow yourself time to grieve. Maybe I am grieving not only for that, but also because I just can't do what I want to do. It seems every way I turn all I'm getting is, No, you can't. No. No. No. When will something be yes and how will I know?

The revival this week was cancelled. I was really looking forward to a great time.

October 23, 2004

The plumb line. Amos 7:7–8. *And the Lord replied, "I will test my people with this plumb line. I will no longer ignore all their sins."*

If we measured ourselves with God's plumb line, we would see that we are weak and sinful. Praying to God for help is the way to start the process toward a life in line with God's standards.

Without God I would have nothing, and surely whatever I would have on my own would be destroyed because the wall on which it was built would crumble eventually. Though the sins I have had to overcome are many, I haven't even uncovered them all yet. God's Word daily is the most important thing to start my day. It helps me find answers for all those behaviors I struggle with from time to time.

It is not easy to meet God's standards without his help. As my lessons have taught me, without God I surely fail and return to the sins of my past. I will carry on and keep asking God to help me overcome the things that stay in the way of the straight path God has prepared for me.

I would like visions of the future or warning signs I could yield to before I go off and sin again. Am I asking for a lot? Yes, maybe, since sometimes we need to fall to remember who can help us. It is my decision what to choose and I choose to follow God.

After I was saved and began in God's Word, I had a problem with my own words and asked God to control my tongue or quicken me when I was about to swear. Now a year later I still slip once in a while, but am very quick to change the next words that come out of my mouth.

God has really brought me a long way, and he still has a lot to help me with. I am like a baby, except I am in the crawling stage where I feel like I have to test what I can get into and get away with. I guess I'm in the state where I'm learning what "no" means.

With God being the only one who knows true love, I need him to show me how to truly love. I am coming to an understanding that before I can truly love anyone, I need to know what it means to truly love God. First John 4:16: *God is love, and all who live in love live in God, and God lives in them.*

I read this devotion yesterday after I put everything away. Now I understand. I have looked for love in all the wrong places and have no other place to turn. I believe God is showing me I need to learn what love means in a whole new aspect of my life with him.

October 25, 2004

Feelings of shame. John 8:3–11. This is the story of an adulterous woman who was caught in the act and brought to Jesus. In the Law of Moses she was to be stoned to death. She was given a second chance to never sin that way again. The ones who brought her to Jesus were told to go ahead and stone her but only if they had never sinned. I find in this a lesson in judgment and a reminder that all men sin. So only Jesus was left there with the woman.

This account reminds me of times when others are quick to show someone else's shame or things they have done wrong. Only Jesus can be fair in the judgment of sins, because he is the only one who is sinless. Also I find the love Jesus showed toward the woman comfort-ing. He chose not to hurt her but to help her.

I imagine this woman must have heard of Jesus. She was probably crying and shaking before him with her life on the line. She must have also been hanging her head, because she got caught. She prob-ably even wanted to run and get out of there.

I remember being a child and doing wrong. I was usually scared of the consequences, knowing they would involve taking away some-thing I desired and had fun with, or a spanking, or loss of taking part in an activity at school or home. So how many times would I get in trouble for the same things over and over? The answer depended on how much I rebelled because I wasn't able to do what I wanted to do. I can think of some things that might have been handled differently; however, the things I had done were still wrong.

The most shame I felt ever was the time I was out partying really heavily, plus I had run away from home, hoping to never be found. My mother and her boyfriend found me in a tent. I was loaded, naked, and with a few guys I knew. It was nearly morning, and I was headed to the (juvenile) system to be taught a lesson. I begged and pleaded as I had heard stories about being there. But the worst part was I wouldn't be free. I was told if I never allowed this to happen again, I would get another chance. But we needed a way to change what had happened.

I agreed to a foster home, since I truly didn't want to be home. I drank most of the time before this. My second chance: I liked the foster family. There was love in that home. I could feel it. But it wasn't long before I missed the love of my mother.

Mom and I were not close. She didn't understand me or what I wanted. I was close to sixteen years old by the time I decided I wanted another chance at home. But I didn't want to go back to school. I never went anyway, and it was time for a fresh start. Time to feel important somewhere doing something.

We agreed I could quit school but I needed to get a job. That was fine. Nothing changed after that. I went back to drinking after work, seeing guys, sleeping with them. I was still the same girl, just in a different area of life. While I was at the foster care house I felt God or some kind of peace. It wasn't hard to be good there.

Today I feel satisfied that God is working in me and am grateful for his timing and not mine. I am like a spoiled kid who wants what I want and now is my time. Today I am grateful God doesn't work that way. If things just happened quickly, then how would I have time to understand what and why? All things happen for a reason, and just like there is a change in season, there comes a time when things need to change. Just like things change in the weather, so I must change in God's due time.

I will no way ever be sin-free; however, with God's help I will at least go on and not continue in the same sins. Never thought I'd have to say I have a problem with sex, and now I have to believe God will help me in this recovery also.

Mom says the things of the past should stay there. On the other hand, I'm in a learning process and must be able to separate my old self and become new with Christ. I need to learn why I did the things I did or do, so I will not continue to do them. Or at least know to ask God to work with me in all I do and that my heart not be hardened. I'm like a child who makes mistakes and needs to learn from them to grow.

October 28, 2004
Receiving forgiveness. Acts 26:12–18. *Then they will receive forgive-ness for their sins and be given a place among God's people, who are set apart by faith in me.*

God's goal in sending his Word to us is that we may receive for-giveness and new life. We find it easier to forgive others who have hurt us than to forgive ourselves for the hurts we have caused. I have problems forgiving myself for things I have done while drinking and even some things done while not drinking, and for when I went for a drink instead of asking for God's help. I am really trying to find out who I am and what I need to do daily.

> Psalm 103:10: *He does not punish us for all our sins; he does not deal harshly with us, as we deserve.*
>
> Isaiah 1:18–20. *Come now, let's settle this, says the Lord. Though your sins are like scarlet, I will make them as white as snow. Though they are red like crimson, I will make them as white as wool. If you will only obey me, you will have plenty to eat. But if you turn away and refuse to listen, you will be devoured by the sword of your enemies. I, the LORD, have spoken!*
>
> Isaiah 43:25: *I – yes, I alone – will blot out your sins for my own sake and will never think of them again.*

This is one of the hardest subjects for me and yet the most impor-tant in this stage of my life with God. When these thoughts come to mind, we should tend to them right away to repair the damage if possible.

Now that I have read that, I know it is of God that we or I should make amends. Lately some past issues have popped into my head out of the blue. One of these came to mind the other day. It was the bad experience of when I was around thirteen or fourteen when I drank and was found with some guys. I mentioned this before when I was writing about shame.

I'm pretty sure the reasons this came up were many as it took me back to my childhood and sexual involvement with my stepfather. All the time I thought he was my real father. Real or step, he still had no right to do what he did to me.

Other things coming up lately are times of sexual activity in careless ways. Truly I am not sure where this is all going except to remind me of the lust temptation carried and how I lost sight of God and sinned again.

Does it really matter if I write all of these things down or is it just enough to know I was not good in God's eyes or in anyone else's?

I am seeking God now and know I may not be in any kind of relationship until he has helped me overcome the past. I believe he will make in me a new and free heart, and he will do it only in his time. I will continue to seek his will in my life.

October 29, 2004

Freedom through confession. Romans 2:14–15. *Even Gentiles, who do not have God's written law, show that they know his law when they instinctively obey it, even without having heard it. They demonstrate that God's law is written in their hearts, for their own conscience and thoughts either accuse them or tell them they are doing right ... the day is coming when God, through Christ Jesus, will judge everyone's secret life.*

In order to put the past to rest, we must stop rationalizing our sins and admit the truth. We are all born with a built-in alarm that alerts us when we do wrong.

I pray all the sins I have done while drinking and being away from God will be forgiven. If I miss any, I am sure my inner self will eventually bring them to mind, so I pray for that freedom from my past. The time has come to move into the future without living in my past. My excuses for doing wrong can no longer be my reasons for not owning up to what I have done.

Lately I have been feeling led to testify on behalf of the changes the Lord has done in my life. I feel very ashamed of the excuses I've made and how knowing right from wrong I still did the wrong. My conscience didn't win years ago. However, through Jesus Christ the answers and courage to change those wrongs are happening now. God's will, not mine.

My way of doing things was all messed up, and all the time God has had to fix me up afterwards.

Got a phone call yesterday from a woman needing respite care for the weekend. I gladly took this on. Then not long after I accepted the job, I received a call for possible full-time placement if I wanted it. I wanted to and I wanted to believe this was the Lord working in my life. What to do about my full-time job I already have? I pray for an answer. Sometimes I wonder if maybe I don't know God closely enough to know his will and whether it's different from my own will. I pray to know!

October 30, 2004

Escaping self-deception. Galatians 6:7–10. *You will always harvest what you plant … So let's not get tired of doing what is good. At just the right time we will reap a harvest of blessing if we don't give up.* Don't be misled. Remember, you can't ignore God and get away with it. You will always reap what you sow!

We cannot escape from any of our wrongdoings. God has made accountability a necessary element for healthy living. It may take time to finish all of the negative consequences of wrongs from the past, but do not be discouraged; in time we will see good crops begin to grow. I made a statement a few times in the past that I surely could drink and then get away with lots of wrongdoings I normally would not do. I must pray I do not get tired of being good. So easily temptation can slip in and cause a disaster. Learning to be good and getting rid of my old way of thinking has been a challenge in itself. Desperately I seek to be free of the awful past I have created.

The people I have hurt and the ones who have hurt me. Truly there must be a way to end the constant battle inside me. First, I know God is good, and I do want to be more like him. The Bible says to admit to someone else the exact nature of our wrongs. Am I too proud to tell people of my wrongs? I am embarrassed I put myself in such situations. I have another saying that what's in the past should be left there.

If this were true, then why do I continue reliving certain things in my mind? The battle is not mine. I give to you, Lord, my past and present and future. You are the only one who can help or do this transformation in me. Let go, let God.

Now this makes sense as to what this new way of life is. I am let- ting go and letting God have all of me. I am reading Our Daily Bread today and these Scriptures are set before me: Isaiah 59:12 – transgres- sions of sin; Romans 4:17 – promise of faith; Hebrews 11:3; 2 Peter 3:5 – God made all things. To the Lord a thousand years is like a day. Before I go on to the next step I must note something. There is one person, for sure, who I need to ask for forgiveness. I must try and mend my past with Robert. It will not be easy to talk with him; at least it never was before.

I committed adultery while we were married and left him without him knowing what he really did to make it so bad. It wasn't entirely his fault. It was my sinful nature to not say no to what I already knew would damage everything.

Robert, I need to talk to you to see if I can make amends for my awful past behavior. First I want to say it wasn't what you did that was wrong. I take full responsibility for my wrong actions. Truly I want to ask if you have it in your heart to forgive me for what I've done and for the divorce it caused. You're probably thinking or want to say what's done is done and in the past. However, I cannot leave that part in the past, until I face the facts with you.

I am back in the Lord's life now, or I should say, he has taken me back into his. This doesn't mean I got off the hook for the wrongs I've done. For a lot of years, after leaving the church, I found the only way to live with my actions was out of a bottle. Today – and I pray forever – I no longer have that desire. Praise God.

Now reality has hit me face to face with all I've done against God's law, and I believe I need this time now with you in order to fulfill the Lord's Word. You've been on my heart deeply, and I pray I don't cause any turmoil between anyone because of the truth. Admitting the truth of my actions is the only way I can be set free from my past with you. I don't know if you understand all I am saying and maybe you won't want to.

Not only did God help me with my addiction with alcohol and drugs years ago, but now he is helping me through the steps to learn to say no to all things not in his will for my life.

Learning that I reap what I sow, from now on I pray I only do

what is good. God is working in my life. The desires of my lusts are handed over to God right now. I will not allow myself to be in a situation I know is not God's will. Daily I must keep in mind that my past behavior is a result of my sinful desires, and I must move on and let God deal with all things in my life.

I have the option of having a person with disabilities permanently in my home. This would require me to quit my job and be home full-time. I pray for God's will and answer.

I just asked the Lord the other day what his plan for me will be, and I got the phone call about Chris, and then a call for the perma- nent person, and now I need God's final answer.

Priscilla is still having a hard time accepting this transformation. I pray the Lord will touch her heart in a special, gentle way.

October 31, 2004

Step Six (AA): Taking time to grieve. Genesis 23:1–4; 35:19–21. We are entirely ready for God to remove all these defects of character.
Jacob set up a stone monument over Rachel's grave, and it can be seen there to this day. Then Jacob traveled on.

The grieving process – whether it be for someone who dies or for the loss of a relationship or addictions or past sexual behavior – is a time needed to deal with the loss in order to move on. Grieving is a continuous cycle in life we all go through at one time or another. I

have always said I never take losing something or someone very well. I believe many times I still grieved over losing my marriage.

About a month or so ago I read a book on coming out of homosexuality. In this step of my life, the book said there is a process we must allow ourselves to go through. My grieving is in the change of relationship with Priscilla, knowing that in God's law we are not to have a man-and-woman-like relationship. This was and at times is very hard after a long time of being together. At first, just the thought of not being as close as we were at one time would bring me to tears. Knowing what God was asking of me felt like I had just lost everything. As I move on with the Lord, I believe he will take me through this part of life as he did with my drinking. Praise the Lord Jesus I have no desire to drink today. Praise the Lord! I am free from that bondage, and God has great plans for me. The reward is so great, but of course, no pain, no gain. I need to obey in all areas of life of which I am being convicted. Today my plan is to press on with Jesus. Don't give up. Don't push away conviction in the heart. If we listen and take that step to change for God, we will experience a new freedom in Christ.

> Jeremiah 17:8: *They are like trees planted along a riverbank, with roots that reach deep into the water.*

November 1, 2004

Priscilla believes I am getting in over my head following God. I have heard that before from Robert, who said I'd be headed for a fall. The only problem is, he was right and I did fall. The only way I will fall this time is if I take my heart and mind off of the Lord Jesus Christ. But I have fallen and I will probably fall again into something because I am not

146

perfect, but God is. Lord, be with me today and always. Even Peter fell and came back again. Today's study is on another chance. That certainly pertains to me all the way. All we have to do is ask for forgiveness and move on. God's grace of forgiveness comes with another chance.

November 3, 2004

Healing the brokenness. Psalm 51:16–19. *For I was born a sinner – yes, from the moment my mother conceived me* (Psalm 51:5).

> *You do not desire a sacrifice, or I would offer one … The sacrifice you desire is a broken spirit. You will not reject a broken and repentant heart, O God* (Psalm 51:16–17).

Saul continued in denial of his sins. If we continue to deny our sins, we are in grave danger of judgment. David's sins were far worse than Saul's, but David was humble and broken about his sins, so God forgave David and offered him restoration. If we are sensitive to our sins and humbly seek God's forgiveness, there is hope for us, no matter how great our past sins are. God will remove any taint of guilt and *restore our joy!*

Step by step God will lead me. I was just listening to the radio and this song was on. I believe this is exactly what God is doing. However, we all have choices to make. I choose to follow God's steps for me.

I am only on step six of my AA devotions. From step one to now a lot has transpired to bring me to the point of learning from my sins to get to where God can help me with gaining joy and peace. I can have these by continuing to learn more from God by his wisdom and understanding and all that follows. Whatever it takes I will fol- low Jesus.

Only God can forgive and change us into what he wants us to be. Only God. I will continue to seek and ask for Jesus to help me, and then I cannot go wrong.

I spoke to Josh the other day. He went to church with his father and what a message of testimony he received. A woman who was in a coma and paralyzed was healed and her testimony is amazing. She goes everywhere preaching of God's healing power. Josh was touched, and he and his father were told something happened in their child- hood that was holding them back. Josh admitted to this and felt the power of the Holy Spirit. I can't imagine what had happened to him other than the way I walked away from God and lived a life full of sin in front of him.

I pray you, Jesus, to touch my son in a special way that he will turn his sins over to you and allow you to save him. We also talked about what God can do, and he seemed to receive this well.

I had a good weekend with the new person, Chris. He is twenty-three and just as cute as can be. I was glad I could help his mother out, and he helped me and will never know how much of a blessing he is. Sometimes we take things for granted in life, not realizing how easily we can lose any of our functions in an instant.

I'm grateful to the Lord that my son is as healthy and intelligent as he is. God spared me the trial of having a child who would have been handicapped in some way or another due to my past history of substance abuse.

November 4, 2004

God's abundant pardon. Isaiah 55:1–9. *Seek the Lord while you can find him. Call on him now while he is near. Let the wicked change their ways and banish the very thought of doing wrong. Let them turn to the LORD that he may have mercy on them. Yes, turn to our God, for he will forgive generously. "My thoughts are nothing like your thoughts," says the LORD. "And my ways are far beyond anything you could imagine."*

God tells us: *Fear not; you will no longer live in shame … You will no longer remember the shame of your youth and the sorrows of wid-owhood* [loss]. *For your Creator will be your husband* (Isaiah 54:4–5). When we give to God all of our past, he will restore us anew and fill the empty places in our hearts. The biggest part of this lesson is trusting and believing God is bigger than all we have done wrong in the past, no matter what shame I have brought on myself, and no matter what wrongs I have done. If I completely turn my will toward God and allow him to take over, he will fulfill my dreams and restore

in me a new heart and a new freedom of happiness.

I believe God is working in me, but all who surround me are just waiting for another fall. If I keep my mind open to Jesus, he can and will fill these empty places in my heart. I did procrastinate, and I did make excuses not to follow Jesus, and my heart did harden for many years.

I pray, Jesus, that my faith in you would be strong, knowing we can see this through this time of trial. People think I am putting too much into my belief and a fall will come. I pray you, Jesus, will be a closer friend to me than those who wait for my failures. Jesus, you know what is in my future, and I pray I will, by your will, stay strong and steadfast to your will in my life.

I used to say to heck with the consequences when I got into trouble and knew I was doing wrong. Now I say to heck with the consequences of being obedient to follow God's will in my life whatever it takes from this day forward.

November 5, 2004

Removing deeper hurts. Jonah 4:4–8. The removal of our sheltering addiction may expose deeper problems. It is all right to let the anger out, but it is also important to let God take care of the real problem. Jonah ran away from the real problem and suffered enough he wanted to die. God's plan for me may not be the easiest way I would want to go, but if I go my way I am sure to suffer. I have found my addictions were covering a lot of my will to do my own thing. Since the Lord and I have gotten the main addiction problems out of the way, now letting go and letting God has led me into a deeper pain of not having the relationship I so wanted. First, I must realize the real reasons for all my hurts so God can take over. Lack of affection while growing up is probably one of the biggest reasons for my fol- lowing into relationships that could not possibly last. Just like God allowed the plant to shade Jonah, he also didn't allow him to stay comfortable in doing his own thing. Just like me. I was allowed to be in a comfort zone, but would not be allowed to continue and do God's plan at the same time while I disobeyed God's instructions. I praise God now that he allowed me the pain I have experienced while

listening to his plans.

God is merciful to those who confess their sins. I'm moving on and trusting God's plans for my life here on earth, although as of today I am not exactly sure what plans the Lord has for me. I do know past relationships with others must go. That means any sexual contact with anyone is out of the question. With the physical aches and pains I'm experiencing, if the plan is for me to return to work, then so be it. If it is to stay home and take care of someone, then Lord, let's get into it. In time I will know the answer to all of this.

November 6, 2004

Discovering hope. John 5:1–15. I started reading a book called *A Way of Escape: Freedom from Sexual Strongholds.* This book contains references to where sexual problems begin and how to end the causes and nature of these different types of sexual desire. This book is part of my process of turning my life and will over to God, the beginning and ending journey with Jesus.

Jesus healed the man who was sick for thirty-eight years. *When Jesus saw him and knew he had been ill for a long time, he asked him, "Would you like to get well?" "I can't, sir," the sick man said, "for I have no one to put me into the pool when the water bubbles up. Someone else always gets there ahead of me."*

Jesus already knows my sickness. Only God could heal me and get me out of alcoholism. I can relate to this miracle performed for this man because every time I got close to the doors to Jesus, some- one always got in my way. But Jesus went past all those people and he knew the man had been desperately trying to get to the pool he thought could heal him.

Getting close to the truth of Jesus is what saved my life. However, just like this man, I had to at least go halfway. Better yet, I had to hit the end and realize only Jesus could help me.

In the beginning of recovery, Jesus and I had been in sessions of healing the damage I had caused. Many times I wanted to give up, but I knew where I would be. To this day, I still believe if I had not accepted the warning signs, I would not have had any more chances to serve God.

We have a compassionate God. He waits and lets us have the desires of our heart, and then he takes us under his wing so, like in the story, no one can hold us back from getting what we do not deserve.

Next is dealing with the past relationships. Now I understand the sin of immoral sexual desire starts somewhere and ends with God. Even though we may do the unspeakable, the Lord is there to help us out of our secret actions. We may not answer here on earth for our spiritual life, but we will answer in the judgment to come. Lord Jesus, make in me a new creation and take away my old nature that I may become new in your image.

November 8, 2004

Removed, not improved. Romans 6:5–13. *Do not let sin control the way you live; do not give in to sinful desires. Do not let any part of your body become an instrument of evil to serve sin. Instead, give yourselves completely to God, for you were dead, but now you have new life. So use your whole body as an instrument to do what is right for the glory of God.* As I am transformed with God's help, I will overcome the temptations in my life.

151

Romans 6:6: *We know that our old sinful selves were cruci- fied with Christ so that sin might lose its power in our lives. We are no longer slaves to sin.*

Years of trying to change or improve on my own have ended in the tragic realization that I cannot do it alone. Frustrations of never doing what is right and always falling back into that pit of self-pity only caused me to go deeper into my sinful nature.

I am deeply disappointed in my behavior yesterday. I was hurting and decided not to attend church. I haven't missed in six months or more. I felt a sense of weakness and I felt like swearing.

The studies I've been doing today are certainly not justifying my behavior: (1) Put God first; (2) Let go of old sin; (3) Character changeis a result of giving it all to God. I also realize I really do need the fellowship of other Christians.

November 9, 2004

Attitudes and actions. Philippians 2:12–14. Pressing toward a goal. *Work hard to show the results of your salvation, obeying God with deep reverence and fear. For God is working in you, giving you the desire and the power to do what pleases him.*

As I continue to move ahead seeking the direction of God, my rewards will be great, and God will strengthen and encourage me. I need to keep working towards God's plan for my future.

I spent some time with Thelma today, and the feelings of lust entered my mind again. However, I did not act on any of those desires.

Last night I read some more in the book A Way of Escape. One part of this really stuck in my head. Sleeping with someone and knowing others have been with that person is just as if we have been with all of those other people. This scares me as I think of my past and how much disease I may have exposed myself to. There are consequences for this, and yet I don't even want to find out what they may be for me. So I am pressing on with Jesus and believing his plan is far greater than I can imagine. This part of my past life, just as my alcoholism, has to go. The bondage of desire must be lifted to press on. *Forget- ting the past and looking forward to what lies ahead* (Philippians 3:13). I will never be perfect physically or mentally, until the day of the Lord's return. Even so, I press on to achieve the best I can and that's all I can do. The more we think of God's Word, the less we'llthink about worries.

November 10, 2004

Step Seven (AA): We humbly asked him to remove our shortcomings. Clearing the mess. Isaiah 57:12–19. *I restore the crushed spirit of the humble and revive the courage of those with repentant hearts. For I will not fight against you forever; I will not always be angry. If I were, all people would pass away – all the souls I have made … I will lead them. I will comfort those who mourn … "But those who still reject me are like the restless sea, which is never still but continually churns up mud and dirt. There is no peace for the wicked," says my God.*

> Isaiah 59:12–13: *For our sins are piled up before God and testify against us. Yes, we know what sinners we are. We know we have rebelled and have denied the LORD. We have turned our backs on our God. We know how unfair and oppressive we have been, carefully planning our deceitful lies.*
>
> Isaiah 55:7: *Let the wicked change their ways and banish the very thought of doing wrong.*

From the beginning of this journey I had no control over anything. I've turned my life and will over to God, and the process has begun. I turned away from God years ago, and I truly believed I would not be allowed back into his grace.

The Lord has let me back and is daily teaching me the reasons that caused me to fall. We know allowing temptations to be acted out will definitely cause a person like me to walk away from everyone. The desires of my heart were lustful and demeaning and caused shame and discontent. I was shamed into feeling I was unable to go to God because of my failures. If I had gone to the Lord first with these short- comings, his plan for me would not have been messed up.

My shortcomings are great. I still have anger, resentment, shame, and am still in a situation that is causing most of this. I have to keep looking to Jesus for answers; otherwise, I am sure to fall.

I still see myself as a baby in Christ and I need to pray the desires of sex will go away because babies don't think of these things. What is still in the way of my peace and joy?

Isaiah 58:13: *Keep the Sabbath day holy. Don't pursue your own interests on that day, but enjoy the Sabbath and speak of it with delight as the LORD's holy day.* There we go. One thing is wrong for sure with me. I hurt today and decided to stay home from church and also had company who doesn't attend church. I stayed away from those I could have shared God with.

November 11, 2004

Giving up control. Jeremiah 18:1–6. *Then the LORD gave me this message: "O Israel, can I not do to you as this potter has done to his clay? As the clay is in the potter's hand, so are you in my hand."*

> Isaiah 45:9: *What sorrow awaits those who argue with their Creator. Does a clay pot argue with its maker? Does the clay dispute with the one who shapes it, saying 'Stop, you're doing it wrong!' Does the pot exclaim, 'How clumsy can you be?'*

If the potter sees a flaw present during the process of molding a piece of pottery to perfection, he starts over. By putting my life into God's hands and getting out of his way in humility, I can be sure the Lord will reshape me into a beautiful person.

God is a wonderful God who gives us the whole earth to prove his handiwork. I am his handiwork, being molded God's way in his time.

Sometimes I get in the way and just want to do what I want. But God knows best, and I need to get out of his way.

Now I live in the light and I feel the conviction of my wrong behavior and lifestyle. This was so hard, knowing that being with a woman was totally wrong, and yet I was doing everything against God and even blaming him for the reasons I was the way I was. This was just another way for Satan to have a hold on me. Now the devil is using others to try and turn my head back into the dark again, telling me I can still do this.

Lord Jesus, I pray you will strengthen me away from temptation and remove me from enemies who would cause me to fall into their darkness. This little light of mine. Please, Lord, help me to get it to shine. I need to remember Romans 6:6: *We know that our old sinful selves were crucified with Christ so that sin might lose its power in our lives. We are no longer slaves to sin.*

November 12, 2004

Pride born of hurt. Luke 11:5–13. *And so I tell you, keep on asking, and you will receive what you ask for. Keep on seeking, and you will find. Keep on knocking, and the door will be opened to you. For everyone who asks, receives. Everyone who seeks, finds. And to everyone who knocks, the door will be opened.*

The honesty of this prayer reveals our weakness and vulnerability to temptation. To harbor anger and an unforgiving spirit when God has forgiven us so much is hypocritical and a roadblock to recovery. We must be persistent and ask repeatedly as the needs arise.

I still need to speak with Robert for some reason, even though I've had a fear come over me to speak with him. Maybe I need to write a letter. I need to move on, and this is one part of my life that needs to be brought out into the open. My sins in the past have been heartbreak for my future. It truly hurts that I might never be married again, and I already know I won't have any more children. At least I have been blessed with Josh.

I just finished writing Robert a letter. I know God has forgiven me for what I did wrong, and I'm sure if I missed anything, he will surely let me know in the right time. I hope I can make much-needed amends with Robert after all these years. I do pray Robert will let God have his way in his life.

It takes a lot to admit my wrongs, but if I continue to hold on to the past by not admitting my wrongs, then I will not be set free. I must continue to look up and ahead to a new life in Christ.

November 13, 2004

A humble heart. Luke 18:10–14. The Pharisee and the tax collector went to Jesus in prayer and the Pharisee thanked God that he was not a sinner like the tax collector. The tax collector humbled himself before God, admitting what a sinner he was, and in verse 14 it says, *I tell you, this sinner, not the Pharisee, returned home justified before God. For those who exalt themselves will be humbled, and those who humble themselves will be exalted.* I pray I will not point the finger at the other person and that I am humbled before Jesus for my own sins. In that way I may then be honored by God.

Lately I have been searching for peace and joy and answers to decisions I have to make, but have found none. Staying in the Word is the only way I have had strength not to repeat sins of my past. I need a touch from God. I feel like I am being tested again. Lord, please reassure me you are still here with me.

In faith, I need to believe only God could and did take away the desires of alcohol. Only by faith he can put aside my sexual desires. Lord, help me stay out of the way so you can do mighty things for me.

I cannot go a full week again without being in the presence of other followers of Christ. I look at these Christians who have been serving the Lord for years and wonder, did they go through all these sexual temptations and judgmental feelings and whatever else I have gone through? How did they get to the freshness of Jesus I so desire? I loved

Jesus as a child, and now I'm just learning to love him as a friend. I have faith that this, too, will be grand.

Jesus died on the cross to save all sinners. God had a plan from the beginning, and we as humans messed it all up. Then God proceeded to the next plan so he would have an intercessor to slow his anger and not to destroy those he created. Jesus came to this earth as a human just like me and subject to temptation. But with the power of God, he obeyed his Father who was and is in heaven. Jesus did not fail in God's eyes or ours, and we are to do our best in obeying once we are saved. I have a hard time understanding how Jesus was so strong and that nothing could take his eyes off of his Father's plans for this world. Why is it so hard to obey and follow God and Jesus' example? There should be nothing I want more than to please my Father.

I lost my trust in fathers long ago, but your Word says you will

never leave me or forsake me. I pray for new insight into you being my Father.

November 14, 2004

Let us draw near and hold fast. Hebrews 10:19–25. Just what I needed to hear. Verse 23: *Let us hold tightly without wavering to the hope we affirm, for God can be trusted to keep his promise.* Then the statement in verse 26: *If we deliberately continue sinning after we have received knowledge of the truth, there is no longer any sacrifice that will cover these sins.*

I am looking forward to attending church service this morning. I pray for good fellowship and that God is at the head of the message to be delivered.

I wonder, Did God forgive me of everything, even after I went and sinned again? Did I let go of all there was, or is there no more room for forgiveness for me? What if I sin again, God forbid. My human self is so disobedient. Does God know I am trying? Am I to be given any more chances? I fear failure and the loss of God again would be too unbearable. I like the song that says, "I don't wanna go back. I want to believe. There is nothing in this world for me."

Christian fellowship builds up and binds us together. Be kindly affectionate to one another with brotherly love. Whatever is not of faith is sin. Believing in all things God can and will do what he desires in my life and in the lives of those around me.

Faith in believing; believing in the Word of God, then cometh his promises. Avoiding temptation. Look up. Look in faith. God promises to take care of me and never leave me or forsake me. Also God will not give us more than we can handle. However, because he gave us minds to make decisions, then I need to ask his will be done in all things I do, or I surely will fail and fall into sin again.

I pray, Lord, that you put in me a new creature and remove my old ways of thinking. Lord, show me how to be a good and acceptable Christian in your sight and for others to see. The old me got attention in all the wrong ways. I pray the new me can stand strong to reach those who need you, God, in an awesome way.

November 15, 2004

Declared not guilty. Romans 3:23–28. Christ took our punishment when he died on the cross for all sinners. *For everyone has sinned; we all fall short of God's glorious standard. Yet God, with undeserved kindness, declares that we are righteous. He did this through Christ Jesus when he freed us from the penalty for our sins.*

Psalm 103:12: When God removes our sins, he does a great job! *He has removed our sins as far from us as the east is from the west.*

Thank God my rebellious acts have been forgiven by the grace of God through Jesus Christ. Years ago I did rebel and left Jesus' side. I pray for the faith that by God's Word I will not rebel in my nature anymore.

November 16, 2004

Into the open. Philippians 2:5–9. *You must have the same attitude that Christ Jesus had. Though he was God, he did not think of equality with God as something to cling to. Instead, he gave up his divine privileges; he took the humble position of a slave and was born as a human being. When he appeared in human form, he humbled himself in obedience to God and died a criminal's death on a cross.*

Lost in my thoughts this morning. I am seeking God's wisdom and still I hear about humility and obedience. Maybe I need a coun- seling session with the pastor. Now that would be humility for sure, to admit my relationship and my desire for obedience at the same time. I am surely being obedient in not continuing in the relation- ship; however, I feel like I am betting against the odds. Maybe I am not strong enough to keep looking up. Resentment has arisen, and I just don't know what to do.

November 18, 2004

Eyes of love. First John 5:11–15. In confidence, if we love Jesus and believe he is the Son of God, which he is, then whatever we shall ask if it is in God's will, will be answered.

> *Even before he made the world, God loved us and chose us in Christ to be holy and without fault in his eyes* (Ephesians 1:4).
>
> *God's discipline is always good for us, so that we might share in his holiness* (Hebrews 12:10).

I can have full assurance God will remove my shortcomings in his time. Pain is not pointless. Isaiah 28:29. This also comes from the Lord of Hosts, who is wonderful in counsel and excellent in guid- ance. God has a purpose in our heartaches. The Savior always knows best. We learn so many precious lessons in every sorrow, trial, or test. Today I have just learned a lesson related to my pain. Jesus knows what I suffer and my sorrow has been great. I believe now it is time to move on for whatever

God's plan is for me. Jesus has heard my many prayers and now my answer has come. God has a reason why I had to suffer deep emotional pain and physical pain also. I stand still on spiritual ground. God will not leave me nor forsake me; that is his promise to me.

Yesterday I didn't read or think on all this. I was just still and rested most of the day. I am not afraid of what is next. I've lived my life in my own will for so long I just needed to stop and rest.

Still, I feel I am always questioning your will for me, Lord. I know it's your will to help me in all things. My desire for sex has gone away, but instead loneliness is at hand. Depression has tried to grab onto me, but I rebuke this in the name of Jesus Christ my Lord and Savior.

November 20, 2004

Step Eight (AA): We made a list of all persons we had harmed and became willing to make amends to them all. Exodus 22:10–15. Making restitution. I suppose this accountability would also include the owing of money for a job that was completed. If this be the case, I sure am behind on debts owed.

I bring all of these debts to Jesus my Lord in prayer. First of all, that I can mend myself from debts owed and free myself from the burden of financial hold-down. I pray for the Lord to help me in all finances to be able to stretch my income to pay all that is owed. I must also consider Danny for helping me years ago in paying a DUI fine so I could be free. I am accountable for my mistakes, and this should be repaid. Now in which order and when and how will I repay?

November 27, 2004

Unintentional sin. Leviticus 4:1–28; Romans 3:23. *For everyone has sinned; we all fall short of God's glorious standard.* Back in Moses' time, if someone sinned intentionally, they had to bring an offering free of flaws to the altar before the priest to be slaughtered. Hebrews 4:14–16: Christ is our high priest.

During hard times and failure, the antidote to all problems is the living Word of God. God knows everything about us, even the things we try and hide from ourselves. God exposes my problems and needs so I may deal with them, with Jesus, promptly.

I pray, Lord, if I am carrying with me any sin unknown to me, that I may have an open heart for you, Jesus, to work with me. Cre- ate in me the person I am to be. I did intentionally sin and those sins have been forgiven by the grace of God. I pray the Lord will chasten me so I will not fall into diverse places again.

December 3, 2004

Scapegoats. Leviticus 16:20–22. In today's lesson the only thing that comes to mind is John and Heidi, especially John, who finds no place for me since I left the sinful ways. As it says, there will be a few who you cannot get forgiveness from, no matter what the difference is in your life now.

Some of the people we have hurt will use us as their scapegoats. Since we have hurt them, they feel justified in sending us away with more than our share of the burden. I need to be careful to not allow things of the past to weigh me down and get in the way of God's plan for my life. Old things are now passed away and all things have become new in the name of Jesus Christ my Lord.

Malachi 1:2: *"I have always loved you,"* says the *LORD.* To love God is to obey God. The other day, while building up the walls in the basement, I stopped and wondered how Noah built that huge ark and what hammer he used. The knowledge of the Lord and his strength must have spilled completely over Noah so he could obey God and do what God had commanded him to do. What faith Noah had to believe such a rain would cover the earth. This takes me to the examples in Revelation and the warning signs we are to watch for to be ready for the time of his coming. I don't want to be left behind. I am turning all over to God to prepare me for this day, which is near. Only a few shall believe and enter.

For about a year now, I have stumbled around smoking, and now the time has come as a sacrifice to Jesus for his birthday to let go of the hold cigarettes have had on me for years. I trust in the Lord that I must obey this command in order to be completely free from my past. I praise you, Lord, for my trials and tribulations, and for where they have brought me in you.

December 4, 2004

Overcoming loneliness. Ecclesiastes 4:9–12. *Two people are better off than one, for they can help each other succeed.*

Loneliness and isolation go along with guilt and shame. Being willing to accept love and concern are a part of the preparation to make amends. With friends and God joining with us to form a triple- braided cord, we will not be easily broken. I must learn to trust oth- ers, to reach out to them, and to admit my need to others. This will give me strength, wisdom, and protection against my dependencies and compulsions.

Some days I don't want any contact with anyone. I don't find much in the Scriptures about isolation but loneliness is covered a lot in the Bible.

December 6, 2004

Forgiven to forgive. Matthew 18:21–35. *Then Peter came to him and asked, "Lord, how often should I forgive someone who sins against me? Seven times?" "No, not seven times," Jesus replied, "but seventy times seven!* I must forgive and forget the debts others owe me and move on to greater things with Jesus. Jesus was telling the story of a servant ask- ing for forgiveness of the debt he owed. The debt was great. He could never have paid it off, but his master showed mercy and forgave the debt. Then the forgiven servant went to one who owed him, grabbed him, and demanded payment. When he couldn't pay it, he had the man thrown into jail until he could pay his debt. When he saw how he had treated the one who owed him, the king eventually did this to the first man, too. God the Father will do the same unto us. As the Lord God has forgiven us, we are to forgive others in the same way.

In thinking about forgiveness, I just saw the movie *The Passion of the Christ*. It brought tears to my eyes to see how you were beaten and didn't say anything foul. Lord, in all honesty, I would probably have been cursing those people or trying to get out of the situation. But not you, my Lord. You said nothing and held true to God our Father in heaven by believing, trusting, and obeying. I don't want to be like Peter when things got tough, and he denied you.

December 9, 2004

The fruit of forgiveness. Second Corinthians 2:5–11. This is about a man who sinned enough that the church pushed him out. This punishment was a judgment against him. *Now, however, it is time to forgive and comfort him. Otherwise he may become overcome by discourage- ment … When you forgive this man, I forgive him, too. And when I forgive whatever needs to be forgiven, I do so with Christ's authority for your benefit, so that Satan will not outsmart us. For we are familiar with his evil schemes.*

I have done things that pushed people away. I have gone to some of them to ask forgiveness. Some forgave; some probably never will. I must keep seeking forgiveness from all so I will not fall back into the trap.

After I fell into the trap of deception, it went on and on for years. I almost believed my way of life was right. May God forgive me for all I have done against his laws of righteousness. Chastise me with the gentle Holy Spirit when I start to do the same things again.

December 21, 2004

Step Nine (AA): We made direct amends to such people wherever possible, except when to do so would injure them or others. Genesis 33:1–11. Long-awaited healing. Seeing someone you've harmed in the past can be trying. It all goes back to forgiveness but there are times the other person still cannot or will not forgive. The trying time for me recently dealt with a sense of forgiveness for a debt owed. The person has passed away without our touching base for a year or so. I owed him money, and I figured he would have wanted to have it for his children whom he adored. The payment was not made in full; however, the gesture was complete.

December 23, 2004

Keeping promises. Second Samuel 9:1–9. King Saul passed on. David had promised when he was king he would one day give all the land back to the ancestors of Saul. Most of Saul's family members were killed, but David searched. And so it was the kept promise was given unto one who was left to inherit it.

This suggests to me that if at all possible, a promise is to be kept, if it be God's will. We must be careful what we promise and in all things be certain it is in God's will.

While I drank I made many promises to stop and also made a promise to return to my life with God. It took years, but I'm work- ing on keeping that promise. Now I am trying to make a promise to quit smoking. My strength is weak even though my desire is strong. On October 22 I had a dream about John. I thought the dream was bringing up my past with the John I knew, when actually it was providing a future. On December 6 another person with disabili- ties, named John, moved in and things have been a trial in one way or another. Readjusting for all concerned seems to be harder than I anticipated. Things are, however, looking up. John has tried my patience in so many ways, mostly because he knows what he is doing.

That's the most irritating thing.

Anyway, my faith in God still is strong. Priscilla is taking our new way of life better and it is getting easier; however, there are times when I want to give back or say let's go back. It's then I need to remember the song again: "I never wanna go back. There's nothing in the world for me."

I must continue to practice this in my mind, heart, and soul in order to carry on. I must obey and now again is the time of quitting smoking. Not successful yet, but have cut down a lot, but still not enough. In a way it helps that John is here, since we really don't want him to smoke, which he would if he knew I smoked. Josh is here to visit and it has been nice so far.

God has brought me this far. I have faith he will continue to guide me in all directions. It's said that only God himself knows everyone's future. I sure would like to know if I am heading in the right direc- tion this time.

Christmas is surely different this year. I am not thinking of gifts or anything related, but enjoying that Christ was born to live and die for me in all the wrong I have done. It's a great thing to be able to be forgiven rather than to be forgotten.

God is great and greatly to be praised. Only Jesus alone could be there for this corruptible person: me.

My heart reaches out to those in the loss of a friend recently, whose death was a shock and has no explanation. This reminded me that there is no time to waste. Anytime, anywhere, the breath God giveth he taketh in the night or whenever he feels fit. We all have come short of the glory of God and all have a sinful nature. However, all have been given a chance to be redeemed with Jesus Christ our Lord. In my heart I do believe there is no time left for me not to have faith and believe God will carry me through all things.

OBEY – Sacrifice of Praise Unto God

FAITH – Forgiveness of SINS

December 28, 2004

A part of me was crying today and another part was dismayed. Felt good to talk with the pastor's wife. She helped me with some feelings of despair concerning my work here on earth. Actually, yesterday I came to terms with the fact that if the money I'm making by taking in people with disabilities isn't enough, maybe I can go into homes during the day and help with others' needs that way. Still, I want to know my calling.

The pastor's wife said I was doing a ministry for Christ by taking on his most precious ones who are as babes. I surely never thought of this in that way. When I take into consideration that John is as a child and Vickie also, then I pray I will do the right things in the way God has planned for them.

Still I need to feel peace with this decision and believe God is in it. How will we make it financially if they decide not to come to my terms?

> First Peter 3:8–9: *All of you should be of one mind. Sympathize with each other. Love each other as brothers and sisters. Be tenderhearted, and keep a humble attitude. Don't repay evil for evil.*

This was today's reading. Wouldn't you know? I haven't been exactly nice lately, more irritated than anything. This addresses my feelings toward John. I do not have a compatibility with him; however, my love for the Lord will show me the light which I desire.

January 7, 2005

I didn't start the new year off very well at all. I am the weakest person ever. A part of me was angry that everyone could go out and drink, have fun, and not come home. The old me was exactly that.

Later in the day I took a nap and the dream I had was sexual. Let go, let God. This lets me know even my dreams are holding on dearly. Yesterday I heard in my mind: "Marilynne, where did you go?

Why are you avoiding me?" I am not sure if this was of Jesus or mejust feeling guilt for not talking with God after the first of January. Where did I go? Am I giving up? What's going on?

I've been tempted to drink. I don't want that outcome. I've been tempted sexually and have given in. I'm just not at all close enough to God or strong enough to walk away. I want what I want when I want it. Spoiled? Yes. Selfish? Yes.

January 21, 2005

I have papers to fill out for long-term disability caregiving, and now after looking over them, I really am not settled with giving them a life story I believe will only damage my future. We'll see what hap- pens next.

January 22, 2005

I read today about being a child of light and not of darkness in the world. Makes sense for my personal things I've been dealing with, realizing I am not the same by any means. All the sins I was involved in are now behind me. Due to the change God has made in me, I have not been close to those sins of my past. I think differently. My trials are the agent of choice. I choose to follow after Jesus.

February 2, 2005

Last week I took in another guy to take care of. Sam is eighteen years old and is still in school but will soon be on his own.

Today I got confronted on the church issue by Sam's social worker. It seems he made it sound like he didn't want to go to church and, well, his rights come in. Here we go. He mentioned speaking in tongues made him uneasy.

It is all different for someone who has never heard tongues. I have always been grateful for that power in God. I don't remember ever questioning and just accepted God in that way with no problem. In fact, if I don't hear the Lord speak, then I think something is surely wrong. Sam is a pretty smart guy but thinks he knows it all. I suppose all teenagers are that way.

It would be so easy to just not do this anymore. It hurts that no one I know or am around can understand God's way. Sure, the church members do, but I am not around them much, or should I say, not enough to feel at ease. A part of me feels as if I am not to be friends with anyone. The only people who go out of their way are those who are of the world. Yet surely I cannot be a part of that.

I don't want to fail God, and I pray I don't. Lord, help me! I have decisions that are going to finalize my life. My job will be here at home permanently. Lord Jesus, I am fearful of my future today. I feel even more unsure.

I don't want to think of this as a 24/7 job. I want to feel more at ease. I am tense and it shows from time to time.

Unfinished business. Philemon 1:13–16. Complete unfinished business before being able to move on. In the story of Onesimus and Philemon, Onesimus had to make amends for his wrongs done to Philemon. God had forgiven him and now in return he had to ask forgiveness of those he had wronged. Bearing grudges against oth- ers is surely destructive. It also fills us with unresolved bitterness. Releasing the past and being free from bondage.

As of today, I have not spoken to Lorrie, Krista, or Jackie since Christmas Eve. I am surprised they haven't even called. Then again, part of me knows why. I just can't be around them because of the way they are.

February 3, 2005

After talking with Mom and then reading some Scripture, my inner anger released and a peace about the situation with Sam and church eased. Fact is, we all have choices and whatever ones we make are ours. I can't make anyone understand God's way in how the church is. I pray when I do ask Sam to go to church that his decision will be yes. In the past, I didn't want anyone to make me go to church. Only I could make the choice to go. What had made me angry was how this was brought about by a social worker. I do know one thing: God helped me through the trial by his words in 1 Peter 2.

Step Ten (AA): We continue to take personal inventory and when we were wrong promptly admitted it. Genesis 31:45–55. Personal boundaries. A fine line between right and wrong sometimes. God knows everything I do, and I have plenty of boundary lines in my life now, based on my past failures and knowing where I can go and can't go. I've vowed before God not to enter a casino, a bar, and to keep distance between old friends. Also a vow not to use foul language.

Before the Lord my God I had taken a vow of a commitment that was wrong. Now that commitment had to be broken, because by the laws of the Lord, it was wrong to exchange vows with another woman. I pray for forgiveness and truly want a new freedom and peace and to have the victory of Jesus be with me.

The day I took those vows, I knew I was crossing the line. I started drinking more and exceedingly so. Life was never comfortable then either. My vow now is to serve the Lord Jesus and obey his commands and ask the Holy Spirit to convict and reveal things to me.

February 4, 2005

Repeated forgiveness. Romans 5:3–5. *We can rejoice, too, when we run into problems and trials, for we know that they help us develop endurance. And endurance develops strength of character, and char- acter strengthens our confident hope of salvation. And this hope will not lead to disappointment.*

For we know how dearly God loves us, because he has given us his Holy Spirit to fill our hearts with his love.

I grow impatient with myself when I continue to commit the same sin over and over again. This causes me to get discouraged, and I grow afraid I may be doomed for relapse. I need to be patient with myself, just as God expects me to be with others. It strengthens me to know that even if I fall, God will be there to pick me up. I must remember no sin is so great that God can't fix or mend me.

February 5, 2005

Dealing with anger. Ephesians 4:26–27. Evaluating how to deal with anger appropriately is an important part of my daily inventory. Recently I was angered by a social worker's words about Sam not wanting to attend church. I was told to ask him first if he wanted to go, but that I was not to make him go. This angered me for so many different reasons. One, he had the nerve to say he didn't want to attend, but worse yet by him telling the social worker this, it was making me look as if I was forcing him to go against his will.

What it all amounts to is that I was wrong. I did make him go in his best interest so he could learn more and get used to the place, but I was wrong in not asking him first. I have learned a precious lesson. I cannot make anyone want God like I do!

February 6, 2005

Spiritual exercises. First Timothy 4:7–8. *"Physical training is good, but training for godliness is much better, promising benefits in this life and in the life to come".*

I have been finding myself lately getting up and right to work instead of reading God's Word first. Then as the day goes on I end up not reading at all. After a week or so of this disobedience, I became weak and stressed. Then I went back to my morning readings. I found I had time for both, and my stress level went down and my body was not as worn out.

Lord, help me to not be slack in learning your Word. Help me to not get sidetracked by those things that are not righteous. Be with me, Lord, in all my decisions and guide me in your path. I pray, Lord, that all those who hear your Word will bow to you.

February 10, 2005

Step Eleven (AA): We sought through prayer and meditation to improve our conscious contact with God, praying only for knowledge of his will for us and the power to carry that out. Second Samuel 22:1–33. A new hiding place. The Lord is my Rock, my Fortress, and my Savior. My God is my Rock in whom I will find protection. He is my Shield, the strength of my salvation, and my stronghold. My high tower, my savior, the one who saves me from violence.

Back when I was drinking and I felt like everything was crashing down on me, God was the only way out. I kept crying to Jesus and then one day I needed to take that first step out, for the Lord was with me all the way to detox. The new mantra from my crying heart was "one day at a time, sweet Jesus." I knew Jesus was there and was strengthened through him to go through the unmentionable: quit drinking. I was tired, weak, and withdrawn. I had tried all the things this world offered, and yet nothing put happiness in my heart. The strength God has given me from that moment forward is incredible, and I'm eternally grateful. I was surely going to die in some way or another, but Jesus saved me, guided me, strengthened me, rescued me, and held me.

February 16, 2005

Powerful secrets. Psalm 119:1–11. The power of hidden behaviors and secrets can work for us as well as against us. *I have hidden your Word in my heart, that I might not sin against you* (Psalm 119:11).

Matthew 6:6: *But when you pray, go away by yourself, shut the door behind you, and pray to your Father in private. Then your Father, who sees everything, will reward you.* I will obey your principles, God. Please don't give up on me! I have tried my best to find you – don't let me wander from your commands.

When I asked Jesus back into my life, I was ashamed of what the power of alcohol had done to me. I was inconsiderate, demanding, and willing to try new things in the world. I did many things I am not proud of. Then my eyes and heart were opened, and I saw my sinful nature. Within time, daily prayer began to become a habit for me with Jesus.

I still have old ideas that resurface from time to time, but now I know who puts them there. The devil has no power over me anymore, for Jesus is working in me. Your will be done, Lord, not mine.

February 17, 2005

Patiently waiting. Isaiah 40:28–31. *But those who trust in the LORD will find new strength. They will soar high on wings like eagles. They will run and not grow weary. They will walk and not faint.*

When we doubt God can really help us overcome all things, we need to remember God is bigger and more powerful than anything on earth. God is also compassionate and loving.

Lamentations 3:25–26: *The LORD is good to those who depend on him, to those who search for him. So it is good to wait quietly for salvation from the LORD.*

The Lord Jesus has done wonderful things in my life. From being an alcoholic – a lesbian – lustful – a sinful person in this world, I can say God has saved me from it all. As long as I shall live, I want the Lord Jesus in every part of my life.

Praise the Lord, O my soul. For the Lord is greatly to be praised. Glory be to the Most High and praises to my King.

February 19, 2005

Friends of the Light. John 3:18–21. *God's light came into the world, but people loved the darkness more than the light, for their actions were evil. Jesus said in John 8:12: "I am the light of the world. If you follow me, you won't have to walk in darkness, because you will have the light that leads to life."*

Right now I have a few friends who, in my eyes, are being deceived. I don't know what to say to them, but I have invited them to next week's revival. I felt moved by the Lord to do so. I can't make them do anything, but I pray, Lord, they will attend.

I have come to terms with homosexuality and understand that in the eyes of God it is not his plan for anyone to live their life this way. The truth hurts, but the Lord has made a way for me to face the facts. I pray now, Lord, for your power to set my friends free, to show them your truth and the way to your light of forgiveness. Lord Jesus, if I might be tempted to sin against your Word, I pray you will quicken my heart, soul, and mind. I truly do not want to go back to my lust- ful desires or my old ways. Jesus, I thank you for bringing me out of bondage of all kinds. Praise and glory be to you, the Most High.

February 22, 2005

Step Twelve (AA): Having had a spiritual awakening as the result of these steps, we tried to carry this message to others and to practice these principles in all our affairs. Isaiah 61:1–3. Our mission. Lately I don't know where my growth in God is. I find a despair of my Christianity. I feel like a fake lately. Is this all real? Who am I? What is going on with my faith? Why are there questions in my mind? I want the free sense of praise and the joy it brings. If these feelings don't leave, I fear a fall. Oh Lord, pick me up. Show me what it is I need. I give all these feelings to you. I hold on to your promises of never leaving me or forsaking me.

February 27, 2005

The battle with smoking continues. Got to the revival today. Lots of people there from other churches. Just great how God works. The speaker was good. The important part was the end of the service when I and others went up for prayer. I've been struggling with smoking, but today I let it to go to God and even threw the pack of cigarettes on the altar. I was relieved and full of peace; sure I was taken from the addiction with no craving for it.

Was disobedient the next day, however, and the battle was back. I tried fighting the desire to quit, but the smoker in me won. Now today I feel a great disappointment in myself and question my faith deeply. No excuse. I am hooked and now I don't want to face anyone at church. I've testified to being free, and I am not.

I feel loads of shame. My inner self is fighting back and forth. I can't give up. I know what God has done for me. I have let the Lord down again. I have justified this habit with stress, and now the guilt is strong and hangs over me like a cloud.

I will go to church but I don't know how I will face the truth that I failed. God didn't fail. I did and allowed circumstances to control my will and desire to smoke. A sin is a sin against what is supposed to be holy and acceptable to God. I am his temple, and I am still destroying his work.

Back on my knees. It will take much more than humility to change circumstances for God's glory. I am a failure.

March 1, 2005

I want to do the right things by the Lord and yet I fall back into the same sin over and over. I went from Friday night thinking for sure the bondage of smoking was broken and the desire to smoke gone, to finding myself Saturday night right back at it. On Sunday, I was feeling guilt and shame and back to my knees again. I made it eight hours and here I go again. Why is this so hard to stop? I pray when it is finally gone, I will know not to ever give in to that fleshly desire again. Jesus has not failed me yet, and he will not fail me now.

I get headaches when I want to smoke, and when I give in to it, the pain goes away but the guilt starts. Because I still have one pack left, I still have a crutch. Thank you, Lord. You know my heart, mind, and soul better than I do. This means you already know the outcome for me. No easy way out, but be with me, Lord, so I can win this battle of nicotine bondage.

March 2, 2005

Talking the walk. First Timothy 4:14–16. *Do not neglect the spiritual gift you received through the prophecy spoken over you when the elders of the church laid their hands on you. Give your complete attention to these matters. Throw yourself into your tasks so that everyone will see your progress. Keep a close watch on how you live and on your teaching. Stay true to what is right for the sake of your own salvation and the salvation of those who hear you.*

It seems lately in all I read that I need to continue telling my story. My question is to whom and where. I still am writing to three people in prison and am glad to witness in any way I can. My question is, what else could or should I be doing?

As the battle goes on I am still smoking, but not as much, even though I am eating in place of having a smoke. I refuse to buy another pack. This one I have left is almost gone. I pray for the will to quit and as one preacher says, ask for the will to quit and the strength will come with it.

I already know it is God's will for me to be clean and pure. My body is to be a temple for the Holy Spirit to dwell in. I can tell when I smoke it's like the Spirit leaves. Sometimes I can't tell if the Spirit returns. My spiritual sense is shaky, since I keep disobeying. I really do want to listen, but I struggle with this addiction more than any- thing. One thing is for sure. I never want to go through this again, so maybe this is why it's taking time for it to go away.

March 4, 2005

The narrow road. First Peter 4:1–6. *You have had enough in the past of the evil things that godless people enjoy – their immorality and lust, their feasting and drunkenness and wild parties, and their terrible wor- ship of idols. Of course, your former friends are surprised when you no longer plunge into the flood of wild and destructive things they do. So they slander you. But remember that they will have to face God, who will judge everyone, both the living and the dead.*

> In Matthew 7:13–14 it says: *You can enter God's Kingdom only through the narrow gate. The highway to hell is broad, and its gate is wide for the many who choose that way. But the gateway to life is very narrow and the road is difficult, and only a few ever find it.*

One time a while back I made a comment that I had seen all and done all in this world that I desired to do. That's not exactly true, because in this world now I do not want to do anything of my own selfish desires. I want to do for Jesus. He has a plan for me, and I am going to listen and obey the best I can. I just need extra help to quit smoking. It is God's will for me to stop.

PART 4
LIVING WITH A GENTLE GOD

March 8, 2005

After finishing steps one through twelve of AA, I am feeling better with my sobriety and realize more today than I did at the beginning of the program how much I need my Lord Jesus in daily living.

March 25, 2005

I went and had a visit with Lorrie the other day. I truly believe it was God-sent. Finally we could discuss what was going on with her and where she stands. God has a big job just waiting for us to do the right thing. Then last night Lorrie and Krista came over and I was able to share some music that might help both of them. It's all in God's hands, and my mind is at ease today.

The past couple of weeks I had been feeling an overwhelming loneliness. The answer is I need to fellowship with others and to feel respected in my walk with Jesus.

Learning to listen to God is not so easy. However, knowing right from wrong is a strong knowledge. We are allowed to make our own decisions, and I have decided to follow Jesus whatever it takes for me to do or not do. I am still struggling with smoking. Actually, I'm not even trying to quit at this time, but I need to.

April 4, 2005

The Purpose-Driven Life. What on earth am I here for? It all starts with God. It's not about me. Everything started in him and finds its purpose in him (Colossians 1:16).

Once again, it's like step one in AA. In order to change my life in the world, the first step was to admit I was and am powerless over alcohol. The answer to today's question is that God is the purpose and reason why I am sober today, and I am powerless over this life of mine. I give myself to Jesus to guide me and show me and lead me into his purpose for me.

I am not an accident. Many children are unplanned by their parents, but they are not unplanned by God. God's purpose took into account human error and sin. We are the most valuable of all God's creation. God says he is our Creator and we were in his care even before we were born.

God has been working in me on my past, and in each thing I faced at a young age. I understand now that he was there and knew I would be okay. He will also be there for my future.

April 6, 2005

What drives my life? I am a product of my past, not a prisoner of my past. God specializes in giving people a fresh start. Jeremiah 29:11: *"For I know the plans I have for you," says the LORD. "They are plans for good and not for disaster, to give you a future and a hope."*

> *You will keep in perfect peace all who trust in you, all whose thoughts are fixed you!* (Isaiah 26:3).

I focus on this one thing: Forgetting the past and looking forward to what lies ahead (Philippians 3:13). Living on purpose is the path to peace.

Made to last forever. God has planted eternity in the human heart (Ecclesiastes 3:11). Earth is the staging area, the preschool, the tryout for my life in eternity.

Since I was made to last forever, what is the one thing I should stop doing, and the one thing I should start doing? One thing I know: I must stop smoking and it is as hard or even harder than when I quit drinking. The truth is I am not trying as hard as I did with not want-ing to drink. That is where Romans come in. The thing I want to do that is right, I fail at and continue to do wrong. By the grace of God I am saved, and I believe this too will have a day of victory. I pray for God to work through me as a witness to all he can do.

Yesterday I got a phone call that AA needed someone to sponsor someone who will be getting out of jail. I almost passed the buck, and then something changed. I said I would go the distance to help this person. I believe God was leading me to answer, and I believe my number was the one God wants to maybe help this person.

April 11, 2005

I should have gone to church last night but didn't. I need God to motivate me on Sunday night. This needs to be a routine for the good of my future. Once a week isn't enough. I need more, and I know it.

April 12, 2005

Life is a temporary assignment. Your identity is in eternity. Heaven is my homeland. Friends, the world is not your home, so don't make yourselves cozy in it. Don't indulge your ego at the expense of your soul. In order to keep us from becoming too attached to earth, God allows us to feel a significant amount of discontent and dissatisfaction in life; longings that will never be fulfilled on this side of eternity.

In my past years I always felt as if I didn't belong here. Well, I don't. However, I am here with a mission from God to serve him and him only. I understand why I just don't fit in. When I used to drink, I just did it to fit in with the crowd and to be accepted for who I was. Where do I fit in now? Right here at home. I am satisfied with just being with myself and God, not like when I wanted people around all the time. Most people I know still party or live the same old life I was in. I need to remember this world is not my home.

April 15, 2005

I was planned for God's pleasure. Yesterday I was out working in an area of our property where Joshua's camper will soon sit. When I was looking around at all the branches to be cut and moved, I realized God gives us so many things to use. I told Josh this and also said we should have our place cleaned up because the Lord has given it to us to use. I felt good in telling him even the little things God notices. It may have sounded to him like I lost it or something, but then he agreed with me. I do turn on music in the mornings and throughout the day, and sometimes I sing along as I meditate on the words. God has been good to me and I really do try to make known his great-ness the best I can.

April 20, 2005

> *For since our friendship with God was restored by the death of his Son while we were still his enemies, we will certainly be saved through the life of his Son* (Romans 5:10).

Just this morning I was thinking about Lorrie and how we used to be friends, and for some reason she hasn't called me and I don't know why. Same goes for Thelma, and again, I don't know why. Maybe I am not to have any friends outside of God's plan for me, or I'm just not friend material. Or just maybe this lesson is what God has ordered for me to become his friend only.

So now we can rejoice in our wonderful new relationship with God because our Lord Jesus Christ has made us friends of God (Romans 5:11).

He is a God who is passionate about his relationship with you (Acts 17:26–27).

Friendship with God is reserved for those who reverence him (Psalm 25:14). What can I do to remind myself to think about God and talk to him more often throughout the day? Yesterday I began talking while working outside. I needed to feel the presence of Jesus, and I did. I also praised God in my heart with verses I thought about, promises of God, and I rebuked the devil who was trying to bring into my mind things from my past that I have been forgiven for. I told God I will trust in him to take care of decisions that have come about recently. His will be done.

May 3, 2005

Just a note of thankfulness to Jesus. Finally I have the refreshment I have been longing for. Actually, for a while I've been having some emotional drawbacks and not feeling like I belonged anywhere. Sunday at church I felt like I wanted something and needed something and didn't feel like the presence of God was with me at all. So the Sunday service was good for me, but the evening service is what struck home with me right where I was – isolating myself, loneliness, causing much discouragement. I will stay true to God for he is just and faithful. I finally got the answer to my despair. I was very close to giving in to the temptations of my past life again. Praying daily in a mindful way with Jesus. Today is good and I believe the Lord is showing me I can reach out and it's okay to do so. I shared my despair with a sister in Christ along with my feelings of not belonging. I am glad I was finally able to talk to someone.

I need to get more involved with church members, and no matter how I feel, it's a must. I went to the women's meeting last night and found I just might be okay.

May 5, 2005

I am called to belong, not just believe. So it is with Christ's body. We are many parts of one body, and we all belong to each other (Romans 12:5). Just recently I started attending all services offered at church. I have been elected to help with decorating ideas for downstairs at the church. The service on Sunday night confirms what I read today. I had been in isolation and wondering where I stood in the church. I attended Wednesday night service also and was glad the Lord placed in my heart a need for fellowship. In fact, I am troubled by my friend-ships outside of church, and here today I read it is my responsibility to face those I know who have not found peace with God. My goal is to be closer to Jesus and today I realize I need to be closer to the people who walk in his likeness.

May 6, 2005

I need others in my life. *Share each other's burdens, and in this way obey the law of Christ* (Galatians 6:2). I think I should call Lorrie and see what's really going on. Forgiving but not trusting is okay. Forgiveness is mandatory. A simple thing is her not showing up for a cookout. She said she would be here for it. She didn't show up for reasons unknown. Bitterness has taken root inside me, and it has to go.

May 11, 2005

Since my last study, Lorrie and I are talking. I also got a call about Don, the new guy, and yesterday had a visit with both John's and Don's social workers. The only rule I asked for and said I wouldn't bend on is that Don attends the same church we do when we go. I won't know until Friday if he accepts this or not. I have to stand firm with God and attend as much as I can. He has a right to say no. If he does, this would mean he would not be moving in, but I cannot sacrifice my living for the Lord for anyone. I pray his decision will be yes and that he might even enjoy the church. God can change this guy's life, and I would enjoy seeing what God's purpose for Don will be.

Started the nonsmoking patch Sunday night. I'm not sleeping well and I don't have enthusiasm in doing this. My energy is lax and my attitude isn't good. I have so far had five cigarettes since Monday and it is Wednesday. So I have failed with the patch. I keep saying this too will pass. Mornings are the hardest. At times I want to give up and not try at all.

Just as with alcohol, I did all things well mostly with a drink in hand. I pray, Lord Jesus, that you help me daily in overcoming the bondage of nicotine and free me in my mind from the desire to smoke. Jesus, I want to live for you and be a witness for you. This is weighing down my testimony for you. I pray, in the name of Jesus, the devil and all things concerning cigarettes will flee from my thoughts. Glory be to God in the most high. In the name of Jesus I am saved.

May 26, 2005

I am going through something now, and I'm not exactly sure how to explain it. What comes to mind is last night's lesson at church to get into the battle with the Lord and don't quit, don't give up, hold fast to the Lord. Psalm 27 was the main topic. I'm not sure if I am living to full potential for the Lord. The victory is already won through the Lord, but yet the decisions to make stand at hand.

Why am I choosing to smoke over obeying what I know in my heart is right – to let go and let God? I've stopped trying to quit, and the joy and peace have left me. I don't feel strong today in anything, but only weak and weary. I'm running but going nowhere. I can't seem to make any decisions.

Saturday I am leaving for Illinois for my sister's wedding. Everyone seems to be with someone, and yet I wonder if I ever will be again. I will trust in the Lord and lean not on my own understanding.

I read this morning Revelation 21 and 22. I received a message from the Lord that I must truly stand strong with Jesus and wait for his coming, but the fear of my failure is always at hand. I wonder if smoking is going to keep me from the Promised Land. I pray not. I truly want to be like Jesus. I want what is on the other side of this. I pray to have the strength needed to overcome this addiction and to see the victory in Jesus.

May 29, 2005

> Psalm 61:1: *O God, listen to my cry! Hear my prayer! From the ends of the earth, I cry to you for help when my heart is overwhelmed. Lead me to the towering rock of safety.*

It has been months of failure in the smoking realm. I lost my desire to quit and seemingly have lost my faith. I have been lashing myself for not having self-control, when the will of the Lord should be my strength. Asking God for counsel and yet lacking faith in his ability to help me.

Everyone I am around this weekend does not smoke, but yet I still have to set aside a place so I can. Sounds crazy and it probably is.

June 18, 2005

Today I felt the need to write a few things down that I had pondered last night. In a year and a half the Lord has led me, guided me, and showed me what real love is. The bondage of alcohol is gone. The life of a lesbian is in the past. And my mouth, well, I'm learning to tame the tongue more. God has removed these blocks in my life and started a new foundation. If smoking is my only issue, then so be it for now. This, too, will be overcome in time.

The word "love" and its meaning is so much more than I've ever known. It's not a bedside manner or a way to get what I want. I'm a new creation and kindness comes from the heart and love means the most in the eyes of God. *For God loved the world so much that he gave His one and only Son, so that everyone who believes in him will not perish but have eternal life* (John 3:16). The greatest of these is love (1 Corinthians 13:13).

July 19, 2005

Months ago I pleaded with the Lord that I did not want to be alone forever. Now I have been sponsoring inmates, and in February I got another person who served time in jail for six different DUIs. Now it is July and we have kept in touch. Letters flow back and forth between us and have been mostly about help God puts on my heart to write to him. Roger has found a desire for me, claiming we may find it to be more than just friends in Christ. Today I find myself in agreement. When the first letter arrived from him, I did feel something, as if God was coming right at me, and the same feelings have resurfaced in each letter. But I can't help but wonder if this is maybe just infatuation.

No pictures, no sexual remarks, just a desire from him to know more of me in Christ. I have to admit to the same associations. I wrote a letter in response except this time I let him know of my past with Priscilla. No details. Just that we were together a long time and that obeying God to end us was hard to do.

I don't know what his response will be. I am trying to concen-trate on God's will for my life, and I do not want to get in God's way. Strange as this may sound, Priscilla made this comment on the first letter from Roger: "Who knows? Maybe you and Roger will have a future together." Where did that come from? I don't want to get my hopes up, however. Today I filled out the visitation in case the time does come for us to meet face to face.

I'm not sure what is going to happen. Roger says so many nice things in his letters. Is this too good to be true? A person who relates on the same level with Jesus as I do? Same interests? I will await Roger's next letter.

July 30, 2005

I woke up this morning with a lot of thoughts going through my mind. The subject was homosexuality. I was thinking of writing a letter – to whom I'm not sure – but in it I would say something about the ben-efit, if you want to call it that, of being in a relationship that way was mostly a mistaken identity. Eventually most people come to realize this at some point. People should know what God has declared, that homosexuality corrupts what he has made appealing. If only people would give the Lord a chance, he would reveal his truth about this lifestyle which the world embraces today.

However, a person may not be ready to hear these words or even give a thought to the fact that being gay is not right. The two books I have read on this topic have been a great help in understanding where God stands in this. Coming Out of Homosexuality is written for people to understand why they got there and how to get out. Restoring Sexual Identity is based on the reason people run to same-sex partners, what God has to say, and what the world makes look good.

I am greatly concerned for those out there, even friends of mine, who need to know the truth and that the truth will set them free. Yes, we live in a country that stresses freedom for all, but the biggest problem is that people leave out God and what God intended for freedom in mind, body, and soul. God also intended peace for us, but without God there is no true peace, no joy, and no freedom. In place of these, people experience bondage and denial.

July 31, 2005

Last night we (Josh, Amanda, Dan, Don, and Priscilla) went to the fair. When we got there I heard someone yelling out my name and it was Dee, whom I haven't seen in at least four years. She and I go way back, and I am not proud of that. She has really let herself go, and I feel a need to help. I've told her I will make a visit and pray the Lord will use the time to work through me.

Also the other day I saw Joshua's first girlfriend who is now mar-ried and has a two-year-old boy. I shared with her what the Lord has done in my life and asked her to come to church sometime. I also said I would love to babysit for her son sometime. That part sounded good to her, but not church; she said she'd feel out of place. I have assured her we all have felt that way but the Lord is able to turn that feeling into comfort. While I don't know what will become of them, I do know one thing: I'm glad the Lord is my witness and not me alone.

The Lord is good and only his timing is perfect, so I will just con-tinue to let everyone know what he's done in my life. In obedience, I plant the seed and God can go from there and he will.

I wrote Roger back and am still wondering what plan God has. Also I have spoken to Priscilla about him and feel that was God's timing. She'll be okay, because the Lord will help and comfort her. I am not out to hurt anyone, but the truth shall set us free.

August 1, 2005

Went fishing last night with Josh and Amanda. I can't express enough to him that he needs to wait with Amanda for relationship. I told him it is adultery, and God does not approve of this. However, I don't know that I stressed it enough. I pray someday Scripture will flow out of me and I'll know where certain things are in the Bible so what I say won't return void.

Church service was good, and the messages were exactly what God ordered. Each time I speak of the things Jesus has done for me, people are amazed, but not enough to want what I have with Jesus. I pray I can be more of a witness for him. My heart cries out for all to know what the Lord Jesus can and will do. Seek. Ask. Find. Why was it so hard for me to let go and let God? I can look back and see only that I truly had to be a person with no other way out, trying everything to find what wasn't out there.

August 7, 2005

I've been seeking God, but maybe I've not actually thought about just loving God for God. I just finished reading the book *The God Chasers*. Part of me wants to jump and yell; the other part is just still within me. Sometimes I feel as if I am learning all of what I should, but it's just not sinking in like in the beginning where convictions were strong. I sometimes think I should or could be doing more for the Lord, and then this shyness about me invades my intentions. I surely do not feel like that person I used to be. I long to do what is right before God, and I do not want to give in to that which isn't of God.

I pray to you, Jesus, for a consistent balance in my character as I become the person you are molding – consistent in you, Lord Jesus, and not to be in emotional turmoil. I seek you, Lord, to guide me in every way each day, and please, Lord, keep me from mine enemies. Lord, use me in your path of righteousness.

August 10, 2005 Based on a book I once read.
First there are some questions to ask myself:

<u>Am I ready for the love I think I want?</u> Yes, but fear of failure is there and not knowing if it will be of God for sure or will I get in the way (flesh).

<u>What is my motivation for desiring a committed love relationship?</u> To be able to share everything, especially God, and all that God has intended for a relationship.

<u>What problems do I think love will solve in my world?</u> Not to be alone.

What am I prepared to give in order to get the love I desire? I want to give all of me to Jesus so he can mold me. Love, understanding, compassion.

<u>Am I willing to make changes in my world to accommodate the man I love?</u> If need be, and if I am guided by the Lord to do so.

Do I know what I want in a man? Yes. A man of God for sure. Someone who loves with God's Spirit. One willing to take care of my needs and desires.

Do I know what I should want in a man? Not really, except he should have the same faith as I do in the Lord.

Are my love expectations love-realistic? I think they are.

If I never found Mr. Right, would I still able to lead a happy and fulfilled life? As of right now in my life I am learning to be satisfied in the Lord. To wait upon him. I am still learning to lean on Jesus. My commitment is to Jesus, and I want him to come first. I still have a lot to learn concerning trust, honesty, and the love of Jesus.

I am not yet ready, so I am going to stay pure for the time being so I am in Jesus' way of thinking. I have already realized I am not content with myself or God as of yet, and that means I am not ready for the man of God.

In the days when the judges ruled in Israel, a severe famine came upon the land (Ruth 1:1). When flesh or emotions rule, I become a prime candidate for famine of the heart. I will no longer allow my hunger to drive me into the arms of those undiscerning of my worth and undeserving of my heart. My relationship with God sets the stage for how all my relationships will pan out.

First commandment: Love the Lord your God with all your heart, soul, mind, and strength. I will allow God to do the work that needs to be done in my heart to make me a whole person, before I pursue love. I need to continue in the Word of God and continue seeking his guidance, wisdom, and strength, and mostly I want to know the Lord on a personal basis.

Isaiah 55:2: *Why spend your money on food that does not give you strength? Why pay for food that does you no good? Listen to me, and you will eat what is good. You will enjoy the finest food.*

August 11, 2005

If I allow my hunger for love to get in the way, I will find love in all the wrong places and will leave the safe place in Jesus by not waiting.

Loneliness eventually passes.

Dig into the Word of God.

I will not allow myself to remain in situations that are not fruit ful or do not contribute to my wellbeing physically, emotionally, or spiritually.

I will consider my heart condition carefully and not be ruled by it. I will make sound judgments and choices not based on my cravings, but on my gifts and my purpose so I may fulfill my destiny accord-ing to God's design.

Sometimes waiting on God is like waiting for paint to dry. It is hard to see progress at the surface because there is nothing visible to compare to. I need to get myself settled with God, the lover of my soul, and then truly my faith will live.

The thief's [Satan's] purpose is to steal and kill and destroy. My

purpose is to give them a rich and satisfying life (John 10:10).

God is great and we are on a journey, a test, a real test, and I think this one has been graded good. I almost fell into the same trap as the old me, but with God's boundary lines I can determine the difference of right from wrong. This is surely a weak area, and now that I know this, God can and will help. He says so and God doesn't lie!

August 12, 2005

I will not compromise my standards and settle for someone who does not walk in agreement with my values, just to have a man in my life. I will hold out for the one who is right for me. *A person who is full refuses honey, but even bitter food tastes sweet to the hungry* (Proverbs 27:7).

I truly have the right intentions of helping others with their jour-ney to recovery. I lost sight of what my goal was, and it surely isn't to settle for second best. Blinded by hunger and fooled by words of deception, I must be free and move on.

I'm thankful to have learned this part of many more lessons to come. Praise the Lord for his knowledge. We move on together.

August 13, 2005

Learning that God does not owe me anything for my obedience! Nor do the promises I make to God earn me any extra blessings.

I will not try to force other people to walk in my light, but will apply myself to being joyfully obedient to the path upon which I have been called to walk.

I should be joyful to be pure for my Lord God and not compromise or go against his answers to me to try to make things happen in my time, but rather be patient for God's timing.

I realized today that I better not bargain with God when I am staying celibate for him. I am not obeying just because I want a man. I am not sure I said to God I would be pure IF.... However, if I did, I take it all back to start fresh. I want to be pure as God intended for me to be from the beginning of life, and I will not let this be a part in my reasons for having a man in my life. The choice is mine, and I choose to be pure in all areas for my Lord Jesus.

It's time to nurture a grateful heart and be thankful for what I already have: rich friendships, a supportive family, people in the church who believe the way I do, and a God who knows my every need, desire, and my heart.

At present, where am I living emotionally? Today things are going better. After church service on Sunday I let go of a lot of distress I was carrying around.

Am I willing to risk stepping out of my comfort zone to find the life I want? Yes. I am ready for whatever the Lord would want me to do. If it is to be alone, I am okay today with that.

<u>What is my main focus?</u> To be able to tell others what Jesus has done in my life and let them know he can do it for anyone who wants it.

My future is in God's hands and I will continue to live in his mercy and grace, for he so loved me and gave his only Son Jesus for me to live in peace and joy, not despair and deception. *If you try to hang on to your life, you will lose it. But if you give up your life for my sake, you will save it* (Matthew 16:25).

August 16, 2005

Living for Jesus is what is at hand. Thank God for his real presence, and Sunday I needed all of him to stand up and not give in to things running in my mind.

There is no going back to the old me, for surely I would die. I like living for God, and I've so much to learn and let go of in order to work for God. I still need to quit smoking, and I just have to lay low on this until the power sweeps me off my feet. My want-to is there, but my mind isn't, and until it is I won't stop.

<u>What things am I waiting to do until I get a mate?</u> I'm not sure that I am holding back, only that it is nice to go places with someone, even just as friends.

<u>What season am I in?</u> I believe I am in a season of knowledge of good and bad, and that God is showing me instructions to become the person he intends for me to be with him and with no one else as of yet.

<u>What purpose do I think God is trying to guide me to before marriage?</u> I believe I have much healing ahead of me and a lot of books yet to read. I will face whatever God puts in front of me and I pray I learn all he gives to me.

August 20, 2005

Thank you, Jesus, for giving me the wisdom I was seeking! Moving into God's favor is what I am seeking, and I will do whatever it takes for my Father who art in heaven to have me be the person he created me to be.

August 26, 2005

I've stayed away from most everyone in my past because it is not spiritually healthy to be around fence-riders for the temptations that would be at hand. Not that I am having any concerns with the guidance the Lord has given me, but on the other hand, where their beliefs are different than mine, I don't see eye to eye. Even Priscilla is struggling with her serving God and still going out. I pray for her and that is all I can do.

August 30, 2005

My mouth has been a bad tool for swearing the past month, and I don't need these ungodly weapons. Lord, be with me in all I do and say. I pray Jesus works this out in all ways. I do feel as if I am being taken advantage of, not only in this, but also in the area of no respect. I've given enough time for Josh to realize I am not the same, and still I get no respect. It is so hard to hold my tongue, and I know I need to.

September 1, 2005

Summer is coming to an end and I'm not ready. I can't say I've had the best of summers, but I can say I've had a sober one. I'm satisfied with this fact. It will be two years that the Lord and I have been treating alcoholism and some days it seems as if I never really had a problem. But I must remind myself I did. The problem was that I wasn't living for God, and now I am giving it all I've got. I pray that every day will strengthen me as I seek the protection of my Father above.

September 14, 2005

It's not easy to stay pure. On Sunday I broke down before church in tears. At first I wasn't sure where the tears were coming from, just that I couldn't stop them. Plus on the 2nd I went out with Lorrie, Krista, and

Priscilla for Lorrie's birthday. I didn't have the greatest of fun. And no, I didn't drink.

I'm really having a hard time fitting in anywhere. I remember having these feelings long ago. Back then I searched for a way to fit in and thought I found it. What I found was the ways of the world, and now I barely fit in there either. I do fit in at church services. I have a peace about me at times, but when I get home it seems to disappear.

Sometimes I want to just give in to myself; however, I realize where that has gotten me all my life. I haven't been reading as much of the Word as I should. I'm going to try and get back on the right schedule with Jesus.

September 22, 2005

I am seeking after wisdom in all things and am feeling a bit of jealousy over Priscilla's closeness with Tabby. I see her looking at her like she used to look at me, whether it is anything or not. It hurts. I don't want to give in to my past way of life. I need God and all the help I can get. Tabby is with Jackie and at this point, if they weren't together, I am sure Priscilla would move in. I have spoken to Tabby about the Lord Jesus and what life is intended to be, and it doesn't include being with a woman. Once again, I don't think I got anywhere in this either.

My testimony should be enough, but the power to change people isn't with me, but with God. I really don't like all the things I've done, but shouldn't some of it show Jesus can do all things? If he can change me, then people should see when I tell them who's responsible for the change. They could have the same things. Since this isn't the case, I will just be grateful God has saved me from any more harm and continue to pray for others.

September 24, 2005

As I read Psalm 119 today I read out loud. A few tears fell in each word I read to the Lord. I'm seeking for God and doing what it takes to follow his commandments in all I do. The ways of the wicked oppress me, and I do seek after all the Lord's strength. I long for his promises to me as a light in my path when everything seems dark.

September 26, 2005

Church was good except Josh is holding on so bad. I pray the Lord to break the hardness covering his sensitive nature. The message was that Jesus should be first in all we do, and we should not look to ourselves for answers. We will not find the right answers that way.

The message affirmed what I had already been saying to Josh, but he didn't move at all. Only God knows his heart, and I pray it is in the right place.

October 6, 2005

Yesterday I went to Spooner where Christine was having a few women from the church over. I was a bit nervous, since I really haven't been with any of the church members outside of church. It is finally time to spread my wings and get out among those who believe the same way I do. The visit went well, and we prayed for Josh right off the bat. I believe God is going to do great works in his life. I sure am ready to witness what God has promised – that all of my household shall be saved. Despite the circumstances, God can do ALL things.

Today the study was on marriage in Matthew 19. I will keep this passage close to my heart for the day God joins me with the right man. How exciting to know it will be God's plan and not mine.

October 14, 2005

I listened to a couple of messages today, one on faith and the other on God not liking excuses when we choose not to obey him. This puts me in a bad way, since I've been using every excuse I can find not to quit smoking. Oh, where is my faith when it comes to this? Where is my willpower of wanting to succeed? What happened to my faith in believing God can help me with this, too? I have to obey God and be holy in order to receive his greatness in my life. What's stopping me? Why do I keep holding on to what is bad for me?

God is good. God is great and greatly to be praised. For he alone made everything including me. Lord Jesus, what's it gonna take? Help me renew my mind to overcome that which hinders my spirit.

In a sense, I'm becoming discouraged. I know what's right, and yet I continue to do what God doesn't want me to do. It's a battle of the mind.

October 15, 2005

> *Instead, you ought to say, "If it is the Lord's will, we will live and do this or that." As it is, you boast in your arrogant schemes. All such boasting is evil. If anyone, then, knows the good they ought to do and doesn't do it, it is sin for them* (James 4:15–17, NIV).

Today's study in James 4 tells me I am sinning when I know what is right and don't do it. How much plainer can it get? Verse 15 states what I ought to say: If the Lord wants me to, I will live this way or that. Verse 16: Otherwise I would be boasting about my own plans. All such boasting is evil. Verse 17: Remember it is a sin to know what you ought to do, then not do it.

How plain can it be? I am a sinner saved by the grace and mercy of God. Why do I have to be so stubborn?

October 20, 2005

A major attempt has been made today to stop smoking. Sunday morning, before church, I watched a pastor on TV. He talked about self-discipline. Next thing ya know, I'm getting ready for church and Priscilla comes in to get Josh a cigarette. I told her to take what I had; I was done.

Today is Thursday and it's been a long week and still the desire to smoke hangs onto me, with a headache swelling in my head and all kinds of emotions. I did laundry, dishes, writing, and devotions, and all these things used to include a smoke. The battle is not over yet, but the victory is on the way. The temptation is still there. The devil tries to get in and make me think, what's the use? But I know what God has been saying all along: my blessings of life are waiting on the other side of this victory.

October 21, 2005

I wanna blame something, someone, anything. I just can't stand this emotional roller coaster. One minute I think it's gonna be okay. The next my stomach hurts, my head is swelling, and I can't think straight to make choices for everyday things. I've tried to talk to God. I can't even voice words. I think I'm even mad at God for my having to quit smoking, even when it is for my own good.

I really need to feel some sort of peace about this. That the choice made was the right one. To be more like Jesus does not mean I can have a cigarette in one hand while I profess God on the other.

Help me, oh my Lord God. It feels as if I will never be free. Take my cross, and I will follow you. On my back I carry the heaviest load of smokes a person can imagine. They are weighing me down, but I can't stop. When I get to the top of this mountain we will burn them in the biggest bonfire and dance the greatest victory ever.

November 10, 2005

Just when I was sure the victory was around the corner at ten days of not smoking, I smoked again. To be holy and just is the aim, but my focus keeps wandering from my inner wants. Now I've sacrificed the victory intended for me. The Lord promises to give us the strength. Problem is, when I was almost there I wasn't seeking the Lord the way I should, and still I don't do all I know is right. I've failed, and that's the bottom line.

December 23, 2005

It's two days before Christmas and I just can't seem to get into the presents and things. I am really thinking about Jesus and Mary, his mother, and the day she gave birth and was able to believe in God. Amazing doesn't describe this well enough.

Still smoking and can't seem to get the willpower to stop.

December 30, 2005

I am headed into the year 2006 and still haven't quit smoking. Lately, too, I don't feel like God is with me, even though I know he hasn't left me. I pray to stay strong and if my temptations stay away, it will be a year since Priscilla and I have been together. Praise the Lord for working this through.

December 31, 2005

As I sit here this morning, I think about the experiences I have encountered. Is there something more I should or could do for God to help someone else battling the same things I did? What comes to mind is the last drink, the last blackout, and where I went to find an answer for the addiction that had taken over my whole being.

I had to admit I couldn't do it and needed help. I walked through the doors thinking, *I've done this before and the outcome didn't last very long*. This time was different. I had come to the end of myself. My cry was real, and it was to Jesus who seemed to be the only answer left. All had failed before.

I remember the woman who took me for my final walk down the hall and away from society. I wanted to kick and scream the whole way, but the words "I can't" made me go through those doors. I had been up since 3:30 a.m. the day before, spent the whole next day with no sleep, no food, and no memory of any of it.

Now it's been two and a half years of sobriety and I still have no memory of the night that changed my whole life. I used to try and fool myself by saying I can quit anytime I want! I will only have a few today. I won't drink tomorrow. But all my promises failed. The reality was that I was and am an alcoholic, and the choice to drink was mine and mine alone.

Looking back at the last day I ever drank, I believe it to be the worst and best day of my life. Severe: the only way I could get any help to begin with was to get a doctor to sign me in. I had been drinking all night, and they wanted me to come to the office. That was the last thing I was about to do. On the way, I yelled, "What's the use of living anymore?" That's all it took. A signature was on its way and so was I. If anything, I knew this would at least save my job. But the best part of all was I was saved, and later on I realized all I went through was for the purpose of helping someone else.

I was through the doors and among people I didn't know. Truth was I didn't know myself anymore without a drink in my hand. All I did was cry and cry. I was losing my best friend. I refused medication the first day, but it was so overwhelming I needed something. Then I slept for a while and woke up wanting a drink. When I realized what I had done I wanted out of there. My mixed emotions were crazy and at some point I thought I was crazy, too.

My cry then went out to a higher power I call Jesus. This cry not only worked for the time I was in detox, but continues today. My cries went straight to the only One who could help. The doctor who vis-ited me gave me a bad bill of health and instructed me to go through inpatient care for at least thirty days, if not more. I was a mess.

Support, willpower, and God were the only ways I was going to make it through the grief I was going through. My seventy-two hours was up. My support group waited for me in the parking lot, and my doctor was totally against my leaving.

Somehow this day was different. I was determined to prove this doctor wrong! I agreed to seek counseling three times a week and contact my family, and go to AA, but I was still leaving detox at my own risk. I don't advise people not to listen to their doctors, but in my case, I had a power much higher than him and what little faith I had, God honored.

I had not attended AA before and surely didn't want to start now, but a promise was just that, and what could it hurt anyway? I also attended counseling, and the biggest eye-opener I got from that was that I was abnormal and never would or could be normal. Abnormal became a joke for me in a good way. People would talk about drink-ing, and I wasn't shy to say I wasn't a normal person 'cause I couldn't do what they could do.

Crying is good, especially when you know who is catching your tears. Those who feel they have to hold back tears should be careful. Nothing will change in doing that, but things will only get worse. Tears are not a sign of weakness but a sign of victory.

One Day at a Time, Sweet Jesus, is the song I sang for my grand-father in church a couple of months before he died. I remembered it well. Every day was now a new day, still with the same loss and grief that overwhelmed me at times, but I didn't drink. My choice every day was not to give in to what the doctor said: "I'll see you back here." What I remember thinking was, *I'll show you. You won't see me this way again.*

January 13, 2006

New Year's Eve we went bowling. I didn't do very well but it was healthy to get out and do something different. Went to church Wednesday night since I missed Sunday, and it was good. The message touched on areas of my life I've been struggling with recently.

Some of the message Wednesday had to do with getting out of my comfort zone. I had gotten comfortable with the income from having John live with us and lacked the trust in God that he had a bigger plan beyond this one.

Plus I had been having impure thoughts. I have to put all those thoughts out of my head and move on with God's plan.

I had been having a hard time shaking off my inner feelings, because I didn't want to let them go. Knowing God would forgive me was one thing, but facing the fact that it might just put me back where God has already taken me from was another. The answers I needed came with the service Wednesday night like the message was just for me.

Praise God for all he's done for me. I want to be ready for what is next.

January 19, 2006

Today I went to L.E. Phillips, a substance abuse services center, to meet with others about becoming a speaker, and I start next week. I haven't gone through all I have not to use it to help someone else. Only God can make my life what he wants it to be. I don't want to get in his way or fall into diverse temptation. The Holy Spirit is there to quicken my thinking.

February 14, 2006

I have spoken two times at L.E. Phillips and both times someone came up afterwards to talk with me. I really have been praying to do God's will. On the way to the meetings my mind is a blank, and I'm not sure what I will be speaking about. I try not to focus on the details of my addiction.

I'm going in the right direction, but I get such an overwhelming fear when I'm headed there. My first thought is that I need a drink, but I need to remember I'm going there to help people.

I haven't been in the best of moods lately, and I have a huge list of why's. I have not been true to my purity. Today I realize that is where everything started to slide back. I will try to be as God would have me to be and not let lustful desires set me back.

I feel spiritually void, but I'm sure that is not the only reason. I have been going to way too many places I know aren't good for me or my spirit. I cannot go into diverse places where the temptation just might be overwhelming. My spirit from the Holy Spirit cannot dwell in such places. I do know one thing for sure: I long for the comfort, convictions, peace, and joy to come back into my daily life.

Every time I seem to feel like I am getting closer to knowing my God and Savior, something pulls me back almost to the point of thinking that awful thought of, *What's the use.*

Fact is, it's worth it, and I don't want to go back. I only want to move forward with my God and Lord Jesus. If you asked me a year ago about my following the Lord Jesus, my answer would be the same. My knowledge wouldn't be as it is today, though. The Holy Spirit the Lord has given me is a special part of me, and I want the closeness back.

My own strength isn't going to get me through. My future depends on my Lord Jesus and the Comforter he has left for me.

Tomorrow I speak again at L.E. Phillips. Once again I don't want it to come from me, but from the Spirit of God within me. Oh Lord, I don't know how people get by not having your help and guidance.

March 30, 2006

I need to go back to Sunday's service. Today I go back into trying to be obedient. My "self" has been in the way. Quitting smoking is a habit my spirit has wanted me to let go of for some time now.

Some will say I am being too hard on myself and maybe I am. The way I feel about it is that every time I give in to the habit, I feel a part of me leave, and along with it peace, joy, and righteousness. Perfect I will never be, but it does say in God's Word to strive to be like Jesus.

God's plan for me is great. I don't know what my future holds except that I will be in the perfect will of God by obeying in the small things. Self-control isn't exactly small to me, but for now, by obey-ing, I will not be demeaning the Holy Spirit who quickens my spirit. The old nature in me needs to get out so the new creature in Christ can bud and bloom.

The devil has tried to find ways to justify smoking and even using Christians to make it not sound like I need to quit. When the Holy Spirit in me and the flesh are fighting daily about this, and when I give in to the smoke, I only feel guilt. This is because the devil has been winning the fight.

I'm here to say today that I am taking back what the devil has stolen from me. With the Holy Spirit in control, I give up my selfish desires to the one and only Jesus who has promised to set me free. Free so the Lord Jesus can use my life in whatever way he chooses.

Rest in the Lord God in the presence of my Lord. This is exactly where I need to be.

March 31, 2006

Yesterday's gone and tomorrow may never be mine. One day at a time, sweet Jesus. Learning to love and forgive is about the hardest thing to do when Krista and Lorrie are out to destroy me. I must take this as a sign that a true blessing is just around the bend of faith. I believe in Romans 8:28, according to God's purpose and will.

My eyes have been opened in more ways than just this. I realize I have lost what it truly means to be a child of God.

LOVE – no matter what, and when I read Colossians 3:12 it is clear to me I haven't showed much of Jesus in my life. God's love is all that I haven't been.

By the grace of God my new outlook in life is in the power of the indwelling Holy Spirit, which will comfort me in my spirit and show me when I am wrong. This is my prayer and my faith, believing the Lord my God will supply all my needs according to his riches in heaven.

Here on earth I pray for strength and know the Lord is in control of my life. I am in agreement with the Lord. I have a lot to learn, and I do stumble and fall. I pray for the Lord to show me what I need to have his wisdom.

When things get tough, heaviness comes over me and I give in to habits. This is the devil and he has no hold on me. I am the Lord Jesus' property, and I will not be condemned for failure when I'm under the blood of Jesus.

Today is a new day. May God shine through me as I step out in faith and forgiveness. Humility is my middle name today. Get the board out of mine own eye.

June 13, 2006

Today my mind has been at a loss for words or anything. Can't seem to find inspiration from the Lord in my devotion. I started out thinking I needed to write Dad a letter, but none of my words were coming out right even while reading Scripture. I don't know. My mind is stayed on Jesus, but to put even this down on paper is a challenge.

I did manage to buy a Father's Day card. It starts out by saying, "May God be with you on Father's Day and always." Then it goes on: "It is

God who knows our every need and hears each prayer we say. It is He who grants us heart's content and guides us through each day; so may it be His gracious will to always give you His understanding and His love and all His blessings, too. Happy Father's Day." Now that I've read this again, I know this is the perfect card and none of my words would be as true as the Lord's promises to each one of us.

My first intentions were to bring out in the open the dissatisfac-tion with Dad's parenting ways. To open his eyes to his wrongs years ago. But now this all seems completely opposite of what God wants me to do. It must be given to God.

I am okay, and as for the damage that once had me in bondage, the Lord has been healing me in every way. I'm still learning how to love and sometimes have a hard time believing the Lord doesn't change. The Word clearly says God is the same yesterday, today, and forevermore. By his Word I will be made whole. This is as true as the Lord my God is true.

Sometimes I must remember where I've been, because I sure like it much better where I'm at, and I am excited to know where I am going.

I lost my grandmother May 27 to the greatest of all, my Lord God. Just to know I will see her again someday gives me peace and reas-surance because the Lord promises us a new heaven and that this earth will pass away.

My grandmother, most precious to me, left behind great and dear memories no one can ever take away or replace. I will miss her, but at least she is happy and satisfied where she is for eternity. Her journey was long and though hard at times, her faith in God holds true her eternal future.

I pray I will always stay faithful to the Lord in all things, that my spirit never leaves me and always quickens my soul for right and wrong. I'm okay now and feel a great peace. God's going to always be by my side.

June 22, 2006

It is early in the morning and I am up again as usual, but reading two different stories: one about love shared for years with a mate and the other about giving rather than holding treasures for self. Both are good lessons and reminders.

The love story is of a man and wife married fifty years. This couple had health problems but remained kind and gentle towards each other. This is the way I want my marriage to be. I always want to have a giving spirit without pride or honor of self. Instead, I want to stay true to the real meaning of life with a future in heaven always in my heart. I've found a love that on this earth could never happen to me.

In my heart is a burning desire to do God's will and to be in relationships that don't hinder my spirit but rather increase a spiritual outlook for all those around me.

Last week my heart longed for Roger. At first you wouldn't think this to be anything more than feelings, but I see in my mind the two of us in a ministry together. This excites me and at the same time frightens me. Is this God-given for him and I to be together or is my loneliness grabbing something of this world that is only a delusion? Well, all things of God are good, and I see good things for my future. I see God opening doors, but I see Roger in them, right in agreement with the Word of God. I wrote to him but haven't heard back. I can rest assured in God's promises and pray for his guidance in whatever he moves in me. Be not of this world but live in the Spirit who will guide, direct, and give peace.

July 9, 2006

A guy named Dave came over to work on the electricity in the house. There seemed to be something between us right away, but he's been with someone for three years. I don't know what is going on but the connection is there. Not sure if this will mean anything or not. He will be back on Thursday.

July 19, 2006

Dave was here last night again and since the last time I wrote we've hugged and kissed. It's hard to say no to him. One thing I still don't like, however, is when he swears with God's name. This changes everything. I need to approach this with boldness and also with wisdom. I am asking God to help me know when to speak and what to say. It's only been ten days, so we'll see what happens.

I think I want this to be, but I also need it to be in God's will for my life and his. The more I think about things, it seems he wants the bed more and more, and this can't happen. I will stay strong in the Lord so I don't get in the way of God's plan in my life.

July 23, 2006

Lord, today is Sunday. I am at peace and still am in your will today. It's been a tempting time with Dave as I have deep desires to know him better. As always, Lord, I need your wisdom and your strength to stand strong on your Word. I don't know where I am supposed to be with Dave, but you do, Lord. If I am not in your will, Lord, I ask you to open my eyes and heart that I might be in your will and not mine.

What more could I ask for in a man except for him to be in church with me or at least somewhere so his life is in your will and in line with your Word, God? I pray today for your instructions and that I will always seek you and keep you, Lord, first in my life.

It just seems if I am in your will everything should not be so difficult. There are roadblocks, and I don't want to stumble through them, if this is not your will. However, if this is a test or trial, I will gladly go through and stand strong on your words and continue to remember you are in control of my life. I also know you never give your children more than they can handle.

You, Lord, are my strength, my comfort, my shield, my life. Without you, God, I am nothing. Thank you for my life in you. I stand on the promises for my divine future. Thank you, Jesus, for saving my soul and for renewing my mind. Lord, I love you. Be with me, Lord, as I continue in the mission set before me.

August 22, 2006

Today I am not sure where my life is. I'm sure of one thing, however. I will follow Jesus, and I will wait upon the Lord for my future blessings.

I really wanted Dave to be the right one, but today I don't feel like I am in God's plan for a life together. So far we have a lot in com-mon but not much in conversation. Mostly a lot of touchy-feely, and I don't want a relationship based on sex. At least I haven't given in to my own desires as I would have in my past life.

There is too much for him to decide, and the most important thing is whether his life is following in God's plans. Only God knows his heart and his intentions. I pray God will do what he will in his life, whether it is with me or not. I need to stay focused on God's plan for my future, and it is critical I stay pure.

I want the plan God has had for me from the beginning. It is going to take all the self-discipline and self-control I can manage while having faith God will bless me as he has promised.

Dave has a few more things to wire in my house and then the time with him here will be at an end. I'm not going to worry about what comes next, because today I'm sure God is in control of everything in my life. Surely goodness and mercy shall follow me.

September 18, 2006

My heart is heavy and has been for two weeks now. I have put myself in a situation I now cannot take back. What have I done? I've laid it down at the feet of Jesus, but I don't feel free. I can't bear the cold-ness it has created in me. A lesson in compromise and a loss of my own respect is now greatly in the hands of God. I gave in to Dave two weeks ago and even on a Sunday, which I call a holy day. Now I have to move on. This is the hardest part of all.

It wasn't worth it. The enjoyment isn't much to talk about. Lust has invaded me only to teach me that it is not what I want my future to be.

Got a message from God himself in church yesterday straight to me and still I couldn't humble myself at the altar. Last night was another message straight to my heart. I moved to the altar but still felt a cold heart. Again this morning a message on the radio relating to what I did. This is bigger than me, and if I don't let God have it all, I am sure to fall deeper than I have today.

What in the world am I to do? God knows my heart. It is trying to clam up and fear besets me. I need to get past this. No way do I want any part of falling down again, especially to the point of years ago. This is not good for me. I don't know what is going to happen next, but I sure want God to be in control, not me.

September 24, 2006

Never thought I'd be able to say I have been free for three years from alcohol, but as of yesterday it has been that long. I tried something different and went to a singles retreat. We had a singing service intro to the weekend, and it wasn't something I fit into. I am so used to really getting into praising the Lord and would like to have seen others enjoying praising God as I do. I have to stick to how God has moved in me and my life and not fall into the mundane routine of others. I had some issues, however, that needed to be let go of and the next day was the opportunity to spill my past all over the four-person group. I just

209

pray the Lord was able to move through me. Everything is going to be all right with me concerning Dave. It is time to move on and let God have my life completely.

Now I know why the message to me from Angie was to submit to God. Jesus wants to be my husband first and foremost.

Today I am not concerned about when or if I ever remarry. It isn't first in my life anymore. However, getting where I belong with Jesus is. One thing for sure: I don't want to go around that same block again.

Tomorrow morning Josh and Priscilla will join me in church. For Josh this will be a first since June. I am thankful, even if it is only today for now. It's a start. I believe God's promise that all will come to him and the timing is his, not mine.

October 6, 2006

Today is kinda different in mood for me. I am feeling discontentment and just feel alone. God never leaves me, but I believe I have drifted farther from him. I want a renewal, a new beginning. However, I am not doing much, if anything, to get there. I had a bad dream that I took a drink and was able to stop after just a couple. I don't want to head down that road again. It's bad enough I've lost my purity for a time. That experience taught me how important being pure really is and what it means to me.

To fall into temptation realizing first it may have been a test and then knowing it was all just me. Nothing other than my selfish flesh to blame once again. I sure don't want to take that path again.

November 3, 2006

Praise the Lord for he is great in all things. His power endures forever! God's promises are awesome and his glory is great. Thank you, Jesus, for dying for me and giving me hope and a brand new life.

Realizing today that God is my God and Father and by the Holy Spirit he has given to me, I am his child. I don't yet understand his love as I probably should, but I pray I will in time. I will not give up, even when I am filled with all the blessings promised to me as a child of God. Only God could and did save me and without my Lord Jesus and his Spirit within me, I would be nothing in the eyes of anyone.

Great prayers are going to be answered in all circumstances I go through today and forever. While the struggles of purity were once an issue, now there is victory. More than ever I want to follow in God's plans for my life. As I begin again to obey and put aside my lustful desires and my selfish behavior, I will have peace and contentment to submit to Jesus.

Making decisions and dealing with neighbors is another part of life where I need to focus on Jesus and not focus on what is coming at me. Sometimes I'm not as obedient as I should be and at times it doesn't seem like God hears my cries. But he does and with each step in faith I take, a victory will be won.

I still go to L.E. Phillips to speak, but I wonder if I will ever be excited about this work the way he wants me to be. It's the getting motivated to go. Once I'm there, God sees me through and each blessing is the greatness of his love for those who are lost and have no hope. My past life is now a blessing instead of a curse.

November 8, 2006

I am believing God for his will to be done in my life. The Holy Spirit moved on me yesterday for the first time in a long time. Well overdue. I was watching a praise-a-thon. I felt the Spirit and pledged Psalm 68:19 for one year. I hadn't done this before, but I can remember my grandmother had much to do with tithing to TBN. I kinda felt as if I needed to carry on by doing what she wasn't here to do anymore. The program had been a blessing to her for many years and to me now. I also asked for prayer for the desire to quit smoking. Well, as usual, I failed that one again. But this year will be a victory over this bondage; it will be done.

Today is the day I go to speak in Chippewa at L.E. Phillips. I start off really not wanting to go, but once I'm there I know God is in control. Even if one person gets the message, the angels sing. So if it is that important to God, then it's well with me.

Life is good and God is great. My life with the Lord is getting better every day. I pray for the strength of the Holy Spirit as I am still in bondage to nicotine. This too will be gone. There will be a time. Soon, I pray.

December 2, 2006

This month is the last of another year that has flown by with some achievements, some disappointments, yet many blessings. This year has been easier than past ones. Still different trials and temptations have taken place. Hard work and labor have resulted in contentment, while still fighting the battle of smoking.

My time is near. I can tell. This addiction is no different than any other, and I am powerless over it. Only God can free me. Why am I holding on to this sin, and why don't I call it for what it is: sin? Even a child in the church recognizes smoking as a sin, and I am to be forgiven. But I have to give it to God in order for him to free me. I can't understand what the hold-up is. I thought I had given this to God but realize I haven't. Question is, why not? Then when I think about all of this, I want to dig in again, knowing I want the opposite. What is it going to take?

This is the season, and the timing couldn't be more right. Now is the day, the month, to be completely free.

The temptations in your life are no different from what others experience.

And God is faithful. He will not allow the temptation to be more than you can stand.

When you are tempted, he will show you a way out so that you can endure.

1 Corinthians 10:13

JANUARY 30, 2005

Hello Roger,

Wayne (who facilitated the A.A. group in Barron County Jail) and I were playing phone tag, and finally we touched base. Since I don't know the circumstances that got you where you are today, I understand if you don't want to share your own story immediately; but when you do, I'll be a lis- tening ear. I am here to help you in any way that I can. First of all, I will tell you a bit of my story so that maybe it will give you hope.

Hello, my name is Marilynne and I am an alcoholic. My alcoholism started with childhood drinking, continued through my teen years, and into adulthood. Then a change happened. I was saved by the grace of God and everything became great. However, I later walked away from my Lord and fell into darkness all over again. In all of those years of drinking, I never professed to be an alcoholic until fourteen years later.

After a few DUIs, being in and out of detox several times, and never going more than a week without a drink, I hit rock bottom. Driving while drunk was one thing, but doing it with a passenger was another. Getting home and not remem- bering anything after leaving the bar was yet another.

One evening ended badly, when I told two of my best friends to get out of my house, among other things that I still do not remember saying. My job was on the line. My house was on the line. My life was on the line. I didn't want to live anymore, but my body had become so tolerant to alcohol that it seemed I couldn't even die from it.

Yet in a sense I was already dead. My personality was now controlled by my drinking. My mind refused to think unless I was drinking. I went to work just so I could afford to drink. I cared for nothing but my best friend: Miller Lite. We stayed together after work all weekend, week after week, day after day. I couldn't go anywhere unless my cooler was full, and if I couldn't have my "friend" with me, then I wouldn't be there.

I decided to get help, but only to save my job. The hardest thing I ever did was to ask for help. I cried and cried to Jesus: "Please help me! Please forgive me!" I had tried quitting on my own, and would do well for about a month, but then I'd fall back again. I was tired and afraid of failure. I used to say, "Jesus, here I am. Take all of me. I can't do it anymore!" From this point on, my words were, "One day at a time, sweet Jesus."

I began every day with Jesus even before I lifted my head from the pillow. I knew I would drink again that day if I didn't ask God for help.

Today, I am fifteen months sober and have never felt better. I have asked God for His help daily, and He is strengthening me. Philippians 4:13 says, *I can do all things through Christ which strengtheneth me.*

I don't want to say that letting go of my "friend" was easy. Even with the Lord's help I still suffered the consequences of withdrawal, and there were many. I started going to counsel- ing. I cried day in and day out for a month, without knowing where all those tears were coming from. Then I began going to a church, where I am still actively involved today.

I want you to know that you are not alone in any of the problems you are facing today. I will help you in any way I possibly can.

I send you my blessings to help in your recovery process. May God be with you. Hope to hear from you soon.

Sincerely,

Marilynne

FEBRUARY 16, 2005

Dear Roger,

God has a great purpose for your life. I can tell this by the way your beautiful heart is revealed in your words.

Church has always been a part of my life; but now, I truly let go and let God do whatever He wants with my life as He takes me through this journey.

I am very much a Pentecostal. As I grew up, I found no sure foundation with any other type of church. I love the way the Lord moves and works, and He works in so many different ways to get our undivided attention. In His greatness, He never gives us more than we can bear, with His help, of course.

From the beginning to the end, He is the same then, now, and forever. But I am so glad that I am not the same as I used to be. On the day when I threw up my hands and surren- dered, I never could have hoped for all the blessings the Lord has given, especially the presence of the Holy Spirit in me.

I was truly a broken vessel. I drank alone a lot, becoming selfish with my beer, my time, and my attitude. I used my phone as an escape – I didn't want to share anything with anyone and I didn't care who I kept up at night or how badly I hurt them with my words on the phone.

The problem was, though I cared for others, I forgot how to be sensitive to their problems. I had lost interest in oth- ers' feelings. I could go on and on about this dark time, but I'd rather share stories about my life now, which is much happier.

Twenty years ago, I got married, had a child, and then got heavily involved in drugs and alcohol. But one day I left my husband, took my son, and headed north to Illinois, where my mother lived. About halfway there, however, I stopped to visit my mother-in-law. While there, I went to church with her. That day, by the grace of God, I was completely freed of my addictions without any withdrawal symptoms. At one point, the doctors had told me that I would probably die, but God had other plans for me.

Just five years later, however, I went back to alcohol. Now, fourteen years after it began, I AM FREE! God never left me, even after I had forsaken Him for a time.

I am getting ahead of myself, but it's so amazing how the Lord works to clean up the messes we get ourselves into. It took me fourteen more years of drinking and messing every- thing up, but in only a year and a half He has helped me to fix what I have broken.

Maybe I'll write a book about what God has done in my life. When I was a young teenager, I wanted to do just that. But I thought I had to go through everything that no one else did, in order to write about it. Now, however, I've had enough worldly experiences that I don't want any more, and I real- ize that my story isn't that much different than that of many others, except that my ending might be much better.

I hope you enjoy the articles that I got from the Grapevine. When I completed detox, I was able to get through my first few days at home with the stories from this book at detox *called Grapevine*.

You have a lot of family who will begin to trust your judg- ment again, and it sounds like you are on the right track towards earning that trust again.

Your song, "Heart Mirrors" is so beautiful. I was touched when I read it and am inclined to see if my church can help get some music to accompany it, if you don't mind. It's clear from the lyrics that you have been through a lot in your life, and I can't help but wonder what kept you in your closet of terror?

I live a busy life caring for disabled people in my home, so my time is not really my own. This is new for me but not new to my heart's desire. Now that the demons are out of the way, I am grateful to be able to help others. With the Lord on my side, this is the new life He has chosen for me for now.

I really enjoyed hearing from you and wanted to let you know I am going through the 12-step recovery process, using the Life Recovery Bible for reference and guidance, and God's help on each and every one of the steps.

Take care and write soon.

God bless you,

Marilynne

FEBRUARY 23, 2005

Dear Marilynne,

How wonderful it is to hear from you again. I love your honesty and openness. It's a breath of fresh air in this stagnant and stuffy atmosphere.

At times, it's hard to realize that life exists outside these walls and that I've actually got a very short time to do, compared to the majority of the inmates. I'm so glad you are grounded in a church and are moved so much to give all to God. One verse I know by heart is 1 Corinthians 10:13, where God says even though we are tempted as all are, He will never give us more than we can bear and always provides a way out so we can stand through the test.

I am embarrassed when I look back, because I gave into the temptation to drink (to avoid dealing with my feelings), turning to alcohol rather than God. I have repented and know God forgives me, yet I am responsible for misrepre- senting my Christian values and throwing all I believe out the window with the first drink. I'm finally in a position to heal my inner-self, work the steps, search my soul, and renew my mind.

I know God has specific work for me to complete. My drink- ing for the last ten years (since my divorce) has really been suicidal. I should have died many times, but God sustained my life through it all and kept me and others from physical harm, for which I am grateful. My biggest inner terror was that others would reject me.

In my childhood I was told my feelings were not important. I believed my parents when they told me this, and so there was no self-expression allowed. On the other hand, we had a family band, and I was taught that no matter what, the show must go on. I was to smile and entertain and look happy whether I was sick or not.

I am sharing this only to set some groundwork as to why I locked everything up inside me. Many things from my childhood were traumatic. In those days (the 1960s), family issues were often hidden, and I couldn't think of exposing what went on for fear of retribution from my parents. While in grade school, one of my greatest fears was that someone would find out that I wet the bed. My mother would humili- ate me, wiping my face in the wet sheets and making me go to school wearing soaked underwear. I felt I was defective, abnormal, and unacceptable.

I only felt acceptable through my music and hid my true self behind my talent and musical abilities. I had many barri- ers to overcome but continued to strive to give all of these to God. I am so glad I have God and other Christians to help me. God's mercy and grace is so incredible.

By the way, I will share more songs with you. I hope you like them and that they minister to you and others. The song "Heart Mirrors" is one of the new tunes God gave me. If you want to share any of my songs with your church, that's okay.

What church do you attend? I frequently attended Red Cedar Community Church in Rice Lake, but have also attended Shell Lake Full Gospel Church, Good Samaritan Church, and Hillsdale Full Gospel Church. I have sung at these churches and others occasionally.

Anyway, I've rambled, but hope I've said something worth- while. Please keep writing to me. Did I ask you if I could get a picture of you? Please (wink-wink)? I'd like that. It bright- ens my cell to have pictures of friends!

I haven't heard back from Wayne yet. It seems like time stands still here. A day seems like a week, and yet I know how time flies when you're out in the world. Thank you so much for the articles from the Grapevine. There is absolutely no Alcoholics Anonymous (AA) literature available here that I've seen and no AA or Narcotics Anonymous meetings. This prison has only been open since April or May and has almost no programs available for inmates. Up to November of this year, the prison here did have outside A.A. groups until

there was a group of inmates who attacked some guards. The whole prison was placed in lockdown status and all outside programs shut down too.

However, I do attend a group on personal responsibility.

It just started on Monday mornings and will go for about two months. I also attend the Protestant church service on Sundays and Brother Bob's Bible study on Thursday morn- ings. I try to watch Kenneth Copeland Ministries each morning at 9:30 a.m., and Benny Hinn at 10:30 a.m. as well.

It is so wonderful that you care enough to write and take time out of your day to share of yourself. Many of the inmates here are so spiritually hungry, while some of them are very angry. It's such a lonely place here and I feel at a loss for words to express the need to be reached. You are a rare and special person to reach out to me without even really knowing me. I applaud you for the risks you are taking in doing that. I've written to many people since I've been here but have received no replies from them.

I hope I don't sound too negative, for I truly treasure every letter I do receive from others. I do know I've separated myself from others in many ways by my drinking, but I have had much support through the prayers of others. Your communication with me has rekindled my spiritual fire and renewed my love for the Lord. It reminds me that each day is a new day. There is light all around me, but I must open my eyes to see it.

I have Bible study in one hour so I'd like to finish my little "book" here. I hope I don't bore you with all my meander- ings and babble. This is a bad place to keep a positive out- look, but I am also fortunate to have made friends with a few here who play guitar and let me share some of my music with them. What a joy it is to sing praises to the Lord! I do pray, if it's God's will, that somehow I can get one of my guitars here or be able to get one purchased for me. I hope you write soon. Don't ever be afraid to ask the questions that you have. I promise I will answer honestly.

I don't relish the thought of reliving the past, but I will let you know all of my past if you want to know. I have grown tremendously ever since my divorce, but I allowed my ex to make me feel useless, undesirable, and not good enough.

God knows I needed to change, and I will continue with His guidance and His strength moves me forward and out of the enemy's snare. I love to read Psalm 91 – actually, I love to read all of the Bible – but you know how certain Scriptures come to mean so much to you. In 2 Timothy 3:16 it says,

All scripture is given by inspiration of God [given life by God], *and is profitable for doctrine, for reproof, for correction* [which I surely need], for instruction in righteousness. I have a song that is called "There is No Wrong Way to Do What's Right." I'll share more in the future. Please keep writing. I hope and pray that I've made some sense with this letter and have answered your preliminary questions.

Your friend,
Roger

And life is what we make it.
Always has been, always will be.

MARCH 9, 2005

Dear Marilynne,

Let's start this out with a huge thank you!! I had to send the stamps back, because they only allow us to buy stamps from the prison canteen. Almost anything can be sent, but they want it to come from the supplier. I don't know what you wanted to send, but places like OfficeMax or any catalog source (even online suppliers) can send non-click pens, paper, scissors (safety-tip), books, and magazines. Books and magazines have to come from a retail source (bought there and sent from the catalog or retail store and the receipt has to be enclosed).

They did allow the pages from the *Grapevine in and Our Daily Bread*. Most everything of a religious nature is allowed in from family, friends, or a church. The rules are constantly changing, but you can send religious materials and such for now.

God answered my prayers for a guitar and I should have it this week. I was singing a version of the song "This is the day that the Lord has made; I will rejoice and be glad in it." I thank God every day for the opportunity to serve Him. I have much work to get done, but I couldn't imagine anything getting done without God's help and guidance. Many times I get stuck in a thought pattern and worry about things, and find it's just my impatience and a futile attempt to control things.

Bad habits or thought patterns can be broken by the power of God, and I am daily letting go of things and trusting God more. His Word promises that I will have my needs and desires met as I am faithful and obedient to His leading.

Your friend,

Roger

MARCH 23, 2005

Dear Marilynne,

Thank you for writing back. Some things that I've shared with you I have let go of, but I still have much to get rid of. I've held on to some things by not dealing with them, and that is part of the reason I'm here today. Though I love my family, and have forgiven them, I still carry some pain with me. God is taking this pain away, too.

I count my time here as a blessing from God and not as pun- ishment. I embrace this time as a gift for me to use wisely and work the steps toward total healing. It can be so easy to dip into the well of self-pity and discouragement, but every minute I'm given a choice and I choose healing instead of self-dependency. It is not enjoyable here (and isn't intended to be), but it gives me another reason not to be complacent or rest on my laurels.

God has inspired me to write music, and most of it has helped me to heal. I have been through, or have witnessed what I've written about. In 2001, God put it in my heart to be in ministry. Specifically, He called me out, chose me, and told me to teach the Word of God. In 2002, He inspired me to share my story of hope with others, and as I learned that forgiveness is mandatory – not an option – He led me to call the ministry the "70x7 Ministry of Forgiveness."

When He first called me, I felt reluctant because I did not feel worthy and knew I was continuing to sin. I realized that I couldn't be used to the fullest until I got rid of the demons in my life, by believing and asking God to take them away. I was sick of burdening others with my lack of responsibility, and with my failure to walk in integrity as God wants.

Being here has made me aware of every defect in my life because I am totally exposed. I am under surveillance at all times – while eating, sleeping, or showering – so there is no hiding, no getting away from others. This is to my advantage, even though it is uncomfortable, because it reduces me to nothing. There's no room for delusion, pride, or ego.

I pray my letters are at least somewhat understandable.

At times I ramble on, but it is precious to me to be able to expose myself to you so you may come to understand me. I totally understand your not wanting to send a picture at this time. I am pleased with your honesty and I like your heart.

I can tell by your personality that I want to be your friend. I have little to offer at this time, but I will always strive to be honest with you. I feel I am being honest now, but I am cur- rently purging myself and have questions about the depth of my honesty in the past. Please tell me exactly how you per- ceive me, and areas that I can change to be a more acceptable person. I don't want to settle for just sobriety. I am willing to do whatever God requires of me to be acceptable in His eyes. Pleasing God pleases me.

Am I making any sense? I've heard of First United Pentecostal Church but have not gone there before. I would be more than happy to check it out, however. I've been back and forth with different churches in the area, but my drink- ing kept me from making a definite choice. I've visited the Shell Lake Full Gospel Church and have sung there once, back when I was married and lived in Menomonie. I vis- ited the Nazarene Church east of Shell Lake with Paul Stone and his wife a few times. Paul is a Christian musician whom I met in the late 1980s when I sang at Barnabas House in Rice Lake. Barnabas House is a Christian coffee house run by Pastor Gene Stodola, who is now the pastor at Good Samaritan Church south of Rice Lake. When I moved back to Rice Lake from Teen Challenge in Iowa, I was part of his church until drinking again separated me from it. I should say that my choice to drink took me away. I praise God that today I choose to heal and be totally delivered from bondage!

In the past, I've obsessed over all the things that I couldn't change. I wouldn't allow myself to claim the total victory over Satan that Jesus' death bought for me. I was stuck then, but I decided I'm not going to stay that way anymore. When I came here I was attending Red Cedar Community Church, mostly because one of my best friends attended, but also because it was close to where I lived and I could walk there. At that time, I didn't have my license. I also went to Joy Fellowship and Hillsdale Full Gospel Church.

None of my friends drank, and it tore them apart to see me keep going back to drinking, trading the promise of God's Word for a bottle that was causing me spiritual, emotional, and physical death.

Believe me, I don't blame anyone for my being here. I know I have a long journey ahead in my life. But I will follow

God's will for my life, praying for the power to overcome any obstacles that Satan places in my way.

I'll also pray for the wisdom to see through God's eyes what is actually there. What I mean is that things aren't always the way I perceive them to be. I developed an uncanny abil- ity to create things that aren't really an issue, blowing things out of proportion. Obsessive-compulsive behavior is one of the many thinking disorders that drinking can create. Every day, however, I am thinking more clearly and feeling better as I trade garbage-thinking for the mind of God. What a blessing!

Again, I am grateful for the opportunity to get to know you and share with you what's going on in my life. Writing to you gives me a way to vent. As I have said, prison can seem unbearable at times, but as God's Word says, He gives us the desires of our heart because He loves us that much (Psalm 37:4). I did not fully understand this, but I knew – and I knew that God also knew – that I wanted to stop what I was doing and get out of the vicious cycle that my actions were creating. I was trapped in a self-defeating mode, but God prevented my death – thus showing me that my purpose has not been fulfilled – and He sent me to this particular prison. I didn't realize why at first, but the Way Out Program here is a twelve-step program deeply rooted in the Word of God, which cleanses our minds so we can focus on God, think like God, and fulfill His will and purpose for our lives. When I first arrived here at New Lisbon all programs were shut down. This is the first outside program allowed back in. Before I arrived here there was a massive riot where cor- rections officers were attacked and about fifty inmates were moved to a maximum prison in Boscabel, Wisconsin. This left empty beds to fill and is why I was moved to New Lisbon.

Am I making any sense? I am known for talking about one thing and then saying something else that's meaningful to me but is about something completely different. So I hope you can understand what I am trying to say. I suppose I could blame the aging process or the sobriety process for that. Terence Gorski talks about P.A.W. (post-acute-with- drawal), a symptom on the plane of recovery that causes disruptive thinking patterns. This symptom can be present for six to thirty-six months after alcohol is not consumed. I think that is what my problem is.

This is the only Wisconsin prison to have the Way Out cur- riculum available, and I think this particular program is a course in miracles. It is designed to remove any blocks in thinking that hinder our ability to be aware of God's love and to convert our minds to think like God thinks, or as close as humans can.

I have come to realize that I am sustained totally by the love of God. Nothing exists in reality that is not God-breathed. When I walk in complete awareness of God, seeing His love and seeing through His eyes, I can also see the imposters and fakes that Satan conjures up. Then

I realize that they are not real and they hold no power over me. When God takes control and I am on His side, nothing can stand against me.

There are many Scriptures that have influenced my life, but I particularly like Psalm 91 and Psalm 121. I love how you have encouraged me with the Word of God. There are many Christians who just refuse to have any involvement with someone who drinks or who did drink. This is profoundly sad, for all Christians need to reach out to those who suffer with any afflictions, whether or not they are self-imposed, as alcoholism is believed to be. I firmly believe alcohol is a con- trolling spirit from hell. Its only purpose is to rob, steal, and destroy *anyone* it can get its grip on. There is an aspect of physical addiction to it, but the mental obsession is the root of the problem.

I've gone for up to four years staying sober, and I thought I was doing well. But I didn't completely exorcise the spirit, and you'd better believe the Devil is patient; he and his demons just wait for the first opportunity to pounce on us and take control. Because of this, it is paramount to renew my mind daily, striving for constant Christ-likeness in my attitude and thinking.

Ephesians 6:11 says we are to arm ourselves with the whole armor of God. Putting on just part of the armor of God will help, but if I (or we) desire total protection from the enemy, the only way is to put on the whole armor. I could probably write all day on this, but I still need to complete my lessons.

I applaud your willingness to be a friend and commit to writing and encouraging me. You are truly a blessing from God. I don't miss the irony, either, that out of all the people Wayne would talk to about writing to is a Spirit-filled born- again Christian. Say "hi" to Wayne when you see or talk to him. I remain your friend and eagerly await your reply.

Thank you for the *Our Daily Bread* devotional. We do get them here but I gave mine to another inmate who will put it to good use. I put smiley faces on my drinking cup (coffee and water only – ha-ha!) so that

I think about you and pray for you because I'm usually not far from my cup!

I am praying for some money to come in so I can purchase stamps and paper and another pen, and will boldly ask if you could keep it in prayer also. When two or more unite in prayer...

God bless you, Marilynne.

Your friend in Christ,

Roger

APRIL 1, 2005

Hello Roger,

Thank you for the card. It is always nice to be appreciated. It's also nice to be uplifted, for even I experience difficult times.

I can see a future for you making CDs for the Lord. With your songs being inspired by God, I believe that this may be what God is intending for you to do. I believe that by your songs you are carrying out His ministry for your life.

It is something to be under surveillance, day in and day out, with every move you make observed by someone. Through this, we begin to realize that we all are under God's sur- veillance in the same way. However, He also knows our thoughts, so there is no hiding place from Him. In Genesis, Adam tried to hide from God after his sin, but he couldn't and neither can we. When my mind starts to wander into past temptations or desires, I remember that Jesus knows my thoughts and knows whether I will make the decision to do or not do something. This may require me to yell out the name of Jesus to get rid of the thoughts that could easily become destructive.

Letting go of the past is a great thing, but in this case it is a good thing to remember from where God me, and the addic- tion and destruction that would come in an instant when I gave in to those temptations and desires.

Love, Marilynne

MAY 5, 2005

Hello Roger,

To answer your question, my birthday is April 4, and I did have a good one this year, at last. Every year gets better and I get younger at heart.

I'm pleased to hear you are standing on solid ground and that Jesus is all around you. Remember, even the times we can't tell He is there, He really is. Don't stop believing that He will never leave us or forsake us. Recently, I went through one of those difficult times like you are facing. Now I know that I was being tested in my faith, tempted by ungodly ideas. Praise be to Jesus: today I have the victory. Other times in my life, I may have given in to those temptations, so I praise the Lord for His words of promise.

If we will walk and not be weary or faint, we will not fall into diverse temptations. I believe that Jesus had been carrying me for a while and then He let me walk, to see if I would fall or stay standing for Him. Years ago, I had similar feelings, but at that time my heart hardened. My past is a learning experience created by my lack of faith and trust. I'm thank- ful today to be able to continue in this beautiful walk with Jesus.

I just read day 17 in Our Daily Bread and am not always on a continual daily program; sometimes I need a few days to let everything sink in so then I can continue. Usually this is guided by the Spirit within me.

It's just like the AA 12-Step Program; sometimes you need to work on one step more than others. The Lord is my leader and my guide, so just like the AA steps, He is taking me through these pages at the pace of baby steps. I am a babe in Christ. Change is great, but it takes a lot of guidance from God for Him to move me in the right direction.

It's so neat to go to church, hear the message, and most of the time feel that it is directed right at me. Sometimes I really don't like what I hear, but if I am obedient to the Spirit, a victory almost always follows. For a short time, it seemed that nothing was reaching me. And then BOOM – a message on isolation; and WHAM – that was me. Since then, I have attended every service and pray to continue attending. I'm excited to have been elected as part of a decorating commit- tee for the fellowship hall. I have ideas racing through my mind and I know the Lord will lead my thoughts, so this is great. When I used to drink, I was always in charge of activi- ties, cookouts, camping trips, and more. This opportunity is for me, and God shows me that I'm needed in this area.

I believe that one of the women in church that wrote my name down was led by the Spirit to do so. Once, I went up for prayer and she came to me and said, "You are being too hard on yourself. God knows and understands all you are going through." Just last week, my mother said the same thing to me, and I disagreed with her! Don't you think the Spirit had a fix in that?

It seems that my work at home is never done. I have been working outside all week getting the garden tilled and clear- ing some more property – lots of work. I used my time in the garden to praise the Lord for giving me the strength to complete it.

It's a big world out here and full of temptation. I pray that God works in your life on the outside especially. The real test of faith lies ahead. May God be your strength in that day. Continue to look up in all things and Jesus will honor us with great rewards.

The battle of alcohol seemed much easier than my battle today with nicotine. I am trying to quit smoking. I had gone up for prayer a month ago and really believed the desire was gone. However, eight hours later I decided having just one wouldn't hurt. Then, I began to smoke more than before, and even though the feeling of conviction set in on me, I still continued to smoke. I went for prayer again and felt like such a loser. The desire to quit is there, but the desire to continue is hanging around too strong. I went and got the patches and they sat there for a month. Finally, I was on my last pack of cigarettes and I opened the box of patches. Today is day three, I've had five smokes, and I need prayer regarding this bondage. I quit once, years ago, with the help of Jesus and have since tried several more times to stop. It's like drinking, but right now it seems harder to let go of.

I don't know your story on smoking, but I do know I want this to be gone for me. My testimony depends on letting go and letting God work through me.

I just felt the need to share this with you. Please pray that the desire will go away and that the willpower to quit will take its place.

Thanks for the card. I enjoyed receiving such meaningful words. May you stay strong in the Lord and may He bless you with His Holy Spirit.

For now I will send just this letter and next time, some articles.

Your friend in Christ Jesus,

Marilynne

MAY 6, 2005

Dear Marilynne,

Well, I finally found out what you sent yesterday. I am not able to keep it but thank you. I have to have everything sent to me by a store or directly from the publisher. I'm working on getting the chaplain to allow me to receive AA materials.

God is blessing me every day and I do have rich resources from the Bible, *The Purpose Driven Life* book, and the mate- rial from A Way Out Spiritual Recovery Program. I've been able to minister to more people every week as they see God working in me and through my actions. I love the Lord and would be lost without His strength and guidance.

Please be in prayer that the prison will be supplied with AA resources and Life Recovery Bibles. Our God is larger than anything we may encounter. He will provide all that is needed for His will and purpose, and I pray that all the inmates will see His glory and desire to live completely for Him.

May you be filled with God's wonderful love and blessed beyond imagination.

Your friend in Christ,

Roger

MAY 26, 2005

Dear Marilynne,

Please forgive me for not responding to your letter sooner. I have been praying every day for your request of deliverance from smoking. Your prayers are answered, for wherever two or more are gathered and are in unison in prayer, God answers.

Remember that even on the days when you do not see the manifestation of the deliverance, it is done, answered, and complete. You are doing the right thing and God knows that. He loves you and your body. The Devil is trying hard not to lose the stronghold of smoking in your life. Remember that all thoughts of degradation and unworthiness are from the Deceiver. Believe in your deliverance and receive the power of the Holy Spirit to stand through the temptations. Read

1 Corinthians 10:13. It has helped me, when I've believed. I am also working on letting many things go, but they are much easier to hide than your smoking! My thoughts do not always line up with God's will for me. I too am drawn to things of the world. You can pray for my thoughts to be holy and pure. I am often drawn to thoughts of being with a woman, partially because I am lonely here.

I want deliverance from sexually impure thoughts about women because it degrades God's creation. I chastise myself on a regular basis, since it's so easy to let the mind stray into dark corners and unhealthy thoughts. I'm not inappropriate or anything, and I do have morally sound convictions about a healthy relationship. However, the other men talk stupidly about the subject of sexual relationships, and I've been strug- gling not to join them in my mind and fantasies. It's really hard to talk to you about this and I really didn't want to expose myself because it's very uncomfortable, but you also took a risk when you shared your struggle with smoking.

For me, the bottom line is that I can try to hide things (God knows anyway) or accept myself as I am, let go, be honest, and change into the image of God.

Being aware of any sin or problem is the first step, which is crucial to change. You are a holy woman of God and that is the only way I see you, through God's eyes of love and compassion. Together, God and I are by your side in prayer and spirit, lifting you up in every conflict or battle. It is God who will see us through every temptation, lifting us up so we will not fall for the Devil's traps, schemes, and devices. We are human and have to deal with a corrupt world and all its influences, but God has all power and is our helper. He will always light our paths in the darkest of nights and in any storm. When you are confronted with any evil desire, get in attack mode and suit up for battle with the whole armor of God (Ephesians 6:11, 18), which will break all strongholds and chains of bondage, for nothing can stand against our almighty God.

I always want to be further along in my spiritual walk than I am, but do I set the bar higher than needed? If you have been growing in the Lord – and you are as I write this – then you are scaring the hell into Satan. He will come at you like a cornered animal, and he loves to hit below the belt.

He knows every trick in the book, since he's practiced for thousands of years on God's people. Remember who you are in Christ Jesus of Nazareth and don't let anyone, including yourself, put you down or bring you down. Look at yourself as God sees you.

Believe His promise of deliverance and know that Satan is under our feet. Claim the victory and keep looking up for God's help, power, and love. Smell the sweetness of His pres- ence, the comfort of His arms, and the shelter of His wings. He is our refuge and the keeper of our hearts and souls. I keep on praising Him as I write, for I see the beauty of Him in your life and how much you mean to God Almighty. I see how much He is using you as a testimony of faith. In the name of Jesus I encourage you to stand fast on your founda- tion of faith, the rock of Calvary, the True Cornerstone of your life. Reject the lies of the Devil and the attacks of the unrighteous.

Trust the Holy Spirit's guidance in your studies and reading, remembering that it is God to whom you answer, not man (or woman), and work at the pace you need to.

I believe you are too hard on yourself and I tend to be the same way a lot. Thank you for lifting me up in prayer. Be encouraged that I do the same for you. I think it's wonderful that you are involved in your church and give of yourself.

On a different note, on the 12th of May there was a fire in Rice Lake, which you may have heard about. It was in the apartments where I was living before I came here. Danny Matthews (the twenty-seven-year-old who died) lived across the hall from me. He used to help me with remodeling and maintenance to pay for my rent, so I was close to him and his girlfriend's son, Mason (four years old), who were also killed in the fire. Often, Mason came over and listened to me sing, which was very precious. I've been working through that loss. I also had all my tools, music equipment, and personal effects burned up.

God's love, grace, and power have helped me through this, but I have shed many tears and have much sadness at losing a friend and a helper, and regret that I wasn't there to help. I am grateful for the time I had with them and I'm grateful for being sober today and having God present every moment.

God has richly blessed me with your letters and friendship, providing for my needs and so much more. I have been pre- occupied and that's why I have not written sooner. I praise God for helping me through the shock and pain, lifting me up and over and above all the circumstances of the fire.

I am working with the chaplain to get AA meetings started and get AA literature available. If anything is sent by you, a church, or AA, it should be sent to Chaplain Teslik with a receipt of purchase. You can donate it to the chapel or earmark it for me. That way, it will get in. In the future, it will be easier, as I am working to get the acceptance policies changed to allow more AA and religious material to be available for other inmates. I love your commitment to God and your desire to help and reach out.

Do not be discouraged; I know your reward will be deliv- ered. As we believe so shall we receive. God is in control!

Love in Christ,

Roger

P.S. Your letters stimulate the Spirit of God to rise up in me. All glory goes to God the Father.

June 23, 2005

Hello Roger,

You probably thought I forgot all about you. I didn't, but it's been a busy time.

Sad to say, I was acquainted with Mason. I know his father and they both attended church with me some time ago. As for Danny, I'm not sure I knew him. This was a tragic acci- dent and a great loss for many. Mason is in heaven with Jesus laughing, singing, and having the time of his life. He was a precious little boy and took to me easily. This year for me has been one of many losses: I just attended two funerals this month and four total this year.

I once said, years ago when I was drinking, that I couldn't handle friends or family members dying. Usually, these sad departures would have been a reason for me to drink. But now, this is a time to be closer to Jesus. We do not know not the hour or day our life will be finished, but it gives me great pleasure to always be ready.

This is a great loss for you, but the Lord gives peace and comfort in sad times as well as happy times.

Only Jesus was able to face every temptation and walk away from each one. We are to walk with Jesus, but we cannot be Jesus. I need to seek Jesus to be able to say no to the tempta- tion of drinking, especially in difficult times. I've also had to seek Jesus to ask Him to remove thoughts and desires that are not holy and replace them with His holiness instead.

Let me share this with you: For fourteen years, I was in a relationship that wasn't the will of God. After being convicted over and over again, I knew the relationship had to end. I prayed and pled with Jesus to let me keep the friend- ship at least. I knew it wouldn't be easy for either of us, knowing the total absence of it would seem unbearable. Still, I was willing to go to any lengths that the Lord would have me go, and I was willing to make any sacrifice as well.

One day, I couldn't take the guilt, shame, and disobedience anymore. I cried out to God and pled with Him to give me the strength and courage to do what was right. The Lord gave me exactly what I asked for and more. Because I obeyed Him, He has blessed me beyond measure. About a month after this, however, I chose to sin again and had to get on my knees and repent. My sinful human nature had gotten the best of me. I finally prayed for the Lord to take away all lustful desires and replace those desires with His love. Jesus has answered that prayer and showed me His tender mercies, His real love for me, and a genuine concern for others. God's grace is always sufficient for you and me.

I wasn't happy about the thought of spending the rest of my life alone, but I knew God had plans for me. Whatever my future holds, it's in Jesus' hands and I will trust in Him, let- ting Him teach me that He is with me always and that I can always depend on Him. He removes the feelings of loneliness when He reassures me that He is always with me. *His Word says, I will never leave thee nor forsake thee* (Hebrews 13:5).

I am still smoking, but one day, I will cross this bridge, and I will quit. I was being too hard on myself and had to remember that *there is no condemnation for those who are in Christ Jesus* (Romans 8:1), because Jesus paid the price for all my sin.

Take care in Christ.

Friends,

Marilynne

JUNE 26, 2005

Marilynne,

I encourage you to stand fast and endure until God's mani- festation of answered prayers arrives. Sometimes deliver- ance is immediate, but all our prayers are answered in God's time. You are delivered from tobacco. I truly believe this and rejoice in it. It isn't pertinent to me that the full manifesta- tion has not yet materialized. It will.

Hold on! Deliverance is coming! That's God's promise. As we believe, we receive.

I only see you through God's eyes and if it ever appears I am not seeing with "God-vision," would you please give me a spiritual slap upside the head? No need to ever become phys- ical. Our mouths, when anointed by God, can move moun- tains. Really, it's God all the way, but God uses us mightily when we totally believe in Him.

I truly believe we were brought together through these letters by God, and that we were meant to get acquainted with each other through letters before we physically met each other.

I am so totally at ease sharing with you that it amazes me. We serve such an awesome God, and if God does unite me with another woman, it has got to be a Spirit-filled, God- fearing woman.

There is no greater pleasure than to share God's love with another, and pray and worship together. To me, a Spirit- filled soul mate would be such a blessing. I look forward with anticipation to see our friendship grow, blossom, and be nurtured through God together. As I said before, you are truly gifted and have so very much to offer. All the encour- agement and love in Christ you share with me is given out to the brothers here in prison. I do love the Christ in you and await your response.

God's love and hugs,

Roger

June 30, 2005

Hi Marilynne,

It's so good to hear from you! I was concerned that you may have been taken aback by my last letter talking about issues with lust. I don't want to ever violate our friendship, but I will always strive to be honest with you. There is so much to learn from each other. I really love hearing from you and you are in my thoughts and prayers every day. I am sorry to hear of your losses this year. We can always replace mate- rial things, but friends are only in our lives while we are on earth. The great part is knowing that though our friends are departed now, we will meet again in heaven. That's glorious!

When I read your letters – and I keep them all – I see the fingerprints of God all over you!

I know God is with you every moment and has His loving arms around you. I can't wait to see you in person. I do love who you are in Christ and you should know I will be a close friend as long as you want me in your life.

You've taken great risks writing to me and your commitment to Christ encourages me every day. I want to know so much more about you. What's important to you is something I really care about, even in this early stage of our friendship. I have no commitment to any significant other, and am focus- ing on what God wants me to be.

I am a son of God and you are a daughter of God through Christ. I will always be aware of who you are in Christ and not violate your boundaries. I'm not sure which songs I've sent to you, but I'm enclosing some more that God has put on my heart to share with you. Please be encouraged by what I write and send you, to seek after God with all your heart.

I also am waiting for the right person to share life with, and am ever aware of changes I need to make (adjustments, if you will) in my integrity and character.

I am encouraged by your letters and never want them to stop coming. Forgive my writing. I try to make myself clear when I write so you understand me more, but I sometimes get too many thoughts coming at once. You are a very, very special person. Don't ever put yourself down. Instead, always look at who you are in Christ. I was way off the mark when I came in here, and rejoice today that I am changing, looking at reality, and focusing on God's will. I was completely blinded before. Even though I wanted to change, I couldn't break free from my pattern of fantasy and unrealistic ways of thinking.

So I give all glory to God for what He's doing in my life, as well as the people here that I can help see Jesus. What I long for is unbridled, intimate communication with people in Christ. I would truly be lost in this place, or anywhere, with- out God to love me through each moment.

I am going to share some things about me so you know me more. I love to hug and be close with those I care about. I am very giving. I like to take walks and build things. I do light remodeling and commercial cleaning. Before I came here, I ran my business out of Blake's Auto Sales in Rice Lake. The owner is my Christian brother and friend. I also sold cars for him. I am always ready to help others. I'm learning how to take care of me, too! I try always to give more than I get.

If we ever become more deeply involved than friends, I want you to know I always try to please and satisfy. I want both of us to feel equal and not used in any way that is uncomfort- able. Please don't be offended by my writing this. If you ever feel pressured by me, or if I ever cross boundaries, please tell me. I won't be offended. As I've said before, our friendship is first. Anything more is a precious gift from God. I place a very high value on our friendship, Marilynne.

I love the way your name is spelled, by the way. When and if you are comfortable sharing a picture of yourself, I would like that. I only have five pictures here right now – my two sons and three grandchildren. I can have up to fifty pictures (no Polaroids), so there's plenty of room for more!

What kind of things do you like to do? How many people do you care for? I know your work is rewarding, but also exhausting. It takes a very strong personal commitment and a dedication to help others. Kudos to you, Marilynne! Where did you train? I am strongly considering seeking work at a group home and continuing in that line of work. I'm waiting for God's direction on that. First things first. I did start to go to college in 1983 to become an AODA (Alcohol and Other Drug Abuse) counselor but didn't complete it.

Oh, the complications caused by drinking! Thank God I'm renewing my mind today. I won't go back to what I was before. Yuck!

In the past, I have enjoyed golfing, fishing, and cooking out – I'm a good cook. Also, I sew and iron, since my ex-spouses didn't. I was married twice before, both times for ten years apiece, and have been single since 1993. I am a hopeless romantic and will commit to only one person. Yes, I vio- lated that in the past, but that is the past and I'm not afraid to commit to one true God and then, to one true soulmate. I am interested in knowing you even more. If you would like, I can get a picture taken of me to send to you. Again, if I make you uncomfortable or our getting closer is more than you would like, please say so. I don't want to lose what we have, Marilynne, but I am willing to maintain our friend- ship at whatever boundaries you are comfortable with. Just write real soon, please. I love your letters and who you are in Christ.

I am sure that Christ will be number one in any relationship God moves us into. He *has* to be the priority for any relationship to work. I pray that God will richly bless you every moment and give you His strength, wisdom, and peace, and that His angels be ever present to assist you through all dan- ger and temptation (1 Corinthians 10:13). Read Psalm 91 and 121 as well. Rejoice, for God is for us!

Love in Christ,

Roger

July 7, 2005

Hello Roger,

I will try to answer some of your questions. First of all, I seek God's wisdom and guidance in everything I do.

Years ago, I had a dream to help young people in some kind of way. Due to my years of wandering in what I call a desert, my dream was on hold until last year. That dream never left me, and when I found Jesus, He held me while the healing took place. Finally, Jesus was able to let this dream fall into place for me. One step at a time, Jesus led me in the direc- tion I needed to go. It seemed that every sermon I heard was directed right at me, and I took it all seriously. I did a lot of reading and disciplined myself in Christ to go in the right direction.

I worked at AMSCO for seven years and my body was get- ting worse. I kept praying, asking the Lord for advice. I had a big house and no one to share the beauty of it with. I finally completed some paperwork to officially start work to help others and was approved. Everything else fell into place, as I had been dreaming.

Since I was sixteen years old, I had worked with the disabled and mentally ill as a CNA, and I found great satisfaction in doing this. I was physically unable to do certain duties at a facility, and I wanted more one-on-one interaction.

When I got my first client it was on a part-time basis only, and I was still working my other job. In December of that year, I was given the opportunity to get a full-time client. That's when I leaned greatly on the Lord, since I had to choose between my regular job or my dream. You'd think the decision would have been easy, but it really wasn't.

I kept on focusing on the benefits, money-wise, of my regular job – insurance, 401k, stability, and time I had already put in.

One Sunday the message at church was from Philippians 4:19: *God shall supply all your need according to His riches in glory.* In February I finalized the caretaking job and quit my regular job, and the Lord has done as He promised.

Last month I was called to have another client, so I have two here at home, and another every other weekend. That is my limit, and it is enough. The Lord will not give us more than we can handle.

I have many hobbies. I just decide I want to do something and then the Lord and I tackle it.

This new home came to me with only drywall. This was an advantage, as I was able to paint the rooms the way I wanted them – with cheerful colors. The basement is still unfinished. However, I've put up walls and made closets and drywalled other places. I don't like doing drywall though.

Remodeling the basement is a winter project, so I went out- side while the weather was still nice, and put in two gar- dens and did some clearing on the land. My son and friends helped a lot with this.

I also enjoy crocheting, which is another winter project. I like a clean house, so that takes care of my mornings.

The Lord has been great to me and I praise Him for all He does. My purpose here on earth is His purpose. He has just begun with me, so I am curious to know what He will do with me in the future.

I'm still in a healing process and still learning what love really is. There is such a difference between how I understand love now, compared to my life in the world of sin, justifying everything I did.

I like boating, fishing, skiing, walking, swimming, and bik- ing. I live on a gravel road so I haven't gotten my bike out yet. Sometimes I like to just relax and do nothing, but this rarely happens. I love to cook inside and outside. I'm glad I like cooking, or else no one would eat around here!

God has a purpose and a plan for me. I plan to stay out of His way and let Him lead me in the direction I should have already gone years ago. Since I can't change the past, I await His hand in leading me each step of the way into the future.

I truly believe He has brought us together for a part in His plan. I am not sure where He is leading us or what His future for us will be. I know I will stand on His promises and His will to be done in whatever the future brings.

For today, know this: If you continue to be open and hon- est with me, I will also be honest with you. May the Lord be with you in all you say and do. I've got to get going, so for now, hold on to what we've got, and may God bless you.

Your friend in Christ Jesus, Marilynne

July 14, 2005

Dearest Marilynne,

Well, my friend, I thought I'd better write right back because I like to get letters back from you so much! I'm very, very happy to have you as a friend. I'm also very grateful that you are doing God's will, that He is supplying your needs, and that you are following God's direction. You have an incred- ibly beautiful heart and I am blessed beyond belief to have connected with you. Your house sounds so nice and I am in awe of your work. I also have a heart to help others and have always reached out every way I could, except for the last ten years or so. Those years were consumed with alcohol-driven thoughts and actions. But I am on the right road now. I've sung at Camp Courage in Minnesota a couple times. Since my teen years, I have sung with our family band at rest homes and grade schools.

My daughter Lisa works at Comstock Farms (CBRF). She, her husband, and three boys have a house in Comstock. Lisa has worked at Comstock Farms for over four years. She loves it there. I sang there a couple of years ago (September 2003) and Lisa was surprised because everyone listened for two hours. She said usually the residents lose interest after ten or twenty minutes. I love making people happy and helping in any way possible.

I've thought strongly about working at a CBRF. I was down at Northfield Center past Osseo a couple of times, doing remodeling and maintenance. I enjoyed it, but couldn't stop the cycle of drinking and

251

ended up in jail for some very stu- pid choices I made while drunk. I'm so glad that chapter of my life is over.

Please forgive me for all the questions. I fully agree that I have to follow God's direction, wherever that leads me. I am totally intrigued by you, and I sense us growing closer, but I don't want to move too fast or be too pushy. I don't want to jeopardize our friendship in any way. I am also in a healing process and need to be perceptive, without manipulating or making things happen. I've got plenty of time to do things God's way – the right way – and I believe in dreams and also in God's promises. Did I make sense there? I pray I did.

I sometimes look back for just a peek to see how I've done things wrong in the past. I wouldn't want to repeat the past or return to that way of thinking at all.

It is so great to live for God and not for myself. Only God satisfies the inner hunger in my soul. I don't want to give the impression that I'm all that great, because I've still got many things I'm working on to be compatible with myself and oth- ers. What I mean is this: I've just come out of a long cycle of not caring if I was alive or not. Since being out of that cycle, I'm becoming aware of the things that offend God and oth- ers. I will never intentionally hurt you, emotionally or physi- cally. It is my heart's desire to nurture and help myself and others that God puts on my heart, especially you, Marilynne. You have reached out across the miles and taken time away from all you do, and I am so grateful for that. If I could, I'd give you a gentle but strong hug of God's love. For now, I just pray that whenever you feel alone, God will wrap you in His precious arms of love, and comfort you and remind you that you are never, never alone. I promise you that as we draw closer to God, we will draw closer in friendship. Wherever God leads our friendship is all right with me. I already care so much about you that your happiness is very important to me. It's important that friends are there to encourage each other at all times. I am also open to suggestions or criticism given in God's love, and I want God's will for us. I'm not afraid of becoming close to you, despite the hurts I've faced before, but it needs to be God's will.

Please forgive me and tell me if I am too nosy, curious, or moving you in any way you aren't comfortable with, okay?

I received an unexpected blessing last week: my younger sis- ter Robin wrote to me. It was the first response I've received since being incarcerated. She is in jail in North Dakota.

Here is her story as I've gotten it so far:

In 1990, Robin was in trouble that got her put in Waukesha County jail. There, she met Debi Christi who led her to the Lord. Robin received ten years' probation and restitution for taking money from her place of employment. She was abused for years by our father, but has gone through counseling.

Now, she is doing well with a top-level manager job in Retail Details, doing point-of-purchase setups for places like Home Depot.

Debi got out of prison in April, after doing ten years for wel- fare fraud, and my sister invited her to stay with her. Debi got a job at a local car dealership in Rhinelander, and after a while came home with a Jeep she said she had leased from work. Robin had a hysterectomy, and when she was well she had to go to Bismarck, North Dakota, to set up a new busi- ness. Debi encouraged her to take the new Jeep, which she did. While Robin was in North Dakota, her boss called and said Debi had phoned him and told him to get in touch with Robin, because the Jeep was stolen and Debi was headed to jail. Robin got her stuff out of the Jeep, put it in a coworker's car (she had a team of workers with her), and went in for questioning. North Dakota charged her and she is waiting for extradition back to Wisconsin to get things worked out. At the time of her letter to me she had no charges against her in Wisconsin. I am supposed to call her on Saturday and she hopes she can come home. If she doesn't answer, that means she's still in jail.

So I am anxious to find out if all is well. Robin has not been in any trouble since 1990. She did all ten years of proba- tion without violation. I don't think she will come out with charges even though she had possession of the Jeep. It's too bad for Debi though.

It brings home the sobering fact of how high the return rate is for prison. I am determined to change during this oppor- tunity God has given me. I will not be a return prisoner, but a victorious son of God as He intends me to be. His grace is sufficient for me.

I know God always gives a way out of temptation so we may stand and be a witness of His power and grace to overcome all things as He strengthens us (1 Corinthians 10:13).

As we believe, we receive. He is more than able to supply all of our needs and wants according to His riches and glory! Hallelujah!! Aren't you glad God loves us? Now that was a good question, right?

I would love to ride bike with you and build our friendship. I will gladly help with all I can. It sounds like you're effi- cient with many things. I also like to cook and I love making things, recycling unwanted items into useful objects. I'll give you fair warning: I'm a romantic (not hopeless though) and like to snuggle (when appropriate). I'm not helpless or hopeless and I would be pleased to help you in all ways possible. If and when it's God's will, I would accept the position of help-meet and soul mate. There I go again! Please don't take me the wrong way, Marilynne. Know that you are in my prayers.

Your friend in Christ Jesus,

Roger

July 18, 2005

Dear Marilynne,

I am writing again because I don't know if I'm sending out the wrong message. At times, I am prone to get ecstatic and feel like I'm bursting at the seams with happiness at getting to know you. I truly sense some things happening in the spirit world that pertain to our friendship. I am much like the young boy who receives a beautiful bicycle that he has prayed for for so long. On Christmas morning, there it is, seeming to have come out of nowhere. He wants to take it outside and ride, ride, ride, even though there's a storm and three feet of snow on the ground.

There you have it. I have prayed for a friendship built on the rock (Christ Jesus) and I don't know where God would have us go with this. Yet, I am encouraged with all your letters. I do want it to be God's will as we follow His direction.

Bringing my optimism and enthusiasm down to reality, I realize we haven't met face to face. Really, appearance is not what God wants me to focus on. In your writing, I see the beautiful, sensitive inner woman that you are, that fears

God, is giving and caring, and listens to the still, small voice of God. That is so appealing to my spirit.

I am not perfect. I am going to lose some weight so I am more pleasing on the outside, but the age thing is in God's hands. But I am also constantly looking at my inner man and throwing out the useless things that choke out the good fruit being planted today. I've prayed for a soul mate that I can grow with, and experience whatever God gives us.

You probably already feel that our friendship is more than enough right now, so please understand that at times I need a "tug at the reins" so I don't rush out into a situation that God has not ordained. I do not want to walk out of God's protec- tive cover ever again.

At times, I'm actually a patient person, but I'd better not get started on that subject. And so, Marilynne, I give you my friendship now, and as time goes on, it will be revealed just what God will have us do.

Well, I want to get this out, so if we have letters that cross in the mail, I will answer questions as they come. Be blessed and know that you are a blessing.

Love in Christ,

Roger

July 18, 2005

Dear Roger,

My complete honesty is a must in this relationship that the Lord has allowed us to share. At church this Sunday, both messages were based on the coming of the Lord, that in all things we do we should always be ready for His return, cleaning up everything in our lives to be without blemish.

Personally, my daily activities were lacking the thoughts of Jesus' return, and this was a great reminder to always be ready, focusing on what would make the Lord proud of me.

That day I was very stressed, but I am thankful for the Lord in so many ways, and it was another reminder of my need to lean on my Lord Jesus for so many things, thoughts, and concerns. I cast my cares upon Him, and when I let God help me, I feel such peace that only comes from Jesus.

I really don't know where I am going in this letter to you!

I believe God has put us in contact for something. I'm not exactly sure if it's just as friends or more, but I do know this: I am anxious in a way I can't explain, waiting for your next letter. When the letter arrives, I'm asking God why I feel all this emotion and anxiety, what His plan for our lives is.

Today, I feel led to be completely honest with you about my past. I am not proud of it and I don't intend to relive it.

257

However, we learn from our past, which helps us to live our future for God.

Not long ago, I told you of my fourteen-year relationship, and that the Lord showed me the seriousness of how wrong that way of living is. I left out the part that I shared this rela- tionship with a woman. Continuing down this path would surely be destructive, and I needed to be obedient to God in all things no matter what.

I fought against the sense of conviction, and felt miserable. Finally, I threw my hands up to Jesus and cried and cried, "Lord, if this truly needs to end, then You will have to help me to end it." The Lord gave me strength, courage, and more. I am thankful to the Lord for teaching me and leading me in the right direction. I know one thing for sure: I'm going to be obedient to the Lord in all I do. I was never good at obedi- ence. I did only what I wanted to do, whenever I wanted to do it. This has been probably the hardest thing of all – *Trust in the Lord with all thine [my] heart; and lean not unto thine own* [my] *understanding.* (Proverbs 3:5).

The old me was so selfish, spoiled, and always got my own way. I didn't care who I hurt in the process. I have now become new and my eyes are open to truth, understand- ing, learning, and compassion. It is another challenge to do things with true love, not for other reasons or for my own benefit.

For a long time, I felt like what the Scriptures describe in Romans 7:14-25. If you get a chance to read this, you will see it was all I was feeling in my life. I intended to follow God, but ended up going my own way. In fact, I'll send this to you copied from my Life Discovery Bible.

By now, you know that I take everything God does for me seriously and believe in all that He will do in your life and mine.

Sorry to hear about your sister's mishap. The Lord has control of all situations, including hers, yours, and mine. Everything will work out. Maybe there is work the Lord intends her to do. We don't know why things happen, but He leads us in all things. That reminds me to share this with you: Many times it could have been me sitting where you are now. I'm grateful I'm not, but we never know. Only God knows what we need. We probably wouldn't be having so many conversations like this if God hadn't planned things the way He has.

By the way, how many sisters and brothers do you have?

I am thankful for my chance to help others with their strug- gles, and most of all I am thankful for God's unfailing love.

May God be with you always and forever. I've given you plenty to take in, so for now I will let God have this and use it for His glory. Praise Him for He is worthy of our praises!

Forever in Christ Jesus,

Marilynne

July 21, 2005

Dear Roger,

I am sitting here, taking a break from my busy, yet relax- ing day. By now, you probably know that I sent the form that allows visitations; I didn't mention that in my last letter.

As the Lord leads me, I like to be ready no matter what he plans. The Lord Jesus is awesome in all areas of my life. So far, the road He has been leading me down is wonderful. I keep trusting Him every day. Sometimes a trial will come along, and I just remind myself of where He has taken me from and that He will lead me all the way.

The more I read and pray – or talk – with Jesus, the better each day seems to be. I've diligently asked Him a few ques- tions, and – though it seems strange to me – I think I have the answers now. I feel the presence of the Holy Spirit so strongly when I hear from you, but I long to know if this is for real. I have to admit that I called my mom and shared your letters with her. Hope you don't mind. Since my mom has been praying for me for years, I figured it was time to share this part of my life with her. All my life I have longed for someone to understand me, and it's amazing to me that I have found someone like that in you, without having even met you yet.

Enough talk about me. You've started computer classes! That's great, and I will be praying for you. I have one at home, but have to walk away from it after just ten minutes. I don't have the patience for computers that you seem to have.

Good luck!

Marilynne

July 26, 2005

Dearest Marilynne,

I know you are waiting for a reply. Cast off all your anxieties and any fear of rejection because I am not at all concerned about what you were before. I love who you are in Christ today! All we ever have is now. Old things have passed away and each day is made brand new in Christ Jesus. I will never tell others things that you've shared with me.

Why? First, my past is not very good, and I also regret many choices I've made. It's eternally important for me to make the right choices today. My heart cries out to God on your behalf, not for what you were, but because of the deep pain and distress you still feel.

I have two brothers, three sisters, and a father who had no time for me, although I know he loved me. When I was thir- teen, I was involved with a twenty-one-year-old man that lived with my family. I was drawn to this person through the gifts and constant attention he gave me. I felt love for him and let him have his way with me sexually. Later, I learned that this was rape and sexual abuse. He was then drafted, and I was heartbroken. I struggled for years with being molested and felt something was wrong with me, since I didn't realize that this man had groomed me to abuse me.

I knew in my heart what he did was wrong, and his desires were purely selfish and they left my mind damaged.

I'm trying to put this in perspective. I have moved on from that issue and pray you will also. Please know in your heart that I love you as you are today.

In Christ Jesus you are now pure, spotless, and whole, and that is the only way I see you. Because of the eternal love God has given me – agape love – you are precious and beau- tiful in my sight because I see you through God's eyes, as should every Christian brother and sister. If I should ever lose God's sight, I pray I would fall under conviction and be corrected. Life is too short to waste time on little things.

I am following God's will for me, and part of that is to nur- ture and build up God's people, respect them, stand in awe of all His creation, and be blessed by the miracles that are happening around us every moment. I cannot waste time in being judgmental or even think of casting stones at others. If I even try that, God is very quick at reminding me of where I've been and how He has forgiven me, and of who I am today in Christ. As a holy son of God, I have to be about my Father's business or all I do is in vain.

So I want to see you and know you more, and to be your close friend wherever God would have us go. I will not get myself in the way of what God wants. I also do not know exactly where or what God will have me to do when I'm out of here, but I must need and want to go in His direction with the rest of my life.

In the back of my mind, I keep thinking that we have seen each other, and that it will fall into place in God's time. I would love to hear your voice. I look forward so much to the day when we see each other and can do things together.

I pray you feel the same. Know this: I will not ever turn away from what you have to offer. Only God can separate our friendship, but I know in my heart He has brought us together for specific reasons and purposes. May God keep richly blessing you and protect you in all you do.

Love in Christ, Roge

JULY 28, 2005

Dear Roger,

I must have shocked you into a lack of interest since I haven't yet heard back from you. Anyway, I have felt compelled to write to you in the midst of my uncertainty.

I've enclosed a card I ran across that touched my heart in a way I can't explain. I feel that God is leading me in this direction. I have gotten used to your immediate responses, so I'm concerned about what you are thinking at this moment. I haven't had these hopeless feelings in a long time.

I've finished the book I was reading, *Every Woman's Battle*. Now I know exactly what God expects from me in my single life and also in a married life if Jesus sees fit for me to have that chance again. Now I've started a new book, *The God Chasers,* and the Holy Spirit is just swarming through the pages. The book, by Pastor Tommy Tenney, is about his search for more of God. I'll try and copy the story so you can read it for yourself. After reading this, I'm aware of how much more I want of God. I know it is possible to have more of Him.

I wonder what will become of our friendship now. If we need to focus on God only, that is more than fine with me. God has a purpose for all His children and I know I am willing to let God do whatever it takes to get me where He wants me, serving Him and Him alone. I need to get back on track focusing only on Him. I need to not be thinking of myself so much and my everyday duties, but to put all my thoughts on Jesus; not just to seek for Him to help me in the messes I get into, but to focus on who God really is. This is what God requires.

I have been scared to be alone. When I say that I am in a healing process, I am not just talking about my life with a woman, but also from a marriage to my first and only hus- band. I feel as I am only now healing from the pain of being married to the wrong person. Since October 2004, I've been progressing in healing my mind and my emotions, and I am finally at peace.

Around December 2004, I prayed to the Lord, pleading with Him to give me another chance to be with happy with a man. I told God I didn't want to be alone forever, but that I also wanted His will in my life, no matter which way He leads me. No matter what happens, I know I will be okay in His love.

Lately, every message at church has been in line for my future and growth in the Lord. In February, I learned what true unconditional love really is. I've read the verses before, but on this day, the Lord taught me that I could love Him and He would never hurt me. I was touched and amazed – I could actually feel His love and power over me. To this day, I cherish His step-by-step teaching and comfort for me when I can't be strong. He is there.

At this point, I know it is God's will for us to continue our friendship. I have read a few other books lately that have been very helpful to me, such as *Coming Out of Homosexuality, Restoring Sexual Identity, Every Woman's Battle, and A Way of Escape.* Only God knows what we really need. In everything I have been learning, He is giving me the wisdom to overcome what used to get me down.

In the name of Jesus, His will be done, not mine,

Marilynne

July 30, 2005

Dear Roger,

This connection we seem to have can only be from God. I was relieved to get your letter. You also have been under God's protection for many years as have I.

I have been praying for God's will to be done in my life. You are certainly not alone in your feelings, and I can relate. I've asked the Lord if this is His will, that he would allow it to happen, and if not, that He would change my way of think- ing. But I have a strong feeling that this may actually be what God has intended for us. Of course, I want to know this for sure.

When I spoke about my anxiety, it wasn't a bad thing. It was more like excitement in hearing from you. I am not dis- tressed, just in awe.

I must share with you about a person in my life. For many years, he told me he loved me. But the timing of things in life changed what might have been. We had been teenage friends, lovers, and confidantes, but one day, I let all of that go and married another man (Robert) whom I hardly even knew. Danny and I went our separate ways. He was a mili- tary man so his travels didn't include me. This is a story of where the grass isn't always greener on the other side. Talk about timing, temptation, and reality.

After about five years, we found ourselves back in contact with each other. He was now divorced and I was unhappily married, but living for the Lord. We began writing again, talking on the phone, and so on. His gestures toward me made me feel wanted and his letters seemed too good to be true. But one day he came to visit where my husband and I lived. He wanted to see if I was being treated the way he thought I should be treated.

The visit went well. My husband and Danny got along fine, and it was uncomfortable for me having two opposite types of people in the same room, but I saw this as a chance to remain friends with Danny.

I'm not sure why I felt compelled to share this story with you. Danny and I are still friends, but in a different way. I keep asking God for His guidance in this friendship. I believe we have been in contact with each other again for a reason. Just as Danny and I didn't know where to go in our early relationship with each other, I am now waiting on the Lord because I don't want to mess up His plan for my life again.

Danny has since remarried and still calls me once in a while, but I make sure to be careful in how he talks to me since he's married. We talk about Jesus, but he is not living for the Lord, although I continue to pray that he will.

I know God has a plan for me because his Word says so. *They that wait upon the Lord* (Isaiah 40:31) comes to mind. Read Psalm 130 when you have time. There are many other Scriptures about waiting on the Lord for His promises, encouraging us to know that all things are possible with the Lord in control. It is exciting to see all that the Lord has done in my life, knowing all He has yet to do.

I want to thank you for the card of encouragement. The timing was perfect. Ecclesiastes 3:1 says there is a time for everything. I lean on the Word to keep myself where the Lord wants me. Perfection isn't my goal, but the knowledge of righteousness is. I want to know more about God, not just for His hand of blessing but for who He is.

There is so much that I want to share with you, and again, the proper timing comes to mind. There is a time to share and a time not to share.

The Lord will give you insight about your future before the time comes. Again, we need to wait patiently on the Lord.

The Lord is molding me and I am comforted to know that the His perfecting me is all for my good. The beauty of the story of the potter's clay comes to mind. We are the clay, and with God as the potter, something good is bound to come out.

I am really looking forward to hearing and seeing your songs put into action. Music is a great gift from God and He loves it when we praise Him. When I praise Him, all cares and burdens seem to lift from my shoulders.

Will you be able to get a driver's license when you get out? I'm not sure how that works. Did you begin that program about drinking that the prison is offering? You haven't men- tioned it lately.

I'm grateful for the Lord and how He can move mountains and hills to get His plan in motion. Recently, I've been seeing people I haven't seen in years, and it's not because I haven't been out. I get to testify for the Lord to these people. The people I used to hang out with can't believe the difference God has made in my life. I pray that God will work while I witness for Him, so they may also know Jesus as their Savior.

I like going to garage sales, and that's where I've been meet- ing these people. I went to the fair in Spooner last night and saw a person I haven't seen in four years. I didn't even know she was back in the area. I will continue to invite her to church with me – to God be the glory.

I still don't feel comfortable sending you a picture of me. It's not because I don't want to, I just think it's best that I don't right now. If it's God's will, you will see me in person some- day, okay?

I need to get this letter out to you so I can get ready for the best part of my day: joining in worship with the Lord and other believers.

May God be with you in all that you do. I pray His hand of righteousness and wisdom be with you every day.

In the name of Jesus Christ our Lord, Sincerely yours in Christ, Marilynne

AUGUST 1, 2005

My dear Marilynne,

I won't make you wait for letters from me. I promise to write the same day I receive yours, okay?

I'm also puzzled at the speed of our relationship. I love you more with every letter you write. I wanted God to introduce me to the woman He would choose for me, and I believe God has a sense of humor because never in my wildest dreams would I have believed I would find you while I'm in prison! God is so awesome. I am full of joy today, and every moment I think of you. I have not yet gotten the form that would give approval for you to visit me, since it takes seven to twenty- one days. You will be added to the list in God's time and plan for our lives, which I believe is for us to be together. The last thing you ever have to worry about is whether I will be your friend. The best marriages are the ones where the two are best friends, and able to trust and express themselves freely without fear of rejection or judgment.

I do not mind you talking to your mother about me. I'm not sure exactly what I said in those letters but I hope I sounded somewhat intelligent! Where does your mother live? You can tell her that I think she has a very wonderful, loving, intel- ligent, and beautiful daughter. I am waiting with excitement for the day we meet in person. I do not view myself as a prize. As I've said before, the inside of a person is far bigger than physical appearance. I love the way you are honest with me and I am honored that you sent in the visitor form. I know that God's timing is always perfect and His will always brings true joy and peace and happiness.

Thank you for the wonderful card. Do not worry or be anxious in any way, because God is in control of our rela- tionship. I know there will be riches beyond measure as we both stay faithful to Him. He is the one who is bonding us together. I will wait for what He has planned and that excites me to no end!

I have a million questions to ask you and I know I could talk to you for hours. I want you to know that I think of you all the time, and I've purposed in my heart to please God in this relationship. By doing so, we will meet God's earthly expec- tations for us.

Thank you also for the article. I was in a Bible study where they used the book The God Chasers, but I was only able to attend a couple sessions and I didn't have the book myself.

I'm going to mail this tonight and I'll let you know where you are on my list for visitors. I realize you may not be able to come, but just to have you on the list means the world to me.

Love in Christ (and also my love!),

Roger

AUGUST 4, 2005

Dear Roger,

First of all, what makes you think that I wouldn't be able to visit you? I can tell you this, that I would not have filled out the papers without intending to visit you; you underestimate me! I believe the Lord has already set the time for us to meet. He put the desire in my heart to be ready to meet you.

Our God is an awesome God and has a sense of humor. I never would have thought of Him picking someone for me that had to spend time in jail. We seem to think alike in everything so far – this amazes me even more.

My mom and other family members live in Illinois. I grew up in Rockford but haven't lived there since I was seventeen. I tried to live there again after I was separated in 1985, but it wasn't good for me. I don't like the busy life and all the traf- fic there. Even though Mom lives in the country, there is still traffic everywhere you go. I visit my mom and grandmother as much as I can and wish I could go more often. I have two uncles who also live in Illinois; one is a Methodist minister and the other one is retired.

It's strange that my uncle (David) went into Methodism, since Grandma is Full Gospel and loves Pentecostalism, and her prayers for me are being answered. It breaks my heart that Grandma isn't able to talk much due to some small strokes that affected her voice. Gram and I were always so close. I could tell her anything and always get a response from her. Now I share with her and only get a look. We celebrated her eighty-second birthday in June.

I try to share with my mom, but it's never the same as it was with Gram. I spoke to my son about you, as well as my mom. When I told him I was planning to meet you, he asked, "When are we going?" I told him I would go alone. He's always been protective of me and just doesn't want me to get hurt again. I am assuring everyone that God is in control because I want the Lord to be in everything I do, especially my relationships.

There are times I wish I could just call you and talk. For now, though, I'll take what I can get and wait for what's in store later.

As for the AA meetings, I usually went to Shell Lake. However, I haven't felt that the Lord wants me to go any- more. I don't like the language used there, or at any other place I've visited for the meetings. People talk good about God and then swear in the same sentence. I think they also use the meetings as their church attendance, and I don't believe in doing that.

I would go if God wanted me to, but I don't want to witness to people that haven't overcome alcohol and only kind of put God into it. I know my higher power truly is God, and mix- ing our past failures with His righteous name all the time doesn't seem healthy. However, my first years I did stay true to meetings and church and I also ran Friday night meetings for a while. God is my sponsor and some people don't get that.

I do miss the casual fellowship once in a while but I get that at church. Going to AA was a must for me, before the power of the Lord fell upon me and took the place of AA. I recom- mend AA to anyone who desires help, and am willing to attend with them. I am on a call list. Wayne has my number and once in a while I get phone calls for someone needing help. I also write to two other guys in prison. They are young and will be in there for eighteen years or so.

I try not to limit myself in helping others because I truly remember how it was to not drink. This world is full of temptations and I praise the Lord for getting me on the right track, now and forever.

I am always in the recovery process, renewing my mind, body, and soul. I want God to mold me and fix what is bro- ken. I read something about being molded the other day that said the Lord may mold you many times to make you into a vessel that will hold the oil.

God is great. I am glad He didn't give up on me. I'm even more grateful that He loves to share His presence with us.

Well, I will leave my presence with you for now, and may God fill your cup till it overflows with peace and joy.

The Lord be with you always,

Marilynne

AUGUST 5, 2005

Dear Marilynne,

Ifeel moved to write more to you. I don't have the answers, only God does. I know God brought us together, but I don't know his full purpose for us. I tend to get more excited the more I know you. I am in prison for a crime I committed, but you don't condemn me for this – that is so meaningful. There were some I thought were close friends in Christ, but because I am in prison, they have chosen not to write me a single word in ten months.

I am incredibly blessed by you writing to me. It is no coin- cidence that I am here. It has given me time to realize fully how transparent some friends can be. We can all get busy, and I fully forgive them. I am not expecting anything from them. I was not nice to be around when I chose to drink.

Nothing else mattered then; I abused people and did all the selfish things an active alcoholic does. I write this only to let you know how much your letters mean to me.

I still have some wonderful friends who knew me in my pro- ductive years and then saw how my destructive course made me lose all desire to live. I am no longer that man, and I don't listen to the devil anymore. In Christ, I still love the friends who choose to have no contact with me. Christ has risen in order that my life can be restored through Him.

Everything that Satan took from me when I listened to his lies could be restored to me if God chooses.

The first thing in my daily agenda is to claim integrity in Jesus' name. Psalm 15 speaks of integrity – being blameless, speaking truth (not lying), hating sin, and keeping promises even when it hurts. And Malachi 2:6 speaks of having moral excellence in principles and in practice.

I also seek God's wisdom for the day. See Proverbs 24:1-6. In our friendship, I will do my part to always be truthful and walk in wisdom, remodeling and rebuilding the parts of me not pleasing to God. I am not lazy. I will do everything that God directs me to do and will listen to Him. I feel I am a miracle of God and He is molding me every day. Marilynne, I don't want to ever represent myself as being any more or less than what I am in Christ.

I am only alive today because of God's love and plan for my life. I want to share my life with someone and I do hope it's you, for you seem so real – almost surreal – and I am awed at the fact that we are meeting this way. Ironically, you are learning more about me faster through our letters than if we had met another way. I understand why God chose this method.

I feel anointed in the area of music and I think you see my hunger to share it. At one time, the music God gave me, along with my other abilities, were a large part of my ego. Now I have laid those things at the cross and wait for God's timing to prepare me before sharing them. I do not want Roger Harrison to get in the way of what God intends for the message, and I will not let Roger Harrison do anything to stand in the way of what He wants for us. I will be happy wherever God purposes my life to go, be it alone or with someone. Either way, I will praise His name because every breath I take is a gift from Him, and you are a precious gift from God. I do not take our friendship lightly. I respect everything we have done so far and will nurture it with all my heart.

When I say I don't have much to offer, it's according to a worldly perspective. I no longer have a credit line and am currently in deep debt because of my foolishness for the past twelve years. I will be filing for bankruptcy when I'm released. Ninety percent of my debts are hospital and treat- ment bills. I am in no way proud of this fact. I do not have any property either, as I gave it all to my ex-wife. I also gave her current husband adoption rights.

All I have to offer you is this man of God, Roger Harrison, and who I am inside today. If I have in any way misrep- resented myself to you, I want to set things in order right now. All my joy comes from God and His riches in me. I have compassion, love, and boldness in Christ. I rely on His wisdom and guidance. All my true gifts are from God and I don't expect anything from you. I know God supplies all of my needs, and every letter from you is such a precious gift. If you don't mind, I may write to you every day. We both need to be aware of what we are doing and that's why I'm exposing myself to you.

Do not be alarmed when I mention falling in love. I love every ounce of God that you display in your letters. You are a precious woman of God and I hold you in high respect for that. We both have many things in our past that are not pretty, but those mean nothing today because that is not who we are in Christ today.

When we share our past, I pray it will be only a peek at how it once was, and that our focus will be on all He holds for our future. I pray that every day we will accept ourselves, change all we can, and expect no less than everything God gives us strength for.

Home is where we regroup, refuel, restore, and reinforce each other for what God has ahead for us. I am speaking quite a bit in plurals, but don't take that wrong. I can see the possi- bility of us and am not at all afraid of it.

Even though I may not be perfect, I see so much in us that may be perfect together and that excites me. Above all, I am happy and care about you so much already. Even if you are only comfortable for us to remain as pen pals, I will accept it. I believe God promised me He would choose someone for me and I fully believe Him for that.

The old man is gone; the new man in Christ is alive. I was previously trying to kill the old man – body and all – but God has sustained me and kept me from harming myself. He has restored my spiritual self and is replacing my previous foolishness with His eyesight and wisdom. Lack of knowl- edge has never been a hindrance for me, but applying that knowledge for God's glory rather than for selfish motives is what a man of wisdom should do at all times.

I try to be in prayer at all times, in conscious contact with God, if you will, and it helps my days go by. I try to find God's purpose for everything I do. If I seem to be wandering at all in this letter, forgive me. As I said earlier, I am writing this in spurts. I started at 5:00 a.m. and it's now 11:53 a.m., and there is so much I want to tell you.

I also want you to know that I do things with intensity and focus. I am a problem solver by nature. I'm also a morning person. Even though many people – especially here – find that characteristic annoying, it is very rare for me to not wake up with joy. In my first marriage, I usually worked until two or so in the morning, and I loved to get up and go play a round of golf around 6:00 in the morning. I'd get back around 9:00 or 10:00 a.m., which gave my wife time to wake up, and then we would do something together. Of course, that schedule was based on the work hours I had.

I am normally a self-starter and that goes well with self- employment. I was going to mention that if I don't finish the OWI (Operating While Intoxixated) program, I will be released on extended supervision subject to the parole board's approval and recommendation of where I will go – like a TLC (temporary living center) or a halfway house, group home, or residence.

Right now, I have no arrangements to go anywhere. A very close friend, Pastor Tim Rust, has invited me to come to Nebraska to visit, but unless I get approval from my parole agent, I can't leave the state.

I will do well when I'm released from here, because I am determined to serve God with my life. At a hearing last October, the judge said he would not allow me to obtain any license for five years, even when

I'm state eligible. But I believe that as I display sincerity in my life and do well as God purposes, the judge will allow it sooner and that my agent will agree.

There's a big river to cross before then, but I am telling you this because you asked about it, and I am being sincerely honest with you. Marilynne, I am an alcoholic and have been guilty of manipulation before. I am aware of this and don't ever want to do that in our relationship. Please let me know if you ever feel pushed or pulled by me and it's not from God, okay?

It's 12:30 p.m. now. I take constructive criticism well. The key word is constructive, which is to repair or build up each other in Christ, not destructive. I know you are not like this, and that's why I know our meeting is part of God's plan.

Ironically, my past relationships were with women who ridiculed me and were destructive. This was much like my father, who did not live for God. You asked about my par- ents' occupations. My father was a multi-talented man with incredible drive. He quit school at fifteen years old, joined the navy, and was discharged after a year because he was underage when he joined. He then joined the army during World War II and fought in Korea and Afghanistan. He was in the service for about twenty years and became one of the original flying sergeants (the army trained him to fly) receiv- ing an Aircraft & Engineering mechanic endorsement given by the military.

1:30 p.m. When he got out of the army he bought the airport in Superior, Wisconsin and built experimental aircraft. Then the airport burned down so my dad and uncle Bill bought Basswood Island, one of the Apostle Islands, and logged it for two years. I was born while they were on the island. One day they were hauling logs across the bay to Ashland when a storm kicked up and broke the binding chain. They lost the logs and ended up going bankrupt. We moved back to Superior and then to Poplar. My parents were divorced for seven years. During that time, my father remarried, did crop dusting, and raised purebred Arabian horses.

My half-sister Gloria was born during this time, but then my dad and his second wife divorced and my mother and father remarried. We moved to Sheboygan, where my father welded and bought a bar. That's when my music career started at twelve years old. My dad also did appliance repair and remodeling, so I picked up many skills from him. Before my dad died, UW-Madison did an aptitude test on him and found he had the equivalent of sixteen years of college educa- tion. He dropped out of school in the seventh grade, but he was able to accumulate skills from the army and by reading books. At age fifty-seven, he died from a heart attack brought on by drinking, smoking, and emphysema. My mother worked at Indianhead Technical College in Sheboygan before retiring to Cumberland, where she died of leukemia at age seventy-two.

My grandfather, George W. Harrison, was a dairy farmer in Eau Claire and then around Fond du Lac. I never met him nor my mother's parents, but only my father's mother whom I loved with all my heart. She died in 1983 in Barron. She led me toward God and always loved me with such tenderness, which I know now was from God.

Well, my hand is getting sore so I'll write more later.

4:18 p.m. Just finished my Bible study in Acts. We're in chap- ter 8. I love spending time in God's Word.

Picking up my train of thought, my dad and mom were hard workers. I am grateful that my mom moved back to Cumberland after my dad died. She was very close to my children and spent much time with my daughter Lisa, which was priceless.

There's something I've been thinking about, but I'm hesitant to share it, because I don't want it to burden you. You have so many other responsibilities, and this is in God's hands, so I only ask you to pray for me. I've had some problems with my right wrist for some time and the doctor here sent me to a specialist in Madison to have it looked at. My wrist and fingers go numb at times and there is a bump in the center of my wrist. The doctor thought it was a cyst, so the special- ist ordered an MRI. It's a benign tumor. The problem is with nerves running through the center of the tumor, and I'm concerned about how an operation will affect the use of my hand, since I finger-pick a lot on guitar. Pray that the sur- geon will have God's direction and wisdom. I will play music to God as He directs me, no matter what happens.

I am so glad that you chose to be a friend to me and that you are even considering visiting me. Thank you again. I'm trying not to cry when I think about what you mean to me – they're tears of joy and gratefulness, of course. I know I will get through my time here and I rejoice that Jesus is in my heart and I am alive in Him.

I am finding myself wondering what you will think of me in person, so I've added daily activities so that I look my best for God, for me, and for my friend Marilynne!

Did I tell you my daughter and her husband got motorcycles this year? Do you like motorcycles? I have ridden before but that was back in the 1980s. I do like riding and walking; but I would also love to just sit on a swing with you and count our many blessings together. Growing old with someone God has chosen for me is so appealing.

I could write to you all day, and that is not like me. I hope I'm not boring you!

One thing you can always count on from me is an endless supply of love and encouragement. I believe this comes from what I have seen God do in my life. He has moved moun- tains in my life as I trusted Him wholly and did what He said. I got hired in Alaska by believing in Him, even though people don't believe me when they hear how God moved to make it happen. I'll explain that in the future.

He made the impossible possible, and He can salvage me – and He already has – from my death grip and I know He is capable of so much more.

I live for and love God, Marilynne. I have gravitated to a state of humility in awe of what God is doing. I didn't think it was possible for my heart to be restored to love again, at full capacity. What a miracle. If our relationship ended right now, I would still rejoice in all He has. But I pray that our friendship continues to grow into the beauty of God's full potential. It's good to be cautious but still always listen to the voice of God. When I get your letters my heart sings with joy, and no one has ever stirred that within me but God himself.

I always pray for your protection, for God to lead you, and for Him to wrap you in His arms of love. I pray for Him to completely heal you of all that needs healing, to give you comfort where comfort is needed, and to be reminded that He sincerely and unconditionally loves you. Nothing can separate us from the love of God. He loves us completely, so raise your eyes to Him and allow Him to flow through you to cleanse any unrighteousness. I will also do the same.

For me, the perfect friendship involves building each other up and always being ready to help each other be encouraged in the Lord. As long as we keep our communication honest and pure, we can always help each other. I rejoice when I pic- ture God using you for His ministry, and when I picture the two of us working together for the Lord…wow! I'm looking forward to possibly going to church with you and sharing our love of the Lord together.

I'm a romantic, so please bear with me and know that I'm not just being led by my own thoughts. God has given me a glimpse of what can be for us, and I know that when we do get together it will be something no one can touch, match, or even fathom. The beauty of our friendship is more vivid every day. It's like I'm seeing the most beautiful colors imag- inable when for years after my divorce I saw only black and

white. All I can say is, thank you, Lord, for all you do, all you are, and all that will be.

Have a day of peace and joy, and if I write too much, let me know. Thank you for showing me God in you. The spirit and presence of God is in your words.

Love in Christ,

Roger

AUGUST 6, 2005

Dear Roger,

With all of these compliments, most people would think you were getting ready to set the hook for the catch! But I'm not most people. Part of me still has my guard up and part of me is in awe of God's plan. I have made a few wrong choices lately and continue to learn lessons about what God's will is for me, especially when it comes to relationships. From your letters I don't have any doubts as to us being able to get along.

Recently, I have been thinking things through a bit, so let me see how I can put this for you. First, it involved changing my relationships and trusting the Lord with them. This was hard to do when I started to really feel lonely and went to the New Year's Eve service alone. Still, I knew I wasn't alone. But by February I was pleading with God that I did not want to live on this earth alone. Yet, if that was His plan for me, then I had to be fine with that. All this time, I knew that I was with Jesus, and I had to learn what love really meant. During the Valentine's Day service I truly felt God's love for the first time and an amazing peace came over me. It was God the Father's love for me. I finally got it and understood that I wasn't lonely anymore, at least not in the same way as I was before.

Looking back at the dates on letters I got from you, I realized that a letter I received from you in February was written the day God showed me what real love was. I am not rushing or getting overwhelmed anymore; I am at ease and realize that everything is truly in God's hands.

I just can't imagine not listening to my Lord anymore. I still kick myself over smoking and I know I can't continue this and be all that God wants me to be. I am frustrated at how hard this habit is to break, when other things that you'd think would have sent me down the rocky road aren't a prob- lem. Praise God for His genuine love and power to overcome anything!

I started something new for my mornings, and I pray it helps fight my smoking. I have a treadmill, although I usually just walk around the house. Now, I've started a two-mile con- tinuous walk on the treadmill, which should strengthen me more than walking and stopping and walking again around the house. I would much rather walk outside, but the flies are too bad.

On TV, I saw T.D. Jakes preaching at the MegaFest in Atlanta, Georgia, and he's pretty good. I'm learning to claim God's promises and tell Satan to get behind the price already paid for my sins – Jesus' blood.

God had a plan, even at the moment of their deception and sin, and so it came to pass. God's timing and our timing are different. His day is as a thousand years and He is really ahead of us!

God knows our future and He waits patiently for us to find out what that future is by repenting of our sins and following Him. He didn't say that our path wouldn't be rough, but that now we don't have to walk it alone if we accept Him and the payment for our sins through His blood on the cross. Praise God for His awesome plan!

I'm also watching Joyce Meyers and I like what she said one day: If something I want to do doesn't line up with God's Word, then I don't do it. I don't know why those words came to my mind this morning, except that I know I need to learn more every day what God is saying and has already said.

One thing is for sure – a relationship without God will not last. I want my desires and God's will to line up in what a relationship for me will be. I have always wanted what is good and pure, but things didn't always end up that way, I realize now. Without God nothing is good and pure. I find my strength in God and I try to obey Him.

In watching these church channels, I realize that these are what interest me now, not the stuff I used to watch. I also keep my radio tuned to a Christian station now and am learning all the songs, just as I used to do country and other types of music. I don't listen to what I used to since it brings up my past again. I don't want to go back to that, so listening to Christian music is my way forward. I don't want any part of my past again. I thought I would miss some things that I enjoyed doing before like dancing, shooting pool, and just hanging out. But I don't really miss any of it now. I still like to dance, but now I dance before the Lord.

Do you get to watch TV? Do they have any Christian chan- nels? What about church services? You haven't mentioned that or AA lately, so I want to know that you are staying on track.

Without the Word of knowledge, we become stale. Today I feel pretty good, but I desire more of God. I need to stay focused on God and everything will fall into place. Favor with God is what I'm after.

Roger, I've got to get some things done before church. It's always great to hear from you. I know the time is coming when we will meet, even though I don't know when right now.

I would encourage you to talk with a godly person about our relationship, as I think it will help. You've heard the saying that something may be too good to be true. Well, it

seems that way for us, but with God, nothing is too good and all things are true! To God be the glory, for old things are passed away and all things have become new – mind, body, and soul.

Thank you for your prayers. I know God listens to His chil- dren, and we are two examples of that!

In the name of Jesus, Sincerely,

Marilynne

August 8, 2005

Dearest Marilynne,

Our God is truly an awesome God! I can't wait for your replies and am starting this letter before I even get your reply. Please don't feel you need to send any money or sup- plies, as I am resourceful and God supplies far more than my daily needs.

Finally, good news on AA here: They will have the first meeting on August 21. That's my daughter's birthday. I am so happy these days. I had resigned myself to being without anyone close in my life, but then God brought you into my life. God knows the desires of our hearts and our sincere desire to serve Him, and He is always faithful and just. He loves to see you and me walking in obedience, and richly blesses each of His children when they do so.

I was asking God recently how come He brought us together and He is showing me some reasons. In my previous rela- tionships, my looks (I'm not ugly, but I'm not Mr. America either), my music and other abilities (such as cooking) are what got me involved with women. But I never felt a real connection between my partners and the real man inside me. To have a precious woman like you even consider me as a close friend, let alone possibly my lifelong soul mate, was beyond my wildest dreams. I've been in constant prayer and thanks to God for His wisdom and His goodness at all He is doing in our lives.

You can't imagine how much you sending in the visitor's form means to me. I am in constant preparation and expec- tation at the possibility of your visit, in God's way and tim- ing, and when it is convenient for you.

All old things have passed away and each day is full of His promises and direction. God has so much for us, and I've been in constant prayer to Him. He is showing me is that I've longed for as a friend that I can talk to honestly without reservation, who will also tell me honestly what God has put in her heart.

Again, I see our friendship as forever, and I truly believe it will be of a depth not known to me before. I can't answer for you, but our letters echo exactly what I've been feeling! Can this be for real? Yes, I believe it's as real as our Creator God is real. I have been so blessed writing and receiving letters that I can barely contain my excitement and joy. PRAISE THE LORD! Our God hears our prayers and is always faithful and just.

I want to answer some questions before you ask them. I am not a know-it-all and I rely on God's wisdom and guidance each day. It's only by His strength and leading that I'm here today. I could be in a worse place than where I am, but the thing that matters most is where I am in Christ. I am still human, but with Christ as my rock and cornerstone,

I hope, pray, live each day to be more Christ-minded and trustworthy. I've been let down by many people in recovery and even in churches. When I look back, I realize it was my wrong perception of reality and who I was that put me in a place where I could be let down. I will continue to be open and honest with you. As our relationship grows, I pray we will both be able to confide everything in our hearts to each other. I have never had such confidence in my life, knowing that something huge is happening between us that tran- scends my understanding. God has been so good to me and to you, and He truly knows the desires of our hearts. Gosh, I could write all day to you!

Now you have heard my voice, and again I apologize if I have stepped over a boundary by calling without your permission. If you should ever feel that you need space, I can give you that and I will respect you always. I really want God's will for both of our lives. At this point, I feel so *right* about us. It's just so good being friends.

They put up the daily mail list and I'm on it tonight, so I will most likely hear from you soon. Please forgive my rambling letter. I have been writing this most of today and it's hard to always remember where I left off. I'm glad to be a small part of your life today. I keep reading your card and it's so true. I will exercise patience, and ask that you be patient with me as I become more pleasing for God's purpose in my life.

Please do what God wills for you every day and all will work for as He purposes. As God's children we are heirs to the throne and to eternity. I will keep writing, and if our letters are crossing, that's okay with me. I just love hearing from your heart! God knows I am forever changed since you've touched my life.

Your loving friend in Christ Jesus,

Roger

AUGUST 8, 2005

Dear Marilynne,

I was so elated to get your letter today. I believe that God has brought us together and I feel it more every day and with every word you write. I listen to everything you say in your letters, and if I mention concern for an issue, it's only because that's how I read it. I truly write in all honesty and I will not hide anything from you, okay?

I cannot believe how happy I am and we've not even met yet! I am so excited to get your letters and hang on to every nuance of your words. You are so incredibly beautiful, Marilynne, and I have to pinch myself at times to make sure I'm not dreaming. I am willing to wait for God's timing, and I know only too well that His timing is perfect and that He predestined our being together for His purpose.

Everything we have been through and brought on ourselves in the past has led to this moment. I praise His name because it's *only* by His mercy and grace that I am alive to write you. As you read this letter, I am praising His glory and name for keeping you from harm and perfecting you into His beauty.

We must always look at each other with God's eyes and remember the beauty inside. If you lose any outer beauty, it will never make a difference to me because *who we are in Jesus Christ is the only important thing.*

I have always had compassion for those less fortunate and have never hesitated to give what I can to enrich their lives. I am not what I would consider a prize right now, at least not by the world's standards. I have been concentrating all my energies on my inner man for the last year, and as I come in line more every day, I know my body will also line up. You have given me so much extra energy that I believe at times

I might be able to fly! (But I won't jump off a building – ha ha!) Actually, I feel like a teenager when I think of you. I ask God what lies ahead and He tells me to be patient.

Please forgive me for calling your number. I didn't expect you to answer, and I don't know if you were even there or if your answering machine picked up. But I wanted you to know you are officially on my call list.

They have many things to do here for exercise, like a track and weight room, but I have not gotten out much to do these things. Mostly, I'm working on my music. I have been so inspired lately and I do what I can to write down what God has put on my heart. Did I mention I think you are beautiful?

I am six feet tall and right now weigh 250 pounds. I need to lose thirty pounds and firm up again, which I will do. I have blue eyes and used to have light brown hair, but now it's gray. I hope I've attained some wisdom in the grayness, but I would dye it and diet if that enhanced any attraction for you to me! I can multi-task and I have the ability to listen but can always use improvement. In our relationship, I try to be aware of what you need from me. I love to be close and I want you to want me around. I give all I can to please. I hope I'm saying that right.

I feel uneasy at times because I've also made mistakes in relationships before, and like you, don't feel that I deserve to be hurt anymore. I'm ready for a friendship that is spiritually rich and God-centered, where we respect each other's boundaries and space, but are comfortable sharing every- thing with each other.

I spoke to my sister Robin, but mentioned only that we write each other and that you are a caregiver. She was very positive about you. She knows more than anyone that my marriages were destroying me, and the last lady I was around was not good for me either.

I desire only the one God chooses. It does not matter in any way what you look like. I would not base my desire to be with you solely on what your appearance is. I desire a true soul mate who reciprocates love and care, with a heart for God's will and plan, and endorses who I am in Christ.

We both need an encourager, someone grounded in God's will and purpose. I've said before that if God chooses us only to be friends (we are already very close, even more than we realize), then I would respect that.

I treasure everything you have written to me. How can I be falling in love with someone I've not seen? How can I know that these intense, deep feelings are real? God is bringing the two of us together in this way not to confuse, but to remove all doubt that it's His will and not ours. I will never degrade you, put you down, or hurt you emotionally or physically.

That's not what I am. I am by no means perfect, but strive to become more Christ-like every day.

I'm reminded of my flesh constantly. I have to admit that I held my breath when reading about your friend Danny, and realize there are many things that crop up, but God is still in control of our lives. I want you to hear from God – not me – that we will be closer as time goes by. I also need you to know that I am not a jealous person. As long as your friendships are God-healthy and not a danger to you in any way spiritually, emotionally, or physically, I will not interfere with what you desire. I trust you as I trust God. I have deep understanding and forgiveness and am working to restore my integrity back to what God wants.

I will wait with anticipation for your next letter. Again, I hope my calling your number did not upset you. It's listed on my visitor form as well as your fire number. I hope you are not uncomfortable with me knowing this.

How tall are you? I have a picture in God's eyes and you are incredible and very desirable, and I can't wait to see you in person.

The OWI recovery program is only in Winnebago, Wisconsin (by Oshkosh), and I'm waiting for my program review. I'm still classified at a medium-risk rating and have put in for an early post release control (PRC), but they're in no hurry to staff me because Dodge corrections put my PRC date in November this year.

My original court papers did not have the earned release eligibility listed on them, so Dodge set my PRC at twelve months instead of six months. They said if the courts send verification of earned release eligibility, I would be staffed early, but New Lisbon could wait until November if they want to. I am aware that everything is a privilege here. I have peace that all things work for good for those who wait upon the Lord. As you mentioned, there is perfection in God's timing. I will be patient and pray that I do not offend you, my dear friend, or make you move away from me, for you are so very important to me. I am going to pray with you right now as I am with you in spirit. *Right now, God, I ask that you keep your hand ever before Marilynne and give her strength this day to do all you would have her to do. And Lord, in Jesus' name, destroy anything that would dare to attack this woman of God and extinguish any thoughts or weapons against her and your purpose for her life. Lift her up and shelter her mind and body and fill her with your Holy Spirit and wisdom so she will know every step to take and know in her heart what you would have her to do today and every moment. In the name of Christ Jesus of Nazareth I pray. Amen.*

I believe totally that God is for us and await all confirmation of this and will be your best friend for as long as you want me to be.

Be blessed today and as Psalm 121 says, look to heaven for that is where our strength comes from.

Love in Christ,

Roger

"His peace passes all understanding"

AUGUST 9, 2005

Dear Roger,

The Life Recovery Bible has a note on 1 Corinthians 2:9: When our lives become unmanageable and we feel as if we have lost direction, we often blame God or feel that somehow He is making things worse. Paul reminded the Corinthians that God had wonderful things planned for them, things even more wonderful than they could imagine. This message is for us, too, if we turn our life and will over to God, he can build a new life for us that is beyond our wildest dreams!

I read Psalm 32 last night while listening to David Jeremiah and this one stuck with me even to this morning. I'm getting serious with God so He can get closer to you and me.

I want to touch base with your concern about your former friends. I learned something related to this from my son., and it's about trust. When Josh was young and even up until two years ago, I drank, and Josh was used to this. I wasn't the easiest person to get along with, and he got used to me staying out late – even though I would tell him I'd be right back – and having someone else keep an eye on him until

I got home. When I quit drinking I realized that he had to regain his trust in me, and now he knows I really mean it when I say something. Your friends, whether Christian or non-Christian, are in the same boat as Josh was with me and it will take time for them to learn to trust you again.

Psalm 31:11 says, I was a reproach among all mine enemies, but especially among my neighbours, and a fear to mine acquaintance: they that did see me without fled from me.

Then, read verse 21: Blessed be the Lord: for he hath shewed me his marvellous kindness in a strong city. Some people wait for us to fall.

When I spoke with you about loneliness, I was talking about friends. My life is not the same now and neither are my friends. God's purpose is for the old things to pass away and all things to become new. I know this is painful for you, but know that God is our comforter. We can't go back and change what we've done, but with God we can begin anew with His Spirit guiding us.

My strength is in Jesus Christ and I thank Him for walking by my side when no one else is. I pray our past mistakes will all be a witness of God's love, power, and faithfulness. I will never completely lay my past experiences down because I want to share with others what God has done in my life and how He is molding me.

Yesterday, I visited a friend who used to be my neighbor. We spent a lot of time together drinking, and she just lost her partner of twenty years. In the two years of my freedom from drinking, I did not visit or call them because I knew what they would be doing. God's Spirit held my hand to keep me from going back until Paul died. Out of all of her friends, she called me on this particular day. I shared with her what happened in my life and tried to comfort her with God's Word. We'll see what happens. Timing is everything.

Psalm 103:3 says that God forgives all my sin and heals all my diseases. Proverbs 16:9 says that we make our plans, but the Lord determines our steps.

Anyway, I've got to get going. I have to meet you. Do I need to tell you in advance?

God bless you.

Friends,

AUGUST 9, 2005

Dear Marilynne,

Anything I write comes from my heart. God has opened my eyes and heart to the way I was. I used to be a womanizer, and I understand that you are wary of jumping into any- thing. I have been afraid of getting close to anyone again. I was in two bad relationships, and in prison, I now see what was really going on and how unhealthy those relationships were. I'm saying this to make it clear to you that I'm not bait- ing you or trying to manipulate you to where you don't feel led by God.

God is in control and it's still a win-win situation for me if I have you as nothing more than a friend. I am grateful to God for this, since I have longed and prayed for a good friend. But I still struggle with not getting my hopes up. In 1996, I started praying for a God-fearing, Spirit-led, faith- ful, caring woman and didn't see someone like that at all in my future. When I divorced I was thirty-nine years old and was convinced no one would ever want me. I was a Christian but wasn't walking like it. It took my coming to prison to lay down my pride and delusional thinking. I didn't like AA because I didn't feel connected to anyone and didn't believe I was worth saving. But I feel a spiritual connection to you, even though I need to keep my focus on God and leave our relationship in His hands. I am still so happy you are coming to visit.

You've raised questions about my lack of faith, and that I should be increasing my time with God in order to hear from Him. I would be concerned if you weren't discerning in this area of my life and how it affects our relationship. I care so much that God remains in this and I would not want a relationship without Him.

Your willingness to write to me is beyond what my prayers were, so anything that develops is a gift from God. Our rela- tionship needs to be God-centered and grounded in Christ.

I pray daily for the bondage of smoking to be broken for you and for you to be set free from it. You will have victory, for the battle is won in Jesus' name. All glory and honor be to God.

Always your friend in Christ,

Roger

AUGUST 10, 2005

Dear Marilynne,

I was re-reading your letter from Saturday and think I jumped to a conclusion at the first reading of it that you were wary of me, but after reading it again I think we are on the same page. God assures me daily not to worry about us but to know that He is in control and His will is going to be done regarding us. I don't want to lose what we have, but I also don't want us to get together just because we're both lonely.

I am pleased with your desire to stop smoking and I have all confidence that God will remove the desire to smoke. Remember this: every facet of your life is a testimony.

We may not understand what we are going through, but God will reveal why so we can share with others. I am not proud of holding the record for the most detox admittances in Cumberland, but if it is used for the glory of God, then who cares? I was told I was the revolving-door AA story in action. I was told that there was nowhere to send me. I was told to write the name of a different hospital on the bottle, because they were sick of detoxing me there. I wanted death and release, Marilynne. But God wouldn't let me die and has brought us together. It is miraculous to me.

3:30 p.m. I just got back from Bible study. We watched a video that Marvin taped in the Philippines. Brother Bob is over there ministering in about forty prisons and Marvin just got back. Our conditions are very nice compared to theirs! They put twenty prisoners in one 10-foot-by-10-foot cell. There are no fences, but all the guards carry M-16s, and if there's any problem, they shoot!

This Sunday, the chaplain said that he would like me to share more of the music God has given me. It's such a privilege to share God's majesty through music. I know lots of older sec- ular songs, but there is no depth of meaning in those songs compared to songs that praise the Lord.

Some days are rough, and I look to God as my source of strength in those times. There are so many bad spirits here, and many may think I'm a little nuts when I smile at their frowns and share Jesus with them, even though I'm not always the shining example of what a Christian should be. Thank you for your words of encouragement; I needed them!

Till later,

Love in Christ,

Roger

AUGUST 12, 2005

Roger,

I've had a few insights recently that you're not going to like. But the Spirit of God is leading me in what I am about to say.

I have been seeking God about this relationship, and I feel I've gotten some answers that line up with the Word of God.

Wednesday night's study at church was about boundar- ies and how to avoid passing over them. Isaiah 55:2 says,

Wherefore do ye spend money for that which is not bread? and your labour for that which satisfieth not? hearken diligently unto me, and eat ye that which is good, and let your soul delight itself in fatness.

The reason I am part of your life is to help you know truth, forgiveness, and God himself. You're right: you can't fix the past, but you have a lot of work ahead of you to make amends for all of it. I do not believe we were ever meant to be together. What God has given you is a chance to make a change in the right direction. The only way this can be accomplished is in your devotion to God. Being truthful and honest is the only way a person can make it with God or anyone.

It's about time you started AA and I pray you put yourself into the program with all your heart. If needed, I will help you with the program. I'm not a quick fix for all the prob- lems you've created in your life, but I can be here to help you overcome them.

Sincerely in Jesus, Marilynne

AUGUST 17, 2005

Marilynne,

I just got your letter that you wrote on Friday. I guess I don't know what to say. I told you that no matter what you wanted to do I would honor that and I was thinking of not writing anymore unless you write and ask something. God spoke to me in my spirit and told me that our letters are not about me and I need to keep writing even if you asked me to stop. He is in control, not me. I haven't written you any empty words, even though I know many empty words and give compli- ments easily. I don't know what you think and it's not really my business. I have been working on myself, I know I have a long way to go, and I have been honest with you.

As I said in my last couple letters, AA is starting its first meeting here at New Lisbon this Saturday and I will be attending it just as I have attended all church functions and Bible studies. New Lisbon prison dropped all outside pro- grams after the prison riot in November of this year. I was moved here because they needed to fill empty beds. I haven't lied to you, but I will be praying for God to show me how I have offended you.

God is showing me things I need to change and He is patient with my progress, and He knows my heart is after Him.

Quoting Isaiah 55:2 in reference to me is insulting to me, and to God in me. I know I'm not perfect, but I am God's child and am under

His protection. I will stand before God at any time and testify that I did not lie to you. I never meant to rob you of anything or take you away from God's purpose. I was shocked because I believed you would visit me, but received a letter of anger from you that denounced our friendship.

If you ever want to write and tell me the boundaries I've crossed, maybe that would explain more. I have never wanted anything from you. Just your friendship was enough, more than I had hoped for. And I am not looking for a quick fix. My hope is in God working through me. I know full well that I've created my own problems and with God's help I will work through them all. Thank you for all you shared with me over the past months. I will pray for you to forgive me.

I never expected anything from you. I asked for a picture, but there was no malicious intent in that request. I'm sorry you don't want to meet me, and I will not write anyone per- sonally from prison again. I trust you and shared more hon- estly with you than with any other, ever. It was a risk I was willing to take, and I'm glad I did, because it has helped me to grow. I thank you for your help and all you shared with me. I accept you as you are. I continue to see you as God does: a pure Christian woman.

Love in Christ,

Roger

AUGUST 22, 2005

My friend Marilynne,

I know you have indicated you don't want letters from me but I am being prodded by God in my spirit to continue writing as a friend. God has shown me that our friendship is not about me and I need to move my motives and pride out of the way. I mean only to share what God puts on my heart. We had our first AA meeting last night and it was such a blessing. I have not seen a big book since I left Barron County last October. Six of us were able to obtain one and

I hope everyone can get one soon. The AA meetings were not held here for a while, so it is a real blessing to have them again.

Do you still plan to visit sometime? I guess I'm not sure where we stand, and if you will write or not. I really thought there were possibilities for us. At the very least we could keep encouraging each other in the Lord. I am sorry I acted the fool. I realize I have much healing and growing to do. I have an ache in my heart because I miss your letters and godly input, but God heals all things in His time.

I should be entering the OWI program in late January or early February. If the judge is in agreement, I will be released when I complete the program. Please pray that God's will be done in all this. You have helped me so much and I thank you for that.

In Christ,

Roger

SEPTEMBER 16, 2005

Dear Marilynne,

Hello, my friend. Greetings in the name of our Lord and Savior. O Lord, thou art my God; I will exalt thee, I will praise thy name; for thou hast done wonderful things; thy counsels of old are faithfulness and truth. (Isaiah 25:1). By him therefore let us offer the sacrifice of praise to God continually, that is, the fruit of our lips giving thanks to his name. (Hebrews 13:15).

I have received no letters from you and hope you will bless me with one in the near future, if time allows.

How is your garden? I am sure there is a lot of work reap- ing the crops you have planted. There is nothing better than fresh produce, which you lovingly cared for and nurtured. I pray everything else is going well for you.

We've had three AA meetings, and I look forward to our fourth one this Sunday. The guys who are coming in have brought big books for everyone and are trying to bring other AA-related materials in.

At my job, I've started to crochet. I've made two baby blan- kets and am making a sweater for a two- to-four-year-old now. It keeps my hands busy.

I am working on my character defects and ask God for help. I don't want to be caught with my lamp only half full of oil like five of the ten virgins in Matthew 25:1-12. It's so easy to be lured into complacency, thinking all is well in my life. I have much work to do. I'm so happy to have received an Amplified Bible from a church in New Hampshire I wrote to a few months ago. What a blessing. When I get out, I would like to get the NLT Life Recovery Bible.

I'm still working through the computer class as well. I've also been off depression meds for almost a year now and it seems like my thinking is clearer now. But I pray for even better days to come.

The spiritual recovery group (12-step based) has been help- ing me focus on God's priorities. There is hope for the blind and the lost.

And the Spirit and the bride say, Come. (Revelation 22:17). *Come unto me, all ye that labour and are heavy laden, and I will give you rest. Take my yoke upon you, and learn of me; for I am meek and lowly in heart: and ye shall find rest unto your souls. For my yoke is easy, and my burden is light.* (Matthew 11:28-30).

Friends in Christ Jesus,

Roger

SEPTEMBER 30, 2005

Dear Marilynne,

Thank you for writing. I read your letter with joy. I am await- ing my program review on Wednesday. Then, I will be trans- ferred to Winnebago or somewhere else. I have less than one year left and so much work to do to prepare for my release.

I am sorry I didn't respond earlier, but my sister from San Diego died of a heart attack last Tuesday. I got mail from my Aunt Lois a couple of months ago and she wrote to me as soon as she heard of my sister's death. I came here with- out my address book and was unable to write to most of my family. But God put it on Aunt Lois's heart to find out where I was (she didn't know I was in prison) and she called my brother and got my address. So I am connected with more family now. My aunt is so very much like my grandmother. It is amazing what God is doing in spite of where I am.

I am grateful that I am sober today and that I found out about my sister right way. Because of where I am in Christ today, I am not overwhelmed by her death. She's the first of us seven children to die, and though it is sad to lose a sib- ling, I am strengthened through Christ and AA. I will get through this in victory.

Love in Christ, Your friend,

Roger

OCTOBER 23, 2005

Marilynne,

Please forgive my tardy response. I had a sinus infection and was barely getting my work done. At last, my son in the Marines wrote to me. What a blessing! He is stationed in Iraq and has been there for about two months.

I am officially staffed to the OWI program in Winnebago and will start there the first of the year.

It was such a pleasure to hear from you. The trees are turning color here and I am so grateful to be alive with Christ as my cornerstone. It grieves me to see men here hurting so badly inside, without any hope. I reach as many as I can and try to plant seeds of God's love in their lives, but I have to leave the rest to God.

I received yarn from my sister for crocheting and now I've got to get to it. At my job we're making preemie hats and booties for the children's network.

Love in Christ,

Roger

NOVEMBER 16, 2005

Dear Marilynne,

I've had an interesting weekend. Sunday I was told to pack up to be transferred to my program at Winnebago via Dodge. So I packed up and took my things to the property department. The property officer said I could take my guitar to church and choir and then stop in after that to pick up my property for the transfer. When I got out of church it was too late to process my things, and on Monday, the Property Department didn't call me. Yesterday morning, I found out that Human Services put a hold on my transfer because they finally scheduled me to see the surgeon for my wrist.

So after saying good-bye to everyone, I didn't leave! God has something planned and I am listening for His guidance about what I should do. I will still go to Winnebago soon, and all will happen as God purposes and plans.

The good part of being here is I am working and will have more time to work with a young man who has been learn- ing bass guitar and Christian music from me. He has a Life Recovery Bible but hasn't used it in the last year he's had it. (We also go to AA together.) I encourage him to get into it, starting by looking up the references to the steps. It excites me to see his growth. When I moved to the unit in March, he was very cynical and rejected many people. But through playing Christian music and the recovery music God has given me, others have seen major changes in his life. All glory goes to God. I am so grateful

God uses me, even in my own recovery and healing process. What a glorious, unlim- ited Father we serve.

Many inmates were upset to hear a hold was put on my transfer and they didn't understand why I wasn't upset! How can I second-guess God's plan? God's timing is perfect. Where I am in this life does not matter, but where God is in my life does.

I will write to you once I get to my next location. I will be taken to Dodge Corrections for one to four days and then transferred to Winnebago. This will likely happen within thirty days.

Your friend in Christ,

Roger

December 13, 2005

Dear Marilynne,

I found out I will start the program on February 27. I also start a job cleaning the main offices and lobby this Thursday. There are only 15 jobs here for 160 inmates, so I know God is watching over me by providing this for me.

Stay strong through all things that may tempt you, and please know that I am interceding in prayer for you.

My son's battalion was attacked recently and ten soldiers died, but my son was spared. I don't know all the details of this but it emphasizes how very fragile our lives are. I pray for protec- tion for my son every day. We are part of God's army and we need to rise up for the cause God has called us to.

May you remember the reason for this season and may God bless you through this time of year.

Your friend,

Roger

December 19, 2005

Hello Marilynne,

Things are coming together! My completion date for the program that starts February 27 will be August 25, 2006, and I'll be released shortly after that.

At this point, I plan to return to Rice Lake where my employment and friends are. I will meet you there. I do believe if it's God will we can be close friends. To be honest, when you said we would never be more than friends, I was hurt. I know that I revealed way too much too fast, and I will not do that again. I still believe we are headed in the same direction and that the timing is right. But staying close to God is paramount for me and that includes sobriety, peace, hope, and all of God's promises for me that will come true.

I am playing guitar for church services and I go to church services too. I'm writing a song that talks about overcom- ers and victory, leaving circumstances behind, and walking victoriously with Christ.

Maybe we can finally meet when I get out. You are a good friend and I don't take that for granted.

Love in Christ,

Roger

January 17, 2006

Dearest Marilynne,

It is the pinnacle of my day to receive your letters. I will gladly help in any way possible to teach and encourage you on guitar. I might even be able to help from here. If there are specific songs you would like to learn, I can send you chords for them to get you started. There are many Christian cho- ruses that are wonderful and easy to start on and I know you will learn fast. My probation officer even asked me to give him lessons when I am released!

I got news today that I am starting my program on February 6 instead of February 27, which will move my release up by three weeks also. Praise the Lord!! I will be out in August instead of September.

In my reading, God brought me to Romans 13:11-13: *for now is our [my] salvation nearer than when we [I] believed. The night is far spent, the day is at hand: let us [me] therefore cast off the works of darkness, and let us [me] put on the armour of light. Let us [me] walk honestly, as in the day; not in rioting and drunkenness, not in chambering and wantonness, not in strife and envying* (KJV). How rich is the Word of God!

Thank you for your prayers, my friend. Know that I pray for your situation at home, protection, direction, peace, health, and prosperity. God knows the depths of your heart and He knows and answers our prayers.

All my love in Christ, Your friend, Roger

February 15, 2006

Dear Marilynne,

On the 14th I got called down to the captain's office and was informed that I am terminated from the D.A.C.C. program. They had reviewed the pre-sentence investigation in which I had disclosed some past act, and now D.A.C.C. staff deems me inappropriate for OWI treatment and is putting me at a higher-risk rating. I am in lockup at Oshkosh Correctional Center pending a placement review hearing. I am not being terminated for anything I've done wrong at D.A.C.C., but for what I confessed to doing thirty-six years ago.

I'll write more later.

Your friend,

Roger

FEBRUARY 16, 2006

Dear Marilynne,

I haven't gone before the PRC board yet. They are going to put me at a higher-risk rating but hopefully just minimum security. We never know what the future holds. I hope and pray you will continue to be part of my life recovery. Maybe it wouldn't hurt to be evaluated to eliminate any doubts. It sucks to have to do ten extra months, but I will make good use of my days and dig into my Bible studies even more. In this world, if any questions are raised about your integrity once you are in the Department of Corrections, you are automatically guilty. That's something for me to remember while I'm here and when I get out.

Since I haven't had my hearing, I don't know where I will go from here. But God will be with me wherever I am. If possi- ble I want to get closer to Rice Lake so I may get some visits. The worst-case scenario is that if I don't get AODA treatment here, I will do it when I'm released in June 2007.

If I can get moved to a work camp I will, and put away money for my release. Not everyone forgives, but God does. I will let you know more as soon as I find out what is going on.

I choose happiness today. My circumstances do not dictate how I choose to feel. Prison and temporary lockup are not nice, but I am happy I'm alive; I'm happy God is with me; I'm happy you write to me; I'm happy and grateful I have any friends at all; I'm happy for all of my children; and I'm happy I am changing every day. If I choose to, I can grow and learn from this experience and become even more trusting and God-dependent. I love God and all He has done for me. Six months is not long; sixteen months is not long. I will grow and mature through this time. God has everything under control.

Love,

Roger

FEBRUARY 26, 2006

Hi Marilynne!

I was staffed here to Oshkosh last Tuesday the 21st. They want me to be evaluated again, but I don't mind as long as I can be staffed to minimum status later this year. Oshkosh has many opportunities for credited courses. I know they have a culi- nary course, botanical gardening course, a computer course, and a woodworking course, among others.

I am still positive God is in control, and I am grateful for every day I have to grow in the knowledge of His Word and will for my life. There are times I want to be out of here, and that's when I stop and listen to what God is showing me.

Then I have to humble myself and realize He is right here with me. His Holy Spirit is in me, and if I have ears to hear, trust, and obey, He will show me what to say and do in every circumstance.

I got the jailers to find me a Bible three days ago. It's a King James New Testament and I am so grateful to have it. Let me repeat what I said in my last letter – I am so excited to hear how God is using you in your ministry. Please know you are in my prayers. You are a true blessing.

Congratulations on how much you are practicing guitar! I may well be taking lessons from you when I'm out! I started on bass guitar when I was ten and a half years old. The bass guitar was bigger than me. I started teaching myself regular guitar at thirteen years old. We played two or three nights a week when I was in my early teens. Now I just love to play and sing unto the Lord. I'll have my daughter send you a copy of some of my recordings from the 1970s. I do look for- ward to playing together with you one day. Keep up the good work.

I got word that as soon as the prison receives the papers from Madison – which is usually less than two weeks – I will be moved to "X" building, where all new inmates of Oshkosh go for orientation. I will do what I can to be released as God wills it.

Again, I am so pleased with your boldness in Christ, spread- ing His love and hope to all who are hungry for God's Word, and even to those who don't know it yet.

God's love to you,

Roger

MARCH 30, 2006

Dear Marilynne,

I was moved to general population on the 20th. I am staffed here at Oshkosh and will probably be here until my release date. I am taking the recommended programs. Oshkosh is twice as big as New Lisbon and offers more programs. My release date is June 19, 2007, but I will get out the Tuesday before, on June 12.

I know a few people here that were at New Lisbon with me, but it still takes awhile to re-adjust. Things will go well because God directs my path and I am in His will.

Happy birthday and God bless you as you enjoy your big day! Love in Christ,

Your friend,

Roger

APRIL 22, 2006

My dear Marilynne,

I have felt your struggles in my own spirit. Even though we are miles apart, I am with you and I pray for you. You are on track and you will have victory over smoking – I claim that in Jesus' name.

I sing in the choir here. It's a much different style of music – more of a gospel hip-hop style, but but very uplifting. This Monday, there is a banquet where the choir will sing. Being here, I realize I have an opportunity to move forward in Christ. There are so many who are lost in here. At times,

I don't feel adequate to be any kind of preacher, as there's much to be changed in my own life. I try to show others the love that God has extended to me. Maybe that will plant seeds to help all the wounded, twisted souls here in prison.

Your words jump off the paper at me and I wish there was more I could do. I know that prayer is effective and inter- cessory prayer is a strong and effective weapon against the Enemy.

I pray God's love will fill you to overflowing today and each day to come, that you will be empowered by the Holy Spirit, and that Satan will be under your feet. We have all the power of God at hand to more than conquer the Enemy.

Always your friend,
Roger

MAY 27, 2006

Dear Marilynne,

Greetings in the Lord! It's always good to hear from you. It sounds busy at your place, but it is good to take a day where you can catch up on sleep, if that's what you need. It's not something that's easy for me to do either. Even here when there is so much time, I don't sleep late. I get up at 6:00 a.m. every day and strive to use my time as God wills.

This institution didn't allow me to keep my guitar as when I was at D.A.C.C. I miss it, but I've found a man who allows me to play his guitar and I am helping him with chords. The hardest part of moving within the prison system is that it takes time to know who is okay and who is not. I don't hang out with those who are bad influences.

Congratulations on your upcoming sobriety date! Three years! That is so good. I know I feel much better not drink- ing. I think more clearly and can focus much better. There are things floating around here, but I'm happy to say I have not been tempted by any of them, even though I know the lengths I used to go to for a drink.

I signed up for AA meetings and continue in my Bible stud- ies and choir and church. There's not much else going on here. I look for miracles every day, and thank God for every- thing He's already done.

Your friend,
Roger

June 7, 2006

Dear Marilynne,

I'm so sorry to hear of your loss of your grandmother. Thank you for letting me know. It is so good that you are sober dur- ing this time, and I agree that God always prepares us for circumstances. I had a heavy burden for your grandmother before I sent you that last letter, and it's incredible how God places people in our hearts and minds so we can more effec- tively pray at the right time. Your grandmother sounds so wonderful. I am reminded of my own grandmother. As I may have told you before, she is the only one who displayed unconditional love towards me growing up, and I think my love for God is due to her involvement in my life. It's such a precious gift to have a God-filled grandmother.

I know this is a time of sorrow and I bear that sorrow with you, but as John 16:20 says, our grief will turn to joy. I have peace when I think of my grandmother in heaven and the joy it will bring to see her again. You have so many precious memories of your grandmother. Though it's hard to lose loved ones, we know their suffering is ended. No more death, sorrow, or pain! It is a joy to know what lies ahead after our mortal death. The lyrics to "I'll Fly Away" come to mind: When this life is over, we will fly away to God's celestial shores!

I am so glad you are on the track of recovery. While it's painful to have death come to those we hold dear, isn't it wonder- ful that we can go through the day without drinking to cope with our sorrow? I will be lifting you up in prayer through this time.

Until I hear from you, know I am with you in spirit.

All my love through Christ our Lord and Savior,

Roger

June 14, 2006

Dear Roger,

Thank you for the card and your prayers. Today I am going to cut up some more wood. It's pretty cool out right now, so I want to get some done before the heat gets to me.

I look forward to your letters. The last couple days I have been at a loss for words, but I want to say that I pray you are as true to God as your words imply. I see a bright and won- derful future for you and a great ministry for the Lord as He leads you. Just think of how far Christ has brought you from one and a half years ago to now. I believe He wants you ready for a bright future serving Him and Him alone – not man or bottle or anything. I really believe He is working on a plan. The thing is, now I'm sure I'm in it.

I've learned a lot since that duel-out about our relationship. This is what it comes down to – I'm no better than the next person, but I think God is doing a pretty good job of mold- ing me into His image. Every day, I'm a new person and I will continue to wait upon Him and delight in His renewed strength in me.

So while we are waiting upon the Lord, we need to be about our Father's business here on earth – do you agree?

May God restore you seven times seventy.

Talk to ya later,
Marilynne

June 20, 2006

My dear Marilynne,

I t's my turn to thank you for the Father's Day card. That was very nice of you. I certainly didn't expect it.

So much has changed in my time of correctional confine- ment. Every day I have the opportunity to grow in God. What a joy to see His love and acceptance! I am very serious about being true to God. I'm far from perfect, but God gives me every opportunity to change. He is helping me accept who I am, what is in the past, what I should work on now, and how to forgive myself. I believe that no growth is pos- sible if we can't let go of what's in our past.

I was moved by your letter. Yes indeed, our Father's busi- ness should be in all that we do and say (Luke 2:49). I need to remember that at all times. I can't say it's any harder to be a Christian here. It's obvious when I'm wrong, as all my actions are seen here, just like God sees them all. Here there is no hiding. When I sin, with wrong words or actions, it's heavy on my spirit. Since there are many around here that curse and live rebellious lifestyles, I have to pay strict atten- tion to my own attitudes and actions every day. I am in prayer for many things and I know God listens and is always faithful.

I received a job on my unit as a "center utility worker." I work with the food line three days a week, and I also clean showers. I get paid at the pay rate of "2" or nineteen cents per hour. It is a real blessing as I can buy shampoo and laundry tokens with my earnings. There is so much to be grateful for if I just listen to God and watch as prayers are answered all around me.

I am getting closer to approval for getting my guitar sent back. There is a new guy overseeing the music purchases, so hopefully, I'll see him in the next day or so to get pre- approval to get the guitar sent in. This is a miracle because guitars have to be new, and I would normally not be able to have my guitar sent back, but would have had to re-order a new one.

There are steps I am working on in a continuous cycle. With my participation in the programs offered right now, I am looking at all areas in my past and making amends to those I have offended by neglect or insult because of my addictions and drinking. At times it's overwhelming, and that's why your letters help so very much. I receive so much encourage- ment and hope from them. I thank God for your friendship.

I am on the waiting list for the AODA Telios Residential Program, and if I do it here, I will start sometime in October. It's fifteen weeks long. If for any reason I can't do it while in here, I'm sure my probation officer will have me in one when I'm released. The probation officer can also order me into programs upon release or any time when on probation.

I have made some very good Christian friends while here and it's good to encourage each other through the daily trials here.

All my love in Christ Jesus,

Roger

JUNE 27, 2006

Dear Roger,

I am at a loss for words today since my spirit has an unusual calm about everything. In my last letter to you I could feel the Holy Spirit leading in every word I wrote. The anxiety I had has finally became calm. I believe it is because of God's purpose and my obedience.

Last week, I could have gone to speak somewhere and the Spirit was telling me to do so. I put it off. The next day a still- louder voice told me I could still go, and once again I blew it off and didn't go. But all I could think about was, "I wonder who needed a word so bad that they might have heard from me." I felt guilty for not doing what I was led to do, so I asked God to forgive me and to give whoever it was another chance to hear what God wanted them to hear – if not from me, then from someone else.

I hope and pray I will not make the choice to say "no" to God again. I'm not good at speaking to crowds, but that is exactly what God is leading me to do. I want to do God's will and I must trust that there is nothing to fear when I obey Him.

Where do we go from here? I don't know, but God is in control. Before, falling in love came with a set of rules to do it my way. But my way only brought all kinds of sin with it. God has renewed my mind, like it says in Ephesians.

We need to talk about when to meet face to face. While everything, including our meeting, is in God's timing, I believe we need to have it set up just in case the time does come. We both have a lot of growing in the Lord to do, but we both know that what we have is based on the Lord, not on looks, sex, or actions. That is a good thing.

Love in Christ Jesus,

Marilynne

June 29, 2006

Dear Marilynne,

I know when the time is right you will come and I will place no expectations on when. If you visit two days in a row (again, not expected), it seems like late Friday and early Saturday could be a good choice, so you can get back home before nightfall. I don't know your schedule, but anything works for me. I'm a rather captive audience (ha ha!), but I am free inside like never before. All praise and glory belongs to Christ our Lord. What a mighty, awesome, and incredible God we serve. He can breathe life into a man and woman that the world would judge or despise.

As you and I stay in God's will, I believe He will continue to bless and restore us. My prayers are more and more of Him and less of me. That's the only way to ever be at true peace.

I will await your reply, my dear Marilynne. Recently, God reminded me of part of the promises that AA speaks of – if I move out of the way, God will do what I cannot do myself, and because of this, I am experiencing new joy and happi- ness that I've never known before.

All the peace, love, and joy to you in Christ Jesus,

Love from your friend,

Roger

July 7, 2006

My dear Marilynne,

What a joy to finally see you face to face! I only wish it could have been longer, but all in God's time, right? You have incredible eyes and I really love your hair. It is finally nice to know what you look like in person. I think of you now more than ever, and I really didn't think that was possible! I apologize for not being shaven. I love the fact that you can be spontaneous – thank you for the hug! It's the first hug I've had since March 2004, and I'm glad it came from you. Meeting like this was very different and I would have liked it to be in a different setting. I'm sorry you were uncomfort- able, but anyone would be. I am so glad you came.

What did you think of me? First impressions mean a lot. I can't wait to be out so we can see each other, talk, and answer all the questions on our hearts. I think God has excellent taste in match-making, and I will wait on Him as our relationship matures, allowing Him to show me what else needs to change. Make no mistake, I am serious about serving God and my feelings are serious about you. I will listen to guidance from God and you to prevent any possible offense or sin that would separate me from God or from you.

Love in Christ,

Roger

July 30, 2006

Dear Marilynne,

I don't have any real questions about what you have shown me in the Scriptures you sent. I spend time in the Word, but I don't have the Life Recovery Bible as you do. I have the

Life Application Bible which has excellent study notes. I will remain in the Word and listen to what God says to me, fol- lowing His will for my life. Thank you for your input. Please realize that I listen to all you suggest and try to stay focused on what is important for recovery and growth.

I pray every morning, evening, and throughout the day as God brings you to mind. I only pray for God's will for you and your life. I remain your friend in Him.

Love in Christ,

Roger

P.S. Got my guitar!

SEPTEMBER 26, 2006

Dear Marilynne,

Hello my friend. I thought I should write and let you know what's going on. First, I am being interviewed for the next AODA program, which will start in October. It's fifteen weeks long and ends in February. I may be released soon after comple- tion, but I will leave that to God's leading as to when it's best for me to get out. There is a grant called Act 109 for Truth-In- Sentencing inmates, which would release me after 75% of my time is served, if the judge agrees. Actually, I already have the eligible time served (June 23, 2004, to September 26, 2006, is slightly over three-quarters of the time). My lawyer said that unless the AODA program is completed, the judge probably would not allow me out. So I am happy I can get into the next group, which will also help prepare me for release. I will suc- ceed and only God deserves the glory for that. Any confidence I have is from God and my hope is secure in Him.

I've prayed very hard to receive the Life Recovery Bible and God is always faithful to fulfill our prayers. An inmate I was talking to told me that he'd written to the chapel requesting a King James Bible with Jesus' words in red. I asked him what the chapel sent him and he said that he'd received the Life Recovery Bible! I just happened to have the Bible he was look- ing for (leather-bound KJV with Jesus' words in red) and so we exchanged Bibles. That was such an incredible blessing. Now if you have passages you feel would benefit me, I have the LRB to look it up! All good things come to those who trust and wait on the Lord.

Love in Christ,

Roger

OCTOBER 12, 2006

Dear Roger,

I haven't forgotten about you, I just haven't felt much like writing or talking.

You have a huge praise going on there now. About two weeks before you got your Recovery Bible, I got a magazine that has offers to buy Christian books. I thought of having the Recovery Bible sent directly to you. I said to God, "Roger could sure use that Bible right now." Then you wrote me and, wow! You've got one! Some people would say that's freaky, but I say, what an awesome God who answers the smallest of prayers. You can just imagine my gratefulness to God when I received your letter.

By now you're either in the program or you're getting ready to start it. If you can take each step one at a time and write down whatever God reveals to you, this helps greatly. It took me a year to finish all twelve steps, but I see the way God worked in my life to get me ready for where I am now.

I haven't gone to speak in three weeks, but I need to go tomorrow even if I don't want to. It's not about me but about what God wants to do through me.

Thanks to the person that traded Bibles with you. May God bless him.

Your friend in Christ, Marilynne

OCTOBER 29, 2006

Dear Marilynne,

The clocks go back tonight. Seven months to go. It looks like the work is up to me since I did not get into the AODA group and won't have enough time to complete the one after this.

God is always good and blesses me with peace of mind. I feel assured that I can succeed with God's guidance, working through the steps with His Holy Word. I've been through treatments, and when I focus on what needs to be changed, God gives me the strength and wisdom to complete the task (1 Corinthians 10:13).

God is so wonderful to me. I feel the changes He has made, and I know that He loves us so much that He accepts us where we are and lead us to where He wants us to be. One good thing is I got a job as lead line server. Now I make twenty-six cents an hour instead of nineteen cents. That comes out to ten dollars more per month – every little bit helps.

I want to encourage you to share your story, faith, and all God has brought you through. I am so very proud of you, my dear, precious friend, and I really want you to fully realize how much I care about you and all you go through every day. Every trial, every temptation, every bad dream, every victory, every triumph, I am on your side, Marilynne, as a prayer partner and friend.

Love from your friend, Roger

NOVEMBER 2, 2006

Dear Roger,

Thank you for the special gift. I am amazed at your handi- work. Do you sew also? When my son was younger he decided he wanted to learn to crochet. It took awhile, but he got the concept, stuck with it, and made a scarf. I encouraged him to start another, but by then he didn't want to learn any- more. He took sewing in school and made a quilt, which I still have. But much changes in life as our abilities grow and we seek out possibilities. *For this God is our God for ever and ever: he will be our guide even unto death.* (Psalm 48:14).

Your friend,

Marilynne

NOVEMBER 13, 2006

Dear Marilynne,

I should have written sooner, but I wanted to send this cross I made (which took longer than I expected). I am so happy that you like the hat, scarf, and mittens. I must deeply thank you for the beautiful card – I love birch trees – as well as the prayer and articles. You have greatly blessed me at a time when I really needed it. I have great expectations as my release draws nearer, and we will see each other and spend time together. God is so good! I finally got on the list to attend AA meetings and am allowed to go to two, Wednesday nights and Friday mornings. This is extremely rare as normally inmates are only allowed to attend one meeting of the three available. So I am very happy!

On another note, be encouraged, Marilynne. I totally relate to the feeling of despair after you speak. The Devil knows how important your ministry of speaking is, and it's mak- ing a tremendous impact on those you minister to. He tries every means possible to bring you down, but be encouraged, because the Devil is under your feet, and God is on your side. He will always provide the strength needed to keep Satan under you. Bruise Satan's head with your heel and claim the victory. You are an overcomer and victorious over all earthly situations. God always gives us the protection, so rejoice, and again I say, rejoice! All things are possible. As we believe, we need to believe big, because we serve an incred- ible and extremely large God. Hallelujah!

All my love in Christ who strengthens me, Roger

NOVEMBER 16, 2006

Hello Roger,

Thank you for the card and the cross. Both are appreciated. God is awesome and is doing great things in my life, as He will continue to do in yours as well. The Lord has taken me through the valley once again and victory has been won, but it will be glorious to be done with this human nature, in the presence of heaven praising God.

A song comes to mind about what we will do when we see Jesus. "Will I be able to speak at all? Will I fall to my knees and worship?" And on and on. What a day that will be when I see Jesus.

In the meantime, I will stay separate from the world but be a witness for God, obedient to Him in whatever I do. The Lord's calling on my life is bigger than speaking. I believe He is preparing me for much greater things that just this. To be honest, I have a vision to reach more people, but it scares me a bit. He is molding me for His work, both now and in the future. I want to help people in their distress, and to see them saved, free from the bondage I used to be in.

Your calling is right in front of you for now and you are being prepared for when you get out. Your music is going to be a great testimony and in fact, it already is. So many are hungry for God but in denial, as we once were. But God knows the heart. God calls each person according to His purpose for their lives.

Hunting season is here and from bow to gun, my son has been more than ready. He already put one deer in the freezer and donated another to a friend in need of food. Saturday is open gun day and he's ready.

Write soon. Keep your faith in God and praise Him daily.

Friends through Jesus,

Marilynne

NOVEMBER 27, 2006

Dear Marilynne,

I pray every day for God's guidance and wisdom in all I do and say, and I pray the same for you. I want God to use you as He sees fit. Today, I am at step one, as I see areas of my life I am still powerless over. I know God will do for me what I cannot do on my own, if it's His will. I've come far from where I used to be, but I'm not looking for half steps. I'm looking for complete deliverance from anything that hinders my walk with Christ.

The song you referenced is called "I Can Only Imagine" and I sing it for you with all of my being. It is so expressive and

I am left speechless at the thought of finally being with our Lord. What a glorious day it will be. When things, people, and more try to press me down, God lifts me above all things as I listen to His words and commandments. You, my friend, are so right when you mentioned that God is going to use you very much. Your life will bring healing and restoration to millions of people as you share your testimony and speak and walk in God's will. I know this from what God has shown me.

Love in Christ,

Roger

DECEMBER 1ST, 2006

Marilynne,
I would like to share the following poem with you:

He is God

*H*e *is the first and the last, the beginning and the end! He is the keeper of creation and the Creator of all!*
He is the architect of the universe and the manager of all times.
He always was, He always is, and He always will be, Unmoved, Unchanged, Undefeated, and never Undone!
He was bruised and brought healing! He was pierced and eased pain!
He was persecuted and brought freedom! He was dead and brought life!
He is risen and brings power! He reigns and brings peace!
The world can't understand Him; the armies can't defeat Him! The schools can't explain Him, and the leaders can't ignore Him. Herod couldn't kill Him; the Pharisees couldn't confuse Him, And the people couldn't hold Him! Nero couldn't crush Him; Hitler couldn't silence Him; the New Age can't replace Him, And Oprah can't explain Him away!
He is LIGHT, LOVE, LONGEVITY, and LORD.
He is goodness, kindness, gentleness, and GOD.
He is Holy, Righteous, Mighty, Powerful, and Pure.
His ways are right; His Word is eternal.
His will is unchanging, and His mind is on me.

He is my Savior, He is my guide, and He is my peace! He is my joy, He is my comfort,
He is my Lord, and He rules my life!
I serve Him because His bond is love, His burden is light, And His goal for me is abundant life. I follow Him because He is the wisdom of the wise, the power of the powerful,
The Ancient of Days, the ruler of rulers, the leader of leaders, The overseer of the overcomers, and is to come.
And if that seems impressive to you, try this on for size! His goal is a relationship with me! He will never leave me, Never forsake me, never mislead me, never forget me,
Never overlook me, never cancel my appointment in His appointment book!
When I fall, He lifts me up! When I fail, He forgives!
When I am weak, He is strong! When I am lost, He is the way!
When I am afraid, He is my courage! When I stumble, He steadies me!
When I am broken, He mends me! When I am blind, He leads me!
When I am hungry, He feeds me! When I face trials, He is with me!
When I face persecution, He shields me! When I face problems, He comforts me!
When I face loss, He provides for me! When I face death, He carries me home!
He is everything for everybody, everywhere, every time, and every way.
He is God.
He is faithful. I am His, and He is mine!
My Father in heaven can whip the father of this world.
So if you're wondering why I feel so secure, understand this . . . He said it and that settles it.
God is in control. I am on His side,
*And that means all is well with my soul. Every day is a blessing, for **God is!***

Marilynne, our meeting is not coincidence. I believe everything we have been through had a small part in preparing us for the future together, you and me in God. He is a God who can take two imperfect people to make a perfect match. He can make a couple that will encourage one another through all trials, stand together as one in Christ Jesus, and share all the joys God has in store as we live in Him. Filled up, pressed down, and overflow- ing with love and happiness in God and us.

All my love through Christ, Roger

December 11, 2006

Dear Roger,

I was reading today's message and would like to share it with you. Hebrews 8:12 says, *their sins and their iniquities will I remember no more.* God is perfect in every way, but in His grace will not remember our sins, and will erase our fears.

This reassuring promise from God eases my heart, soul, and mind. It is so comforting to know that God is a God of sec- ond chances, though others are not so willing to let go of the wrongs we've done.

It sounds like I will need to call you "Grandpa" soon. Congratulations! What a blessing to have heirs in life. Maybe you'll be able to be a part of their lives in God's time.

By now, you are probably on step two. Remember to ask for God's forgiveness in each step. *Trust in the Lord with all thine heart; and lean not unto thine own understanding* (Proverbs 3:5). I pray that all you learn from God in each step takes you to the freedom of complete deliverance for the rest of your life. Whatever happens with us when you get out, always put God first in everything you do and say.

Have a Merry Christmas. I pray that God will comfort you during this season and bless you in the New Year.

Your friend,

Marilynne

JANUARY 5, 2007

Hello Roger,

I woke up this morning with you on my mind. I hope every- thing is going well and that your faith in the Lord is strong today.

Happy New Year! I spent New Year's Eve at church. We had a service with praise and worship time afterwards. We brought the new year in with the song, "We Have a Mighty

God." That is exactly what He is – mighty and wonderful in all things. I am still getting used to the new me in Christ and the difference from the old life I lived. It shows that nothing is gained without the sacrifice of self. It seems I have a smok- ing demon trying to stay on board, but I know Jesus can take this away. All I need to do is give my life over to the will of God. It sounds easy compared to all the Lord has already done. In this case, it's easier said than done. I can't explain it, nor do I understand it. One thing is for sure, I'm not giving up until I am set free, no matter how much time it takes. I just thought I'd share with you what I am facing today.

Here's a testimony of God's way: at church on New Year's Eve, I testified about the mission the Lord has given to me in speaking to others who have no hope. Later that evening, a man that is new to the church asked if I did public speaking. Of course, I said not really, just every Wednesday. He asked if I was the one who gives out notebooks with a word of prayer. To my surprise, he had gotten one of those notebooks – it had changed his life and it gave him hope.

It goes to show that we never know where our testimony can help someone discover a new beginning. You know, it's awesome when we obey God's will in our lives. I don't know what my future holds, but God does, and this was a way God has worked with me. This Wednesday, I didn't have any fear or excuses for not testifying. It's amazing. The Lord's will in my life is awesome and I believe He is getting me ready for His work now, more than ever.

You also have an awesome testimony, and I know that God is using you, both now and later. Keep your mind and soul open to God to clearly know His calling in your life. Beyond dreams and visions, God is always in control. His plan for each person's life is already established according to His purpose.

Your time will be done before you know it, so I pray the Lord will give you insight about His purpose for your new life and new beginning. Stay strong in God's strength. May His wisdom lead you into His divine understanding, renewing you in mind, body, and spirit. *Without faith it is impossible to please Him* (God) (Hebrews 11:6). Faith as a mustard seed can and will move mountains. Be of good courage and dili- gently seek God's face, power, and instruction.

Thank the Lord for His many blessings and may His prom- ises fill you with overwhelming grace and mercy. Our God is awesome and mighty.

I believe everything happens for a reason and all in God's season. You've been in prison because I believe that's where God could reach you the best. I believe everyone deserves a second chance. The Lord gives many more chances than we would. I used to be the person that said, "My way, my wants, mine, mine, mine." My way only led to destruction, but each time I was given another chance. It takes a lot to give our- selves completely to God, to realize He can do a much better job in our lives. We cannot do anything right unless God is in complete control.

In all things seek God. He is all-powerful in everything, and that covers all our concerns.

May the Lord bless you and keep you,

Marilynne

January 6, 2007

Dear Marilynne,

I got your letter on the 3rd. What a blessing to hear from you. This Sunday I am sharing some of the message, and the inmate that has been organizing the service has asked me to take over since he is leaving soon. I've been playing guitar at the service and sharing some songs, and it is all such a blessing. There are many negative people here, but I pray for them and lift them up to God for only He can change them. I ask God that they change what they need to so they don't fall into the Devil's snares. I ask God for His guidance and wis- dom in all I say and do to be a blessing and encouragement to those who aren't saved.

There is much I'm not sure about when I get out. The Department of Vocational Rehabilitation should pay part of my tuition, and I may have funds available because I was in prison. There will be ways to help as long as they know I'm sincere in my change and commitment to live a new life. I will always have to deal with my past with people I meet, but I know that true friends will see what I am now. If I'm living for Christ, that should be enough. It's a miracle that I am even alive today, and all the glory belongs to God for that.

Be encouraged and blessed, Marilynne. I will be praying for you every day, my friend.

Love in Christ,
Roger

JANUARY 9, 2007

Dear Marilynne,

Thank you for your letter. You are intertwined in my three- fold desire: to do God's will, to know God and myself bet- ter; and to know you more and help you as God guides, and we develop a deeper friendship. I feel our friendship is deepening. I want you to be honest with me and for me to feel mature enough in Christ to hear anything you say and appropriately respond to it.

I am praying hard and long for my total deliverance from anything that separates me from God, as it also separates me from recovery, relationships, and freedom. I pray mul- tiple times a day for your deliverance from smoking, fears, and the trials you face. There's no way to overcome anything without releasing it to God, as He has the power to dissolve anything to nothingness.

God is so good. I am grateful for the gentleman who shared with you how positively rich and life-changing your ministry is. You have gifts that flow out of you through Christ that are life-giving. Keep sticking to it for God's glory.

I am trying to un-focus on my fleshly desires (food, comfort, and more), as all are self-serving. I get down and moody at times. When I really look at what I'm not doing about it – like giving it to God or being grateful for all He's done – I am spurred into action to do what I can. Many have it worse here and some might have it better, but nothing changes in any of my situations until I first adjust my attitude to gratitude or, better yet, to a Christ-minded state of freedom. Remember 1 Corinthians 10:13 and stand on it. I have said this as encouragement to breathe life into all areas of attack in our lives. The Bible is our foundation, so we need to stand firm on the Word of God.

Love in Christ,

Roger

JANUARY 24, 2007

Hello Roger,

I hope everything is going well for you and that your strength in the Lord keeps growing.

I have been overwhelmed with a lack of desire to do any- thing until yesterday. What a terrible place I have been in, not even able to speak to God or praise Him. I don't know how I would have made it without a few words of encourage- ment from a person from church. She called a couple of days ago because I hadn't attended church since New Year's. It was the first time in three years I've missed so many Sundays in a row. I didn't want to talk or even listen, but she's persis- tent. I haven't shared my struggles with anyone, but she just gave a seed of thought and God took it from there.

I praise God that I didn't fall into a place of destruction but took heed to instruction. God is good, and today grateful- ness and mercy are on my side. She had great concern for me and with good reason. Even though she doesn't know what

I was facing, God did. This may sound out of character, but I was even trying to hide from God, trying to get away from everything and everyone. When nothing worked, God came to my rescue. I tried to stay in bed to not smoke, and depres- sion set in. Peace, joy, and thankfulness were leaving me quickly. But I realize I can't run and I can't hide, and I don't want to go there again.

Mercy came running and I've grabbed it, praying for grace. It's not that I relapsed or went back to my old ways. It was all about trying too hard in the wrong ways to quit a nasty habit that won't steal what Jesus has given to me.

I'm okay now. I know I'll be all right and everything will fall into place. God's plan, His timing, His everything. I am His.

Your days probably seem to be getting longer and your time is shorter. Know this: God is our only source of strength.

His great mercy and grace are sufficient for everyone. I know God has great plans for your life and I pray you stay focused on Jesus when you step out of the boat. Peter had the faith to walk on water until he took his eyes off Jesus. Someone recently told me that we start to sink when we look away or think we can do it alone.

I'll write more later.

Friends through Christ Jesus,

Marilynne

January 27, 2007

My dear friend Marilynne,

Thank you for your letter. I knew in my spirit that there was something wrong, and I've had you constantly in prayer for a few weeks. Thank the dear lady from church for me, and I thank God for her persistence and love.

You are a very, very important vessel of God, and I would like you to know that I will always stand in the gap on your behalf, whether or not I know what's going on at the time. Remember that the Devil has no authority, no power, and no right to attack you. You belong to God. Hold on and stand on His Word for deliverance. Suffering may last for a day, but joy cometh in the morning (Psalm 30:5). You are in continual growth and nothing can separate you from God's love.

Love in Christ,

Roger

February 1, 2007

Dear Roger,

Thank you for your letter as always. God's ways are not ours. His thoughts are not the same as ours. His timing is always right. God knows our every thought. I used to think about invasion of privacy when I thought about His knowing my thoughts. Today I pray that my thoughts are pure and righ- teous as the Spirit leads me into a new season of purpose.

It's great that you will be taking the college course now, and it would be great for you to be able to get into an AODA program. I know Barron has starter classes, but if you can find one place to take all the credits, that would be great. I thought I would get myself going on classes in Barron, but my desire to do so has left. It doesn't seem to be what God intends for me.

I can't recall which Recovery Bible you have. Mine is the Life Recovery Bible, New Living translation. It doesn't really mat- ter as long as you are not just going through the motions but really getting what you need to get out of it. Do you know what I mean?

It took me a year to go through all twelve steps, to really get all the old stuff out of my heart, soul, and mind and bring in the new. Maybe I need to start over to be sure I didn't miss something.

Isn't God great? Sometimes a bit of a valley isn't so bad.

At least I can say that now. I really don't like those times, though.

I think I am more on a countdown than you are. Five months to go. Wow. You've come a long way, and I am glad to be a part of your recovery. May God stay first in all that you do.

If you decide to go to college, is there a program to set you up with housing and finances? I don't know how things work for people who had to serve time. Let me know. I know that all things work together for good for those who love the Lord and are called according to His purpose. If this is God's purpose, then no man can stand in the way – God will make the way.

As for material things, I can help you out when you get out in your place, wherever that may be. Are you still working there? I think it would be good for you to finish the steps before you are released. Stay focused!

May the Lord bless you and keep you strong in faith. May your strength be renewed daily through Jesus Christ. May God do His will in your life. Stand strong and firm on the Word of life. God spoke the world into place, and He will speak your life into place also.

Friends,

Marilynne

FEBRUARY 8, 2007

Hi Marilynne,

I talked to the social worker here, but I really don't know where I'll be allowed to go when I'm released. I am going to finish this twelve-week course in preparation to attend col- lege, but I don't know where I can go. The probation officer controls all those decisions, but God will make a way if it's His will. For my part, I will be ready. I will probably go to a temporary living program; there's one in Rice Lake that keeps you until you have enough to rent an apartment.

I want to get this card and rose to you, praying that you are more blessed and happy every day.

Love in Christ,

Your friend,
Roger

February 10, 2007

Dear Marilynne,

I pray that you like the rose I sent. I sent it in God's love and as a symbol of our friendship, with no expectations. The red rose is significant as I see God's love represented in the color red. He gave His only Son to bear our scars and red signifies the blood Jesus shed for us. Red is also a symbol of the respect I hold for you as a friend. Red is also a symbol of courage. I see so much courage in your walk with God. For example, I see it when you speak to groups, sharing true sobriety and the joy and happi- ness only Christ can bring into our lives as we submit to His authority.

Finally, red is a symbol of the passion we express in our lives for the things we love. I see the passion and desire in your letters to serve God and do His will. I can feel your commitment to Christ leap off the pages when I read your letters.

There was a pastor that told me a few years ago that a con- densed version of the Bible is found in Romans 6, 7, and 8. There's a lot to be found in those chapters, but it has been hard for me to digest. I know I need to continue submitting to God and listen to what He wants for me through His Word. I am very excited to hear of your speaking to and inspiring others.

I am anxious to get out but I know I need every moment here to prepare for what God wants me to do when I'm released. There is much uncertainty, but I must trust God completely and con- centrate on my inner man.

God bless you, Marilynne, and may His love ever surround you.

Love in Christ,

Roger

February 26, 2007

Dear Roger,

I'm back from vacation and it seems as though I need another one. We went to Epcot, MGM Studios, and Walt Disney World where we had a family picnic. I enjoyed the day of the picnic most of all. My brother and his wife both work for Disney. They made the meal and planned the day at the park. My dad showed up and we enjoyed the day. We went on paddle-boats and saw live alligators just a few feet away. I enjoyed most of my time with my niece and nephews, but I'm glad to be home now.

I've gone through some depression recently. I finally went to church yesterday and quit hiding from God. It's hard to explain on paper where I was at, but God is again number one in my life and I am ready for Him to keep molding me.

The dirt of sin was in the way, but by God's grace, mercy, and my repentance and renewing of my mind, He has given a spirit full of peace and comfort.

Sin is sin, no matter how small. It's dirt, and I never thought going to a casino would put so much dirt in the clay (that's me) to break me down to nothing in so many ways. What I thought at first was harmless almost cost me my future with God. Bitterness, depression, and anxiety about gambling all defeated me.

I was giving up to give in to the world and all that God had freed me from. Praise the Lord that my heart did not harden to self-will and selfish desires, which would have meant complete destruction. A speaker from Onalaska with God's wisdom brought forth a message only God could have given in my time of need. That morning, at first I didn't go forward for prayer, but still the tears fell where I sat. There was no victory until the evening service, which set the words of God in place for my life. The message in both services fit exactly where I was. God isn't done with this vessel. I humbled myself at the feet of Jesus and cried.

Just when I felt I was about to give up and walk through life as I did before, God came to my rescue, but still left the choice to yield or become hardened. Thank God for the church He has put me in. A new day, and another step in this life of His promises.

I'm telling you this so that you stand firm against the wiles of the Devil and know that God is still molding you into the vessel He has intended from the beginning.

Where are you in the steps now? How is school prep going? Have you heard any good news about your release? What programs will you have to finish when you get out? Will you need transportation to where you're going when you're released?

You've come a long way in the past two years. Let God lead you and direct you. Open your heart and mind to His ways and lean not on your own wisdom and understanding. Our ways are not God's ways. Only God knows best what we need. He supplies all according to His glory and honor.

Friends because of Christ Jesus,

Marilynne

MARCH 3, 2007

My dear Marilynne,

Warm weather is in sight and the snow will soon be gone. I knew you were in a rough spiritual time before you wrote, as God had me on my knees in prayer for you. Even when I don't know what others are going through specifically, I know God is faithful to hear our prayers and cries of pain and need. Only God can truly meet those deep needs.

I am taking two more classes in addition to the back-to- college class. One is four days a week about re-integration. It will answer all my questions about release and help provide documents such as a birth certificate, and a social security card. The other class connects me to the job center network and résumé preparation. I am grateful for anything that better prepares me for my release.

I don't have anyone committed to providing transportation, but I am not sure of my destination or whether my probation officer will pick me up. I will know very soon (within thirty days) and you will be the first one I write to. If you don't object, I may call you one day soon toll-free and talk to you briefly. Before long, I look forward to seeing you face to face, my friend.

Your friend who loves you through Christ,

Roger

MARCH 31, 2007

Dear Marilynne,

Happy birthday, my friend! I hoped to hear from you before I sent this, but I'll update you about where my probation officer is considering sending me. I talked to him last Monday. He said that since I don't have a residence lined up or finances to secure an apartment, I will probably go to Triniteam Halfway House, which is in Eau Claire.

I am so looking forward to getting out, and the halfway house is not a bad option. I will be able to get treatment, obtain employment, get plugged in to a church, and get a place to live when I've saved enough. I will not know until I get out if my probation will transfer to Eau Claire County, as many want to move there for employment. I am leaving the big things to God and asking for His wisdom in how to prepare each day.

I hope to see you and pray that we grow closer in friendship when I'm out. It may not be easy, but I know God has a plan and I will be obedient to His will. It's exciting to finally be nearing my release date. I am on step eight now. Step five was the hardest one, but the most cleansing. I have very far to go, and I am grateful for God's love and mercy to see me through the valleys.

Please let me know how it's going. I pray for you multiple times a day.

Your friend, Roger

APRIL 3, 2007

Dear Roger,

How are things going? Are you still preparing for your release? Have you found out anything more? I am doing okay. I have cut down my speaking to once a month. I push myself to go, but after I leave I always have a good sense of how it went. It still takes all I've got to go. I still don't like speaking in front of people, but I know it is what God wants because of the way I feel after I leave. I wonder if I'll ever get used to it or have a greater desire to do it. I don't know.

I am happy that you will have a chance to start over, and it won't be long from now. I believe you've changed and I give God credit where it is due. The true light is where we go on our journey. We must not give up on God's promises and never try and hide from Him to satisfy self. I believe that is the key to staying victorious in Jesus. We put Jesus first in all things. That's where I've fallen, but I'm not going stay there because I know God's grace is sufficient for me, even when I don't deserve it. You might say I've been waiting for God to harm me in some kind of way to straighten me out, but I've been told that isn't how He works.

The weather was so nice yesterday that I worked outside clearing brush and started a fire to burn it. Not a good idea since I didn't have a permit. The fire department came and I got a fine. The old me wanted to grab a drink then, even after all this time of being sober, which would be the worst idea ever. I had worked for eight hours and just when I finished, they showed up. I can't get away with anything.

Sunday's service was about where I've been in the past. But like the apostles, I'm leaving that behind. Do I want to be of the world? No. I've been there and nothing in it made the peace with God so real. God has taken me through so many things, and yet I hit this rocky place (dealing with an addiction to gambling) and just want to hide. I ask myself why I always have to get on my knees, but when I don't, I get hardened in spirit. Please take my advice: when you have a thought that isn't of God, from God, or for God, get rid of it immediately. Don't be like me – ignoring the Word of God for too long, and not letting the Spirit guide me.

Read the Word even when you don't feel like it. Choose to praise God when wrong thoughts come to your mind. These are the things I didn't do for so long. Sin is still sin even if it's only a thought.

Well, let me know what's going on and I will make it a part of my schedule to come to Eau Claire to see you.

Sincerely,

Marilynne

April 6, 2007

Dear Marilynne,

Please forgive my strong letters exposing my feelings for you. I really want you to know that I care for you first as a friend, and I am willing to back off and keep our lives separate, interacting only as friends.

I would still encourage you to speak to others as God leads you. It's hard for me to talk to large groups, but I can sing and play all night! I love singing to the Lord. It's a big part of who I am. Music has always been important to me, and since I dedicated it to Christ, it is a true blessing now.

I've completed the reintegration classes and finally got back into computer classes. I've been trying to reach who I can by phone to arrange a place to live in Rice Lake, but have had no success yet. My probation officer is considering Eau Claire initially upon my release. But I won't stay there if Eau Claire County doesn't take my case. There is public transportation and an AODA halfway house in Eau Claire, so it may be a wise move.

I have finally forgiven myself for what I did that put me in here. Those who were victims of what I did have also for- given me. I wasn't able to do this until I participated in the programs, so I know God wanted me in them.

I will be involved in AODA and other groups as appropriate, or as my probation officer directs. I'm never going to return to prison. My goal is first to please God in all things and carry a message of hope and encouragement to others who suffer. I need other people in my life and would like for you to continue to be one of my closest friends.

I will have major adjustments when I get out and start living again. I was spiritually and emotionally dead before I came to prison, and your input and friendship has helped me so much to get this far. This is a major transitional period in my life, and I will not allow fear to enter. God's wisdom and peace will rule so that I can be all He purposes me to be for Him.

I'll close for now.

Love in Christ,

Roger

April 17, 2007

Dear Roger,

Thank you for the birthday card. I feel like friendship is hard for me to obtain and keep, so I appreciate our friend- ship even more. Time will tell what God's plan is in the future for us.

Staying focused on God's plans for my life is a trial as I go through a valley of temptations. In Christ, I will rise above this, but I need to learn not to go around the same moun- tains again. Gambling is such a hard temptation to over- come, but with God's wisdom and strength I will get past this. I tend to be a disobedient person and choose the wrong things more than the right ones. If I just speak just the name of Jesus, sometimes that helps me to know that the battle with temptation can be won. Failing to do this takes me to a place where I can't see a good future. When the flesh and the spirit go to battle, I will either fall or rise to that which bonds me with Christ.

Me, myself, and I. What a bad combination without the Father, Son, and Holy Spirit. I am vulnerable to this world, but I love the Spirit that God has given me. All that is of God is good, but this flesh of mine wants to do just the opposite, ignoring what is right and doing that which is not good.

That's when I have the choice to choose the Spirit of God over the me-myself-and-I flesh that is no good at all.

I say this because I still struggle to rise above the things that look good in this world that I know are not. I've been trying to hide from God. Funny, isn't it? He is everywhere. He's in the middle of the casino too! I've even said things like, "just this time then I'll quit," only to have my mind in a place where I will be sure to do it again.

Love,

Marilynne

APRIL 23, 2007

Dear Marilynne,

My heart is grieved to hear what Satan is trying to do to you. I am standing on God's promises and proclaiming total victory from whatever is tempting you. 1 Corinthians 10:13 says, *But remember this – the wrong desires that come into your life aren't anything new and different. Many others have faced exactly the same problems before you. And no tempta- tion is irresistible. You can trust God to keep the temptation from becoming so strong that you can't stand up against it, for He has promised this and will do what He says. He will show you how to escape temptation's power so that you can bear up against it* (The Life Recovery Bible).

The Devil can put thoughts in your head, but he cannot read your thoughts or plans. He can see your actions, but only whether his influence is successful. Satan wants us to hide in a corner and stay in sin. That's why God wants us to come to Him with our sin and confess it. God already knows exactly what we are engaged in, but when we come to God, Satan loses again!

I am not preaching at you, Marilynne. I don't see myself as any better or more qualified. We are both children of the Most High God and Satan will be put in his low place as God gives us the power and authority in Jesus' name to kick the Devil, his filthy thoughts, and his puny demons to the curb.

Marilynne, we are all selfish at times, me included. I am not surprised that Satan is attacking you just before I am released from prison. Satan is not stupid. God revealed over a year ago what you and I can do together in prayer. When Satan is threatened, he attacks. If you were not a threat, he would not be trying so hard to trip you up. Nothing you do will turn me away from being your friend. And nothing can separate you from God's love. If we sin, God's only require- ment is repentance and a desire for Him to fix us.

I can't wait to see you again.

I love you in Christ, Marilynne.

Roger

MAY 10, 2007

Dear Roger,

I am just as excited as you are about your release and con- tinuing in life with God. I also look forward to talking with you. In fact, if I could just call you right now, I would.

I know that all I have been going through had to be taken care of now, not later, so that this will be behind me and God's plans for the future can move to higher ground. I pray that this valley is not one that I will face again. The storm is letting up and I praise God the storm will be defeated. I talked with the pastor's wife and confided in her what I was going through. It wasn't the easiest thing I've done. When it seems that storms will bring my world to an end, praise the Lord for those He puts in our lives with wisdom and com- passion. I can look up to God, but I still need to get to that place with Him and His Spirit to release the selfish me and get it out of His way.

What you wrote about being friends when you get out doesn't surprise me. Nor does the part about being a hus- band, but only time will tell what plans are in God's future.

I asked the pastor's wife to pray about what our future may hold. I want to do what God wants, and right now I know He wants me free from things of this world.

I received your gifts and they are very nice. Thank you again!

When is your release date? In Eau Claire, there is a Pentecostal church you might consider attending. I wouldn't want a church service to be anything but God himself in the presence of His people.

I expect a call from you when you get out. I want to know everything that is going on with you, okay?

Until I hear from you again, stand strong on the Word and let it fill your thoughts. Pray, pray, pray. God's will be done, not ours. To God be the glory.

Marilynne

MAY 17, 2007

Dear Marilynne,

So good to hear from you! I've had more answers about where I'm going. My probation officer sent reference letters to Triniteam Halfway House and Rice Lake's transitional liv- ing program, but there are no guarantees of acceptance from either place. He said he would have somewhere for me to live, but I should have a backup plan in case things don't work out. I am again praying hard, and I know God will open doors and help me through all circumstances. Greater is He who is in me (see 1 John 4:4). Thank God for all situations.

I will arrive in Eau Claire about 6:00 p.m. on the twelfth of June. I leave here at 9:30 a.m., so I have a long day but plenty to do on the bus. I can't wait to see you, my friend.

God answers all our prayers and is with us every step of the way. I am so grateful that He lifts us up when we can't stand or find our way, and that His love endures forever. Every single day He reminds me that when Satan lies or tries to remind me of my past, I am forgiven (you are too) and that Jesus' blood cleanses all the unrighteousness of past and future sin. It is so important for me to go daily to the foun- tain, to the Holiest of Holies where my God is, and drink of His righteousness. I ask for the Holy Spirit's fire to burn out all unclean thoughts and help me focus on my God, my one true love, Jesus Christ. Because of Him alone, I am forgiven. It's for Him I must live, or everything is in vain. Everything is going to be all right. I am grateful that our God, who is faithful, brought you through that difficult time. I pray that through every time of trial, you will be richer and more alive in Him. I pray that for me as well. I know all things are pos- sible through Christ who strengthens me (Philippians 4:13). I have hope in God's will for my future, so I place my future and treasure in His perfect will for you and me.

Thank you for the phone number, and yes, I will contact you. I am still awaiting instructions on where I will be headed. I don't have a ride yet from the bus stop, but I will get wher- ever I'm going with God as my co-pilot. If I call you for a ride, don't be surprised! But I don't think I will be stranded.

I know people closer to Eau Claire to assist me, but I'll call you anyway. At the very least, it will be an opportunity to pray with you and give thanks to God for all He has brought us through.

There are exciting days ahead! Please drop me a line and I'll let you know as soon as I know where I'm headed. I may have work at Blake's Auto Sales, but his son Eddie may be work- ing for him. But God's got it under control, so I will let Him drive and be prepared for the journey into another day He has prepared.

Love and hugs,

Your friend always,

Roger

MAY 21, 2007

Dear Marilynne,

Hi my dear friend. Every day, I look at what I can do to better prepare myself for getting out. What a rich blessing to know I have friends to help me, since I can't do it alone.

God's mercy and grace and love are what I need most, as well as His love moving through others. I am so ready to spend time with you, Marilynne! What a mighty God we serve!

May 23

I was hoping to hear from you, but all at the right time. I was given the privilege to sing at the Bible study last night. On Tuesday nights, a husband-and-wife team from Brother Bob's ministry sing and preach. One Tuesday a month they allow inmates to bring a four-minute message or a song to share.

Well, Jerry and Amy found out I am leaving on the twelfth of June and asked if I would do three songs on the fifth of June. What an honor! I don't want anyone else to feel left out, but I am humbled that I was asked to do this before I leave. I will give all glory to God and ask His will in preparation for what to sing and say.

May 26

Thank you for your gifts – your cards, stickers, and devoted friendship are so dear to my heart. I also embrace the pre- ciousness of freely sharing Jesus Christ with you. I don't always make the best decisions, but with God's hand before me, I pray my daily choices will be guided by the Holy Spirit.

I just got a certificate from my Friday morning AA group in recognition of three years of sobriety. And I give you many thanks for helping me in recovery and personal growth, both as a Christian and as a man. I'm certainly not saying I am without flaws, but I thank you for loving me – or something about me – in Christ. I've needed God most, but I never want to lose you, Marilynne. So I hope and pray that God guides me so Satan has no room to move in. As we remain in Christ, nothing will separate us.

I am going to Triniteam Halfway House in Eau Claire. I will talk to my probation officer on Tuesday at 1:00 p.m. and I'll know all the details then. I'll send you instructions on how to get there, but it's easy to find. I can't wait to talk to you and see you.

In Christ,

Roger

MAY 28, 2007

Dear Roger,

It must be exciting to know the date you're finally going to get to move on with your life. I am excited that you have come so far since you went to prison.

...all things work together for good to them that love God, to them who are the called according to his purpose (Romans 8:28). I am not concerned because God supplies all the needs of His people. The timing is from God and you may not know anything until the day you leave. But He has a plan and you will know it in His time.

The days are numbered and the time of release will be here before you know it.

This weekend, my mother and her husband are coming to spend a week with us. I have no idea what we will do with all that time together.

Until I hear from you, be strong in the Lord for He is our strength. Look not unto you own understanding but lean on the Lord.

God bless you,

Marilynne

June 1, 2007

Dear Roger,

It's getting really close to your release. I don't know how many more letters are going to get to you before you head out of there. I guess that depends on if they give you your mail right away. I will write as long as I can – until June 7th, okay? After that, I will wait for your call and whatever is next.

I'm glad you finally know where you will be living. Just remember to make the best of every situation and be strong in the Lord. He will see you through to the other side if you endure.

It is a blessing you will be able to witness. Let God be your guide in what you say and everything will work for good, and God will be glorified.

I am amazed at what God has done in you and pray He will continue to move in your life as well as in my own. I've

learned so many things about myself in writing to you, and I am sure God is in our midst as we write back and forth. We are truly friends in Christ. I don't know where our lives are headed, but I am ready to find out. You may not even like me in person! I am very headstrong most of the time, but in a good way. However, I am also selfish and set in my ways.

Having a friend is special in many ways, but I don't have that many friends that I am close to or even spend time with. At one time I had many around me all the time, but that was then, and now I want friends in Christ. You and I have Jesus in common, and that makes you special in both God's eyes and mine. Without Jesus, there would be nothing to discuss. Know what I mean?

June 2

Last night we went bowling in Chetek, and a few people I hadn't seen in a long time were there. I didn't know they were there, so when I saw them I had to remember that I am a Christian and asked what would Jesus do in this situation. We talked a bit, but I was reserved. Then a couple I once partied with showed up. Boy, I felt out of sorts, but I was once again reminded to be like Jesus in all I do. People from your past are waiting for a fall so they can pick you up and put you back into the life you had with them. I need to keep in mind that only Jesus can get us on the righteous path. It is so important to stick to God despite what our nature would otherwise do.

I pray I am making sense to you. You will have your own encounters and situations with those who won't believe you've changed. Some would rather be your savior than go to the Savior Jesus themselves. Despite the awesome changes that have taken place, people will always be waiting for the moment to remind you of your past life, so it's important to be as Christ-like as possible. It only takes one swear word and people will condemn you. It will be four years of sobri- ety for me and people are still checking out what I am drink- ing when I'm out. Surprise! It's not what they wish it would be. Praise God.

Just remember that your past can be used to help others in your future. Stand firm for Jesus, giving Him all the glory.

You might have time to write once more, and then I'll see you in person. Hang in there with confidence in Christ who can do all things and holds each future in His hands. I pray for you that God may bless you in and through this life's journey.

Talk with you soon.

Marilynne

JUNE 7, 2007

Dear Marilynne,

A few more days! I'm looking forward to just talking on the phone with you, not to mention seeing you without the con- fines of prison. My heart is leaping for joy and I have men- tally already left this prison! I am on stable ground spiritu- ally and emotionally. That is because of the changes God has made, and because of our incredible friendship. God's Word is in my heart. Deep respect and love for you, Marilynne, is also in my heart.

I have not received the halfway house rules yet, but you will be on my list as a visitor. I don't know what hours visitors are allowed or how regulated it will be at first, but it will cer- tainly be better than here. The halfway house is on the north end of downtown Eau Claire, right across from the post office.

Don't be surprised if I write a few more letters before I leave. I do love to write to you. Today is my last day at my job here. I am looking forward to a real job again, and even a mini- mum wage job sounds good after making twenty-six cents an hour! As I stay in His will, all will go as God directs.

Wow. It doesn't seem like I'm actually getting out of here. Oh yeah. On Tuesday when I was to share three songs, it turned into seven songs! God was moving and it was a blessing to share what He put on my heart. There are many special people here and I will leave a piece of me behind. To reach the lost and hurting people is what ministry is all about.

Well, I need to get this in the mail, but I will probably write another letter this weekend and then I'll talk to you some- time Tuesday.

You are in my thoughts and prayers, dear friend. Till later babe.

God bless and keep you,

Roger

July 28, 2007

Dear Marilynne,

My heart stopped until I talked to you tonight. Before that, I was numb with only God present. I know exactly who I am in Christ and how important it is to seek His kingdom first, because all power, strength, love, wisdom, grace, mercy, and forgiveness comes from His throne. Apart from Christ, I am nothing. It's only in seeking Him that anything is given. I love God with all of my heart, soul, and mind and I will not hold onto anything that displeases Him. This was really a test and quite the reality check, huh.

God has been so good to me since I've been out, though I've done nothing to merit His favor. When I say you are a gift from God, it does not come close to conveying how I feel.

I care so much for you that I would let you go, but I can't envision not having you in my life as my close friend and companion.

What glory will tomorrow bring? What beauty lies around the next sunrise and sunset? I want to watch the sunrise with you and the sunset, the moon, the stars. I want to run in the rain, sing in the sunshine, and bask in the presence of our dear, precious Lord with you. As God directs, I long to share everything with you.

God knows you completely and knows exactly who you are. Just as I want to always please my Father in heaven, so I long to be a blessing and pleasing soul mate to you, Marilynne. I can't write the depths of my feelings because there is no good explanation.

Let us see every delay as an opportunity to grow closer to each other and to God. If something like a pass is not accepted, let's embrace it as being part of God's timing and learn from it. We will have all of our lives to share together, and these first days are a short time to plant and cultivate what our future with God and each other may hold. Because of my past, I may not get every request granted, but I am praying for God's wisdom, understanding, and direction in all things.

I pray for God's favor, power, grace, and mercy to open the right doors and close the wrong ones that would lead away from God's will.

Love,

Roger

July 31, 2007

Dearest Marilynne,

Hi sweet eyes! Here we go!! God's timing has always worked for the best. I will not mess up what we have with my own will, and I pray God gives me the strength every day to wait. I pray to wait for the right time when everything we have unfolds before our eyes. From the very beginning, God has given us something that should be triple-underlined as unbelievable, right? The beauty of all we are connected in – spirit, body, soul, heart, and mind – is only possible through God. Many people talk of a soul mate; but we are that and so so so so so much more! That's evident in the fact that God knows us both. He knows every hair on our heads (not as much on mine), and he knows we would not have connected on our own, so He interceded, and created a miracle. The miracle is only starting and will continue until our last breath on earth, and through all eternity in heaven. Unfortunately for me, I can only be devoted to you on earth, for in heaven we will both be busy at the feet of our almighty Creator and King in continual worship. I am such a lucky man and I praise God for all He is doing. I will see you tomorrow, my sweet precious one.

It's 11:39 p.m. and I can't get to sleep. Thank you for the pens, shaver, paper, and shaving cream. I am humbled by your generosity – it means so much to me. Anything you give me has deep meaning because it's from you. I probably sound silly, but this is so new to me. Tomorrow is a new day, a new month, and I am expecting miracles. God is giving me such peace.

I am transported to a place of glory and stillness when I'm with you and nothing else matters around us. It's as if the world for a short moment disappears and we are in a trans- lucent place where the air is purer, the sun is purer, the wind is sweeter, and there is sweet solitude. God's grace, favor, and power are in our presence. It's all for the kingdom of God.

I dreamed of finding the one that God set aside and prepared for me, even as I am being prepared. I dreamed of that some- one to share everything with, to hold until death takes us to glory, to pray with, to share hopes, dreams, and desires with. God has made that dream come true in you, and I accept it with humility and gratefulness.

Love,

Roger

AUGUST 1, 2007

Marilynne my dear,

I thought I'd check out your letter – quite brief, but I understand.

Wow, God's love is coursing through me. While I was rid- ing my bike, I thought of you and found myself groaning! I said, "God, what is this?" He showed me that this is what I was designed for – you. Just as creation groans for Christ's return so He (God) has placed a desire in me for you that supersedes anything I ever thought possible. It is a holy desire given for God's glory. A big part of this is that you opened up and allowed me to come closer. It doesn't work with only one participant, right? You are the one God has prepared me for. As I've said, I will wait on the Lord in all things. But boy, I never thought it would be so powerful and awesome. Groaning while I'm riding my bike just thinking of you? How is it possible? I've always been rather passionate in what I give my heart to, but not like this. Sometimes, I'm surprised you're not running away, but now I know it's God. I really thought I'd be alone the rest of my life. But what does God do? He puts an angel in my sight and says, "Give her your love and heart because she will know exactly what to do with every desire and need as you grow together in my Word and purpose in your lives." To top it off, God is giving you complete control of me as you stay in Him, as we are so much more than soul mates. Can you feel it? Can you feel that deliverance coming? Freedom from the world, in each other's arms, in God's very presence. All glory and honor goes to God. I won't forget that. How can this all be possible? I don't know, but God does. He wants to move in us and I am going to let Him take us wherever He wants. I love you so much, in ways I never thought possible, and in depths I've never imagined. I thought it would never come into existence, but God's promises are true. His Word never fails and He never changes. Till later. You know that won't be long. I've got you really bad and in Christ, that's goooooood!

Love,

Roger

AUGUST 6, 2007

Marilynne,

I will wait as long as it takes for us to know that the time is right for all to come together. I know that every second I wait will be worth what God has planned for us. I don't want to rush this either, even though it is sooooo hard being away from you each day. In time we can be together at our discretion.

Later,

Roger

AUGUST 17, 2007

Roger,

On September 22, 2003, I wondered how God was going to take the mess I had gotten myself into and do something about my ongoing alcohol and drug addiction. I wondered how He would get me out of the rock bottom I had gotten myself into. I had no idea how I would make it outside the detox center I had already tried before.

Nothing made sense anymore. I couldn't fix the mess and I was afraid of where I was headed. I threw my hands up in the air to God in faith that He could hear my cry for help with words only He would understand, because the cries in billows of distress are as an animal in pain. I was hopeless. It seemed that I was on my last leap, and I couldn't see anyone to catch me. Somehow, though, a new hope came over me two days later. I had no idea where my life was headed, but on September 24, 2003, I left the detox center. The doctors said that leaving so soon would surely result in my return- ing there in six months or less, if I was lucky enough to even make it that long.

In that moment I told myself, one day at a time with Jesus. I left the center, carrying the hope of Jesus with me, remem- bering those words from a grandfather who had gone home to be with Jesus many years before that.

I took the leap and God has been blessing me ever since. I set forth in a new direction, a God-given journey, with faith that can dissolve any and all mountains. What more should we expect than the best from the only true heavenly Father God who can do all things? It has been four years since then and I expect only the best of God's blessings.

There were people who didn't believe that I would ever change. Roger, I don't expect anyone to believe the difference in you or me now. Jesus never said this would be easy, but God is awesome and holy. No one can see Him unless they seek to see. We are both in God's time. We can share our testimonies to glorify our Lord who has completely changed us, preparing us for His will in ministry. This has been His purpose for both of us from the beginning of time.

We are soul survivors by the grace and mercy of God our Father and have been given another chance in life to have what God intended. The thought of you and me in ministry shows me that only God could create such love and desire between two such unlikely people. It was unlikely that we should be united, but with God all things are possible.

I was thinking about how God's plan has been coming together all along – you went to jail, and I was your sup- port. Look at all of this from then until now, and everything makes perfect sense. We are what God wants for His king- dom, to help those who seek a greater power. We are here to let them know how to get the God of all things into their lives. Of course, you already know this is true. This is what God has already done.

With love,

Marilynne,

AUGUST 27, 2007

Marilynne,

My love, I just read your letter. All my dreams are officially coming true, just as my precious Lord and Savior has promised for twelve years. Not in my timing, but in His perfect timing. It is soooooooo hard to wait, but God has shown me how important it is to wait for you, my only love, yes, you. You are the one who lights my fire, who has my heart, who I will wait to know more, who I wish to spend all of my days on earth with. I, Roger Harrison, love you, Marilynne.

Now happiness is more than just a word – it's a reality!! Now love is real. Now everything is in color. Now I am real and I have purpose and I have a home. I love you with everything I am. No barriers. No limits. No end to the possibilities as ALL THINGS ARE POSSIBLE WITH GOD. I LOVE YOU MARILYNNE TO NO END.

Love,

Roger

SEPTEMBER 5, 2007

Marilynne,

I can't be reading your letters here because everyone's won- dering what's wrong with me sitting here in tears. You are so incredibly awesome and beautiful and I don't understand this love. How can it get bigger? But it does, with every breath I take and with every beat of my heart. I have to see you, and I'm so darn impatient. God help me, for I love you so much I would swim upstream to meet you even if there was no river or water. You see, I have faith in God. It is His business to provide the way, and my job to swim.

I love you tweety pie!

I can't stand to be without you. I'm counting the days, the hours, the minutes, until we have time together. Know what I mean? How I love you. It gets so strong that I was getting mad at God because we aren't together yet. How crazy is that? He (God) said, "Be patient, for I am preparing things you have not seen yet in visions or dreams, things so spectacular that the world will be in total awe and know for an absolute fact that I, Jehovah Jireh, have placed you and Marilynne together for all time on earth and no one will any longer question your togetherness and your love, because it is birthed in the I AM. The God of all and everything." So I am being quiet and letting God have His perfect way. Whew! Talk about humble pie. I should know better by now than to question what God is doing, right? Look up, baby, for God has everything in His control, right down to our very heartbeats. I love you, Marilynne. I want to hold you so badly it hurts.

Roger

SEPTEMBER 20, 2007

Honey,

I miss you so much. I'm not sure why I can't reach you by phone right now, but God is in control, and I pray you are all right. I am so looking forward to this weekend and every day in the future we can spend together. I want you by my side every moment. I will talk to you later, my love.

Roger

SEPTEMBER 24, 2007

Dear Marilynne,

I am so happy for you, for who you are in Christ, for how far God has brought you, for your faithfulness to Christ, for your commitment to change, for your love of life, for your compassion for others, for your unfailing search for righ- teousness, for wanting only the very best that God has for you, for wanting door handles turned so wear and tear is reduced, for reducing water use – why waste it anyway? I am so happy for you putting up with my idiosyncrasies (silliness, pouting, quietness). I'm working on me and so is God. Quite the job, huh? I'm amazed at all God has done in your life and your pastor was so right: you worked through some incred- ibly hard issues and came out renewed, reborn, refreshed, and rededicated to the purpose that God has for you. I am so grateful to be your man, your love, and a part of your life. Count me as one wholly devoted to making sure you always have something to smile about, something to laugh about, and a shoulder to rest on, to lean on, to cry on, to love on. I am so in love with you, it makes me want to shout, to laugh, to cry, to sing from the rooftop, to let my voice ring across the miles with the absolute awesomeness of our love and our lives together, joined as ONLY GOD COULD DO. I am totally devoted to you, to us, to all God has intended for us. All joined with the cords of God's perfect love and care.

I just want to hold you right now and every moment. Our togetherness is about to be finalized, to become a time where we don't have to be separated for any reason. I want to wake up with you every single morning the rest of my life. I want to lie down with you every single night FOR THE REST OF OUR LIVES TOGETHER. NOTHING LESS WILL DO. I LOVE YOU, AND GOD IS CRAZY ABOUT YOU, MY LOVE.

Love,

Roger

P.S. Happy sobriety day. FOUR YEARS – HOW AWESOME IS THAT?

October 8, 2007

My sweet Marilynne,

We have a date, it is for real, and I am not afraid to jump. I am confident that our God is in control and has predestined this marriage since the beginning of time. What an incredible union God has put together.

The former town drunk, of all people, to marry the for- mer lesbian, of all people! It is no coincidence, no accident, and no stroke of luck. It is the perfect will of our God who so loves us that HE JOINED US TOGETHER IN A WAY NO MAN COULD HAVE CONCEIVED POSSIBLE. All things under heaven and earth shall obey the will of God and line up with the Word of our most holy, just, and true God. The reason we were brought together is only start- ing to manifest itself, and it is so so so so awesome it takes my breath away. I WILL NOT LET ANYONE OR ANYTHING COME BETWEEN US EXCEPT WITH GOD'S PERMISSION, OKAY? I TRULY LOVE YOU AND WILL DO EVERYTHING IN MY POWER THROUGH CHRIST WHO STRENGTHENS ME, TO MAKE YOU THE HAPPIEST WOMAN AND WIFE IN THE WORLD!

You are who I want to wake up to, who I want to sleep with, who I want to have and hold for all our days on earth until the day of the Lord comes. I LOVE YOU AND ONLY YOU.

We are meant for each other and Satan will not steal any more from us. We are one in Christ Jesus who so loves us. I am so happy with you. We need to always be honest with one another. I can't wait to be closer to you, and I am so look- ing forward to being married to you. It is so rich when we're together. Everything makes sense and everything is right with you and me. I can't explain everything, so I'm not going to even attempt to. To wake up next to you – I want that for the rest of our lives and I know in my heart that God does too. Our ministry is life-changing and He's starting with our lives first. Can't you feel the awesome glory and presence of our God when we're together? I do and I know you do, too. I love you in every way.

Your fiancé/husband-to-be,

Roger

OCTOBER 29, 2007

Roger,

I'm unable to sleep, so I've gone from praying to watching TV, realizing we are days away from our future together. To think that just a couple of years ago this was all just a vision, a thought, a you've-got-to-be-kidding kind of dream. Now it's a reality and I'm wide awake with excitement. I would much rather call you and talk for the rest of the night, but I'm not able to do so.

I loved you long before I said it aloud or even to you. I shook my head at the very thought of falling in love with someone I had never even met in person. I longed to meet the one who had captured my heart (that's you), and set a beat so strong I couldn't contain it. I have since seen a wedding, a ministry, and a full life with God in every step.

Then again, I shook it off and thought it would only be in my wildest dreams, that something so crazy as this could ever happen. Tonight I am so ready to be your wife, your friend, and your all.

God has been preparing us to be together for some time; I have no doubts about that. I know God gave us those dreams and visions for this very reason, for our upcoming day that will be the beginning of our wonderful future together.

Praise God for our sisters and brothers in the church. I am so thankful to God for having such a special family for us to lean on in these special moments.

I am thankful that you are going to be my husband. I saw it and didn't want to believe it. I'm grateful for the awesome God we have and how He has taken our lives and molded us to be as one in all things we do together. Jesus Christ, as our strength, will move mountains, build bridges, and give hope to many. Each day, I will remember those days I didn't doubt it and realized this happened by faith in a God who changes hearts and creates new creatures in Jesus.

We are God's vessels and He is our potter. With Jesus all things are possible; there is nothing that our Lord cannot do.

Sometimes we have things to mend, and that is okay. Stay faithful and true to our God and praise Him for moving us beyond our past mistakes, so that we strive together in a future with God. God has prepared me to be all you want and ever need as a best friend and wife. As long as God is first in all we do, we will prosper and be disciples of God.

Roger, I love you, and I am so happy I stopped running and trying to look for the "perfect outside" person for myself.

You are perfect for me and I know our love is the greatest I've known on earth. God is love. Our God that lives in each of us has a perfect connection through us and has become the best part of who I am today. We will love each other through eternity. You are my one and only, now and forever.

Love,

Marilynne

OCTOBER 30, 2007

Dearest Marilynne,

I am more amazed every single day at how much I love you. It's because of the love God has given us for each other and for Him, more and more and more until I don't think I can handle any more. Then God gives me another tank of your precious sweet love and affection to fill up. Nothing others have tried to give comes even close to the love and compas- sion I feel from you. That is because it's from God and from your heart, even from places you didn't know you had inside you. I love you.

Love and kisses and hugs,

Roger

CONCLUSION

First and foremost, I had to admit I needed help. I was tired of going in for help and ending up in the same life I wanted to escape. So I cried all day to Jesus every day. I could not live one minute without my best friend, which happened to be my drink.

I would need more than AA. I would need church. I attended the same denomination that worked for me before, which was Pentecostal. I remembered the healing I received before in my life from drugs. I needed healing from alcohol.

My healing began but not without hearing messages I could have walked away from regarding the truth about living in same-sex relationships. Part of me wanted to walk away from the message, and the other part of me wanted to let go and let God, but I still thought I was beyond God's favor.

I continued to attend church and the day came when I fell to my knees to be saved from my life of sins, but I still did not know how God would take this mess and turn it into good. I was in a relation-ship, but it was killing my spirit to do what I knew was wrong. I was living the Romans Scripture. I wanted to be good, right, and please God, but I was barely staying sober.

Keep pressing on, Jesus. Every morning I would wake up to say, "One day at a time, sweet Jesus." Keep me sober. Give me strength. The Lord placed on my heart, in his timing and his grace and mercy, a book to read to help me come out of homosexuality. I stayed in church, and that led to reading another book about restoring sexual identity. When the relationship ended in 2004, the renewing of my mind and spirit lined up with God and his plan for my new life. I was free and I no longer faced the addictions that once took over my life. I am now married, and my husband and I are in agreement that God has joined us together.

God is a wonderful God, and I am by all means an example of what He can and will do if we give it to Him and really give it all up. Giving up that relationship was the hardest. I am in a church now and am a new creation. Yet my old ways are still tempting at times, and I pray I will never walk away again with a hardened heart.

I now have a home business taking care of disabled adults, and it is exactly what one of my desires was years ago. The Lord is still work-ing on me. I relate to Romans a lot. My life seems to have revolved a lot around wanting to do good, but ending up doing wrong. I pray Jesus will always win when I am tempted now. I now am able to give my testimony on different occasions and am always open to telling others how great our God has been to me, and will be to each of us who choose to let go and let God. Recovery does happen.

Thank you for allowing me to share what God has done in my life so far. The Lord is not even close to being finished with me. It's time now that I thank him for taking me out of bondage in such a step-by-step way. This program has been such a blessing, and I pray every message given will touch many in need of Jesus, or for those who have strayed, it's never too late, until God says so.

God bless you in Jesus' name.

Therefore if any man be in Christ, he is a new creature: old things are passed away; behold, all things are become new. (2 Corinthians 5:17, KJV

ABOUT THE AUTHOR

Marilynne Harrison and her husband live in northern Wisconsin, in the small town of Shell Lake. Aft er overcoming drugs, alcohol, and a same-sex relationship, life seems almost normal. Without a doubt it would have been an unhappy ending for Marilynne's life had God not intervened. Because she so clearly knows that her victories are a gift from Him, Marilynne boldly released her journals, written during the most trying days of her life, out of which this book was taken. Her primary purpose for sharing her uttermost secrets is to encourage others also struggling with drugs, alcohol, and/or same-sex relationships. Th is book serves to provide an example of a person who overcame a blatantly wrong lifestyle, and today lives a clean lifestyle, worships God, and fellowships with other like-minded believers.

Review this book on Amazon
Like LSP on Facebook

RESOURCES

Twelve Steps and Twelve Traditions – by Alcoholics Anonymous World Services, Inc.

Our Daily Bread – by RBC Ministries

Coming Out of Homosexuality – by Bob Davies and

Lori Rentzel Restoring Sexual Identity – by Anne Paulk

Managing Your Emotions – Joyce Meyer

The God Chasers – Tommy Tenney

The Bible – New Living Translation

www.ingramcontent.com/pod-product-compliance
Lightning Source LLC
Chambersburg PA
CBHW062321120626
46553CB00015B/60